REFORMED FAITH AND POLITICS

Ronald H. Stone, Editor

REFORMED FAITH AND POLITICS

Essays Prepared for the
Advisory Council on Church and Society
of the United Presbyterian Church in the U.S.A.
and the Council on Theology and Culture
of the Presbyterian Church in the U.S.

Ronald H. Stone, Editor

The University Press of America
Washington, D.C.

PREFACE

This volume is a collection of essays on the relationship of reformed faith to politics. It is the result of a two-year process within the Presbyterian Church in the United States (PCUS) and the United Presbyterian Church in the United States of America (UPCUSA). Requests from Presbyteries in both churches in 1981 to respond to concern over political activity by the religious right intersected with work already under way in the UPCUSA to rethink the relationship between faith and politics.

An editorial board of James Smylie, John Mulder and the editor met with staff members Jorge Lara-Braud and Dean Lewis to outline the original plan of the volume. Upon receiving suggestions from the Council on Theology and Culture of the PCUS and the Advisory Council on Church and Society of the UPCUSA, the work went ahead. Seminars in the summers of 1981 and 1982 at Ghost Ranch Conference Center in Abiquiu, New Mexico, brought ministers and laity into the process of discussion and planning. A further seminar is planned for Ghost Ranch in the summer of 1983.

Writers completed their essays in 1982 and, after their work was accepted by the respective councils, the project was ready for a final editing. During the same period, the development of recommendations for policy positions and a background paper for the respective General Assemblies (or a reuniting General Assembly) in 1983 carried the subject's concerns to the churches.

Some essays commissioned for the project could not be completed in time for publication. The essays were selected with four related groups of readers in mind. They vary in the technical knowledge needed to appreciate them from those for scholars in the field (particularly the essays by Paul Minear and Louis Weeks) to the rest which are easily accessible to educated laity, ministers and students in college or seminaries. The reformed political ethic is complex, and the volume reflects that complexity. It is hoped that the collection will serve as a resource for study of reformed political thought in local churches throughout the country. Though the collection does not fulfill all of the aspirations of the original editorial committee, it represents the concessions ideal plans make to reality in both publication and politics. If the reception of this volume justifies the endeavor, a second volume developing further Biblical resources, historical reflections, and church-state issues is projected. All of the essays were written originally for this volume except Jane D. Douglas' address at the Purdue meeting of the United Presbyterian Women (July, 1982) and "Introduction to Reformed Faith and Politics," which also serves as the background paper for the 1983 General Assemblies or the reuniting General Assembly of the two churches. As the introduction grows out of the other essays, it is a conclusion of the process as well as a general introduction to the essays.

Though the essays are diverse in perspective, as a collection of essays on this theme from reformed Christians appropriately reflects pluralistic perspectives, there are common themes. The political ethic of reformed Christians is a commitment to the vocation of citizens in politics. The ethic eschews simple solutions. It distinguishes between faith and politics, but aggressively relates the two. The political realm is subject to the sovereignty of God. Politics is a primary mode of Christian social ethics for reformed Christians. They recognize the sinfulness in politics, but they are upheld by the rule of God to work hopefully in the political realm. Out of faith and the hope it nourishes, they respond to God's love to work for justice.

The movement of the book is from a general introduction to the book drawing on all the essays, to three contemporary Presbyterian perspectives on the relationship of faith to politics by David Pryor, Donald W. Shriver, and Anne Austin Murphy in the concluding chapters. The introduction is followed by a statement on faith and politics by George Chauncey. Next the Gospel of John is examined for its perspective on the problem by Paul Minear. Essays four through six examine the new Christian right and liberation theology. Essays seven through nine look at the historical and contemporary issues of church-state relationships in the context of the broader faith-politics relationship. Chapters ten and eleven examine domestic politics and world politics from the disciplined inquiry of two political scientists, before the three concluding chapters speak to questions of the agenda before the Presbyterian churches.

The essays are offered as Christian political thought for our time. They will need to be reformed for another time. My prayer at Christmastime, 1982, is that this thought will help us move into future time where our children and students will see better than we have how to relate Christian faith to politics.

CONTENTS

CONTRIBUTORS

1. Ronald H. Stone is Professor of Social Ethics, Pittsburgh Theological Seminary, Pittsburgh, Pennsylvania.
2. George A. Chauncey is Executive of the Washington Communication office of the Presbyterian Church in the U.S., Washington, D.C.
3. Paul S. Minear is Winkley Professor Emeritus of Biblical Theology, Yale University, New Haven, Connecticut.
4. Peggy Shriver is Assistant General Secretary of the National Council of Churches in the U.S.A., New York, New York.
5. George Marsden is Professor of History, Calvin College, Grand Rapids, Michigan.
6. Albert Curry Winn is Pastor of the North Decatur Presbyterian Church, Decatur, Georgia.
7. Jane Dempsey Douglas is Professor of Church History, School of Theology at Claremont, Claremont, California.
8. Louis Weeks is Professor of Historical Theology and Dean of Louisville Presbyterian Theological Seminary, Louisville, Kentucky.
9. John C. Bennett is Reinhold Niebuhr Professor Emeritus and President Emeritus of Union Theological Seminary, New York, New York.
10. Dorothy Dodge is James Wallace Professor of Political Science, Macalester College, St. Paul, Minnesota.
11. Alan Geyer is Executive Director of the Churches' Center for Theology and Public Policy, Washington, D.C.
12. David Pryor is a member of the United States Senate from Arkansas, Washington, D.C.
13. Donald W. Shriver is William E. Dodge Professor of Applied Christianity and President of Union Theological Seminary, New York, New York.
14. Anne Austin Murphy is Professor of Political Science, Eckerd College, St. Petersburg, Florida.

INTRODUCTION TO REFORMED FAITH AND POLITICS

Ronald H. Stone

The Crisis

The question of the relationship of *God and Caesar* is not a new issue, yet it arises today with a fresh urgency. All human communities have had to resolve the problem of the relationship of the deepest religious loyalties to their practical decisions about government. The solution of one society has never prevailed over all of humanity. In our day, the crisis between religion and government has disturbed regimes in Central America, Iran, Afghanistan, and Poland. Recent politics in the United States of America has been energized and disturbed by new forms of Christian political activism. Religious divisions have contributed to political conflicts and war recently in the Sudan, India and Pakistan, Israel and the Arab countries, Lebanon, Northern Ireland, and elsewhere. Currently, political leaders and scientists are taking serious account of religious forces. As religious leaders and students of religion have learned, their religious practices have political implications which they cannot ignore.

As members of the Presbyterian Church, we know that the sovereignty of God and the service of God are of utmost importance in our lives. We also know that the practical exercise of politics, the process by which we govern human life, interpenetrates most areas of our lives. Questions of life and death, whether considered on the global scale of peace and war or the personal scale of human rights on abortion, have both theological and political dimensions. Both God and Caesar are involved. There will be no peace without politics. There will be no answer to the vexing questions about abortion without politics. Human history through which God works to realize divine purposes is subject also to the politics of human beings. These humans act out of a mixture of religious judgments and political judgments.

So we are inevitably political and religious. The *God-Caesar* question will not let us go. The question flows through scripture. We are confronted with a variety of solutions. God moves Joseph into a position of authority in Egypt. Then Egypt oppresses Israel. God leads Moses out of Egypt and the confrontation between Yahweh, the Lord of Moses and the god-king Pharaoh disrupts

[1]

Egypt. The tribes of Israel are joined in a religious confederacy to resist the Baalistic city states of Canaan. Kingship is granted Israel only reluctantly by Samuel for he sees the rejection of the Lord in the institution of kingship. Prophets and priests struggle to work out a solution to the problem of religious loyalty and political loyalty. In Amos the struggle is between the prophet of God and the priest of the court serving the king. Through periods of political success and political failure, from David to the exile, the question is not absent. The Jewish struggle for pure religion breaks out into political conflict with their Greek and then their Roman masters.

Jesus himself from his birth to his death and resurrection was involved in the politics and faith controversy. The stories about his birth involve promises of the overthrow of the established order in Mary's Magnificat and Herod's perceived threat to his rule in the birth at nearby Bethlehem. His death is an act of political execution and his resurrection a surprising victory over the political order that attempted to quell him.

Luke described the charges brought against him by the elders as "perverting the nation," "forbidding tribute to Caesar," and the proclamation of "Christ a King" (R.S.V. Luke 23:2). The three synoptic gospels related Jesus' own avoidance of the trap about paying taxes. Confronted by the disciples of the Pharisees and the Herodians he avoided affronting Rome or Judaism by saying, "Then render to Caesar the things that are Caesar's and to God the things that are God's" (R.S.V. Luke 20:25).

Political thinkers have had to deal with the meaning of this aphorism in varied historical situations since that day. What is appropriately owed to Caesar, and what is reserved to God? Different political orders work out the issue differently. Jesus himself only avoided the verbal trap of his enemies. Soon he was to surrender his life to the representatives of Caesar. Could there by anything on earth more completely God's than the life of Jesus? Yet it was laid down before Caesar. The Gospel of John makes it clear that Pilate, the representative of Caesar, was acting under God's authority. Pilate, overwhelmed by the issues of the crowd's religious-political convictions, finally acquiesced to the crucifixion. The saying of Jesus of rendering to Caesar and to God points toward the need for a distinction, but it fails to draw the line for Christians or for Jesus, himself.

Religious faith and politics are not the same reality, but they cannot be separated. On Biblical grounds they cannot be separated, though distinctions can be found. Empirically they cannot be separated, for many of the political conflicts of our day involve dimensions of faith.

Political authority, like water, is ultimately from God. Neither water nor political authority are gods, though in certain cultures both have been worshiped. Governments, like irrigation canals, must be organized by people, the breaking of either can create chaotic conditions. Often both canals and governments must be changed. Paul was confronted with Christian extremists in Rome who were tempted in the name of Christian freedom to be careless of political authority. His response in Romans 13 has protected political authority with religious legitimacy to both the health and detriment of the people.

[2]

Every person must submit to the supreme authorities. There is no authority but by act of God, and the existing authorities are instituted by him; consequently anyone who rebels against authority is resisting a divine institution, and those who so resist have themselves to thank for the punishment they will receive. For government, a terror to crime, has no terrors for good behavior. (NEB, Romans 13:1-3)

These words seem hard to those of us who are conscious of our own religious liberty which comes out of a history of revolution. The Calvinist revolutionary, John Knox, understood: "For government, a terror to crime, has no terrors for good behavior," to be foundational to the argument. Therefore, when a group of people were a terror to good people, regardless of their claim, they were not God's government and they were to be replaced. Usually, however, the text has buttressed authority and recognized the high place that governing authorities have in God's work. Too seldom has attention been given to the sentence preceding 13:1, "Do not let evil conquer you, but use good to defeat evil" (12:21). The last sentence in the section on government is also relevant, "Love cannot wrong a neighbor; therefore the whole law is summed up in love" (13:10). Paul, expecting the end of history, had a problem with Christian extremists and he ordered caution about challenging government. He, himself, of course, challenged it unto death. His advice to the Romans was meant for their time, but it has relevance to our time. He urges us to regard proper governmental authority as serving God and to see government in the context of good defeating evil. The summary of law, rightly conceived, is love.

The early hearers of the Gospel according to John anticipated martyrdom as Jesus and his disciples were martyred. The background of the New Testament is religious and religious-political conflict. The New Testament concludes with the saints oppressed by Rome and the overcoming of Rome in an apocalyptic vision. Thus, Scripture provides a plurality of answers to the question of the relationship of faith to politics.

Church history shows that the church has attempted many solutions to the God-Caesar problem. The early church defied the state's idolatry, and it was persecuted. Often it still is persecuted. Ascetics withdrew from the state. In small communities, the church still withdraws. The Roman Catholic, medieval church attempted to run the state for Christian purposes, and Christians who would run the state are still active. Martin Luther tried to maintain the church distinct from the social realm, recognizing that God governs both realms. In practice, often the church became subservient to the political needs of the rulers. John Calvin tried to reform the state while recognizing that the state is not and cannot be the Kingdom of God. The church in reformed lands was tempted to establish a theocracy where it had the power.

John Calvin taught and political history affirms that no one form of the state will serve different peoples best. Governments must correspond to the limits and possibilities of the population. Social science confronts us with a variety of models of solutions to the God-Caesar issue. Beyond recognizing and describing the

[3]

plurality, social science can help only a little in our search for the answer to the perplexities in the relationship of the God-Caesar problem.

Consequently, the search for wisdom for Presbyterians regarding the faith-politics questions begins in a recognition of: 1) the inevitability of the issue, 2) the importance of the issue, and 3) a variety of answers to the issue in the study of the Bible, church history, and social science. All three sources will provide wisdom. The Bible particularly will provide controls to the options that are open to contemporary Christians in their resolution of the problem. From our history we learn of a particular Reformed way of perceiving those scriptural controls as well as a style of political action. Social science, also, helps us understand the contemporary problems around the issue and describes alternative consequences of certain choices.

The crisis of the relationship of faith to politics involves not only religious issues, but the changing political scene. The American political system is troubled.[1] The national leadership has been highly unstable with Dwight D. Eisenhower, 1952-1960, being the last President to complete two terms in office. Others have been assassinated, retired under criticism and intra-party conflicts, forced to resign under clouds of political scandal, or defeated at the polls. The 1980s may be a time of political upheaval characterized by fundamental debate and change.[2] The media, the reform of the primary system, the computer, the Political Action Committees, the new religious-political groups all impact a system characterized by political apathy toward and suspicion of the political process. The American political system is an old system which has evolved greatly and which is undergoing intense strains. Four issues which the last two General Assemblies have addressed in substantive ways raise questions about the system's ability to resolve problems. Can the United States' political process handle the issue surrounding the energy issue for a just and sustainable future? Is the system adequate to meet the needs of the urban population of the country? Can a just migration policy be developed with all the pressure groups and fears around the issue? Finally and most important, can a just peace be secured which will reduce the terror of nuclear destruction? All four issues, addressed theologically and ethically by the church, will require political leadership which does not seem to be on the horizon. Fundamental questions are on the national agenda, but most political leadership seems to be ducking, refraining from leading, settling for oversimplified media answers, serving special interests, and concentrating on re-election.

The Ambiguity

The complexity of the relationship of faith to politics inheres in the nature of politics as well as the demands of faith. The classical political philosophy as articulated by Aristotle, in the fourth century, B.C., regarded politics as the governing for the good of the people of the city. Politics was a branch of ethics. Thomas More in the sixteenth century continued this theme in his writing of *Utopia* as he portrayed an ideal society. Caught up in the religious-political controversies of his day, the author was martyred. Socrates and More both represent a view of politics as ethics and both paid the ultimate sacrifice. An alternative view is perhaps best represented by Nicolo Machiavelli, a relatively religiously indifferent thinker of the sixteenth century in *The Prince*. Here politics is basically the search for and the maintenance of power. His views too had their forerunners in the writings of the Greek political thinker, particularly the cynics. In this view politics is a relatively amoral skill of ruling the people. Neither view in a pure form is sufficient. Ethics and politics are not united, but neither are they completely separate.

Reformed Christians understand this political ambiguity as rooted in our human nature. We are inevitably sinful in our political actions. All of our political actions reflect our own self-interest or our own perspective. The best hopes for our political life reside in knowing of our sin as well as the sin of others and acting accordingly. We may still be called to martyrdom. The willingness for martyrdom is essential to Christian political action.[3] Not only Jesus and the apostles, but countless Christians have taken this route. The refusal to compromise on ultimate issues is a mark of Christian participation in politics. A recognition of our own sin, however, guards us against a willingness to force others to martyrdom and points toward the need for compromise and prudence in political action. Sin in politics, both as a distortion of our created goodness and as the refusal to live in love, is not to be celebrated, but to be recognized as the context for repentance, change, and transformation. Knowing that we exist in a violent world we try to be peacemakers striving to realize God's peace or *Shalom*. Our tools for achieving peace are awkward, still as the Bishop of Hippo in North Africa, Augustine, taught at the beginning of the fifth century we must use these imperfect tools. Faith gives a context for knowing that God wills people to live together in trusting, wholesome relationships. Hope provides a motivation for engaging in a politics of expectation that life can be more just. Love requires us to respond to the love God has shown by loving service to the neighbor. These central Christian virtues transform but do not annul the way Christians in society try to order society through moderation, courage, wisdom, and justice.

Reservation and Commitment

Until the founding in the twentieth century of frankly atheist states, most earthly rulers in Christian civilization have been Christians. Maybe they were not thoroughly Christian, but they were baptized and most confessed themselves to be Christian. Christianity since the overthrow of official idolatry has been frankly quite political. The Christian hopes and values of their populations nurtured the politics of these societies. The societies were not secular, they were religious in Christian terms. Still the Christian faith could not be reduced to politics. Memories of prophetic distance of religion from politics were never completely eclipsed. Monastic groups withdrew from the politics of the state, though in both Eastern and Western Christendom they would return to reform politics. Clergy would demand and receive some exemptions from political responsibility. Religious visionaries would reawaken again and again the hope for a Kingdom of God which was different from political kingdoms. A faith with even a somewhat dim memory of Jesus could not equate Roman rule or its motley heirs to the kingdom which Jesus announced.

Christianity along with Judaism and Islam is among the most worldly of the world's religions. Yet, there was a reservation about political involvement which remained. The human spirit could not be satisfied with the peace of the city of the earth; it sought the peace of the city of God. A person caught up in the love of God knows that earthly justice is usually only rough justice. It is not enough. We pray for the coming of the Kingdom of God daily in the Lord's Prayer, recognizing that these kingdoms or republics or people's republics are not God's fulfillment of human community.

Western Christianity in both its great Catholic and Reformed traditions is committed to political action. But it also has a reservation about political action. All of life is not politics. There is a freedom to the human spirit too great for any of our political organizations. The neglect of the religious reservation about politics has led and can lead to a religious fanaticism in politics. The human spirit, the imaging of God in humanity, is too free to be satisfied in any political settlement. Knowledge of the greatness of the human spirit as well as knowledge of human sin must help Christians to affirm a religious reservation about politics as well as a commitment to politics.

Two Roots of Political Thinking

In the closing days of the Weimar Republic, in 1932, Paul Tillich reflected on the relationship of faith to politics. The new pagan, political cult of Nazism threatened to overturn the weakened republic which was also under attack by communism, and by a collection of conservative political interests. Tillich's essay, the "Two Roots of Political Thinking," made a contribution to thought which is still relevant. He argued that traditional regimes often were founded upon the sacralization of political systems in root myths of the society. Ancient Egypt and Babylon were characterized by myths which supported divine kingship, religious hierarchy, and wove into the myths of creation the divinely ordered present government. Religion and politics were one with politics favoring a particular religion and religion legitimating a political order.

In Israel, prophets arose who criticized the political order in terms of their understanding of God's covenant with Israel. Amos, for example, witnessed to God judging all nations by justice. Also he held out the possibility of repentance or change for the political order. The present rulers were not merely to be legitimated but they were judged by justice and there was a sense of movement or expectation to history. By hearing judgment new, better order could be established.

Consequently, one root of political thinking was the myth of origin involving worship of the Mother or Father land, the sacralization of kingship, and the blessing of customary rule. The second root of political thinking had a sense of movement to history and evaluated rule by a standard of God's justice; it was the prophetic critique of a sacral politics.

Despite a tendency of the middle ages to sacralize the Papal-Caesar settlement the Western world kept alive the second root of political thinking until it broke forth again born by the movements of Renaissance, Reformation and Enlightenment. Democratic politics, capitalism and socialism all contained this movement of historical expectation and the centrality of justice or political ethics.

The Weimar Republic was an expression of this second root of political thinking. However, it was not strong enough given economic depression to withstand movements based on the myths of origin. The monarchists expressed the myth of origin, but they were enfeebled by lacking a sense of historical expectation; they were just trying to return to the past. The forces supporting the Weimar settlement seemed to lack sufficient respect for the truth of the myth of origin. They were critics of the past without deep roots. The Nazis expressed a romantic myth of origin with a sense of future transformation in the dream of a Third Reich. They had the power of a myth of the past and a myth for the future, but they had no sense of justice nor any critical understanding of human reality.

Democracy depended upon critical reason, but in a period of world-wide depression it was a weak opponent to romantic, pagan myths of ancient Germany united with a promise of a political messiah and a transformed future. The churches both Protestant and Catholic were politically inept. The liberal cultures' institutions of universities, press, moral-cultural institutions were in disarray and unwilling to fight for the weakened liberal culture. The fury of romantic myths and the fighting cadres of the Nazis overwhelmed them.

Protestants were too willing to abandon the political realm and Catholics were too willing to compromise with an evil regime to maintain their prerogatives. The democratic, mixed-economy of the Weimar Republic could possibly have defeated the Nazis with more sophisticated understanding of the need to maintain a promise of a better order with justice and a willingness to fight the rising tide of barbarism. The churches, however, would not fight and could not understand.

From this essay, we can conclude that the liberal republics of the Western world are weakened if they do not understand the need for maintaining a sense of the myths of origin. Myths of origin in our day are expressed in terms of civil religion. But civil religion is not strong enough in periods of stress unless it maintains a sense of expectation or future promise combined with a strong commitment to social justice. Justice cannot be only the agreement of a society to order its life in a certain way, but it must be grounded in the conviction of the reality of a sovereign God who requires justice in periods of stress as well as times of affluence.

In our society, the civil rights movement, particularly as it was led by Martin Luther King, Jr., combined the affirmation of the American myths of origin in the Declaration of Independence, the U.S. Constitution, and the American dream with the demands of justice for the oppressed and the poor. The movement combined a willingness to fight, though nonviolently, for justice with a grounding of the fight in the democratic ideals of the country. The sense of expectation that the country would change toward fairness toward its oppressed was vital to the success of the movement. When it lost its expectation with the assassination of King and as the movement surrendered the nonviolent strategy, it clouded its ideals to the point that its achievements were limited. Myth, critique of myth in terms of justice, and sense of expectation are vital to the expansion of further democratization in the liberally oriented republics of the Western world.

Theology of Liberation

The most exciting contemporary movement to relate politics to faith is that of the theology of liberation. Theologies of liberation have grounded their theologies in various social movements. Commentators distinguish between women's theology of liberation, black theology of liberation in its various forms of Caribbean, North American, and African theologies, and Latin American theology of liberation. All these forms of liberation theology identify with the social-political causes of their respective movements and engage in theology as critical reflection for and upon these historical movements.

The success of the Sandinista Revolution in Nicaragua and the role of theologians in that revolutionary movement attach an urgency to the examination of liberation theology in Latin America. The Latin American form of liberation theology has arisen from theological reflection upon new forms of Christian community. Thousands (perhaps a hundred thousand) of "grassroot," basic Christian communities have grown in Latin America in the last two decades. These basic Christian communities unite for worship, Bible study, social analysis and mutual support. A fascinating example of their dialogic work together is recorded in Ernesto Cardenal's four volumes of *The Gospel in Solentiname*. Here one can learn how peasants, artisans, poets and priests studied and lived together. The reality of suffering under the Somoza regime is dramatized through peasant voices and accounts of martyrdom. The process of a developing Christian political consciousness is revealed. Eventually the Bible study, the social analysis, worship, and mutual support lead some to participation in armed revolution. Now the two priest brothers in the dialogue, Ernesto and Fernando Cardenal, are members of the new government. The United States is trying to undermine the new Sandinista government, fearing Marxism and larger unrest in Central America. The long history of United States' resistance to revolutionary movements in Central America dominates U.S. policy. The Somoza family whom the Sandinistas overthrew had been U.S. clients. The stage is set for a direct conflict between U.S. policy and believers who do liberation theology.

The battle on the foreign policy level is also an intra-church battle. Pope John Paul II fears and criticizes the development of a popular or people's church. His own politics and theology incline him to distrust Christian common fronts with Marxists. He warns against ideological distortions within the popular church, meaning the basic Christian communities. He appeals for the recognition of the authority of bishops in the church. The struggle is not only of popular Christianity versus hierarchical Catholicism. The struggle goes on within the hierarchy as well, as the results of the Bishops' Councils of Medellin and Puebla reveal. The Protestant churches of Latin America fragment, also, on the issue of political involvement to change the present system. Thus Christianity in Latin America, supportive of the present social situation of terrible poverty, extraordi-nary wealth and military repression, is thrown into confusion.

The social reality out of which Latin American liberation theology has come is that of degrading poverty and military oppression. The liberation theologians have abandoned hope for help with development from the developed countries under the present structures. They see the relationship of the developed countries to the poor countries as one of the rich exploiting the poor and enforcing that exploitation with whatever means necessary.

Five central themes of liberation theology are: 1) God is on the side of the oppressed; 2) In Latin America, oppression is systemic; 3) Participation in lib-eration is a work of salvation; 4) The church must become the church of the poor; 5) Theology is critical reflection on the project of social liberation.[4]

An engagement with the movement articulated by liberation theology can help Reformed Christians to: 1) Rediscover their own history of political in-volvement with the poor; 2) Rediscover the political dimensions of neglected portions of the Bible; 3) Reexamine the connections between Calvinism and capitalism; 4) Remember that Calvinist Christians are committed to social re-form.[5]

Comparative reflection upon the Calvinist heritage and the emerging work of liberation theology, then, helps us to rediscover our own social ethic and to challenge our complicity with suffering and murder in Latin America. Calvinism has some cautions to offer the liberation theologies. Theology is about God and it strives for universality. The doctrine of sin is central to any theology and particu-larly to theologies of politics. In Reformed theology scripture is primary; it in-forms experience.[6] We can say with liberation theology that theology must in-clude critical reflection on the liberation of the poor, but we must say it in light of the whole of scripture.

Reformed theology in dialogue with liberation theology is helped to hear afresh its commitment to transform the world. Reformed theology will still insist that the Kingdom of God is always relevant to political change, but not the same as political change. It cannot give up its insight that politics is ambiguous while calling for a theology of politics to serve the poor. Reformed theology insists upon a religious reservation about politics that disinclines it from affirming uto-pian politics while affirming a politics for change inspired by the Kingdom of God.

The New Religious Right

Religion thrust its way into American politics of the 1980s with surprising vigor. Religious rhetoric usually had been a part of political campaigning. In some regions of the country it was politically important to be religiously correct. Most successful politicians learned early that, even if they were not religious, it was smart to appear religious near to election time. However in the election of 1980 conservative, particularly fundamentalist, religious leaders organized voter registration drives, T.V. political campaigning, political rallies, and direct-mail campaigning that startled the nation. The conservative religious leaders utilized all the tactics the moderate to liberal religious leadership had exercised over the years and added an increased capacity to raise funds, a more sophisticated utilization of T.V., and computerized lists for frequent political and religious mailings that outshown the tactics of their opponents.

Liberal Senators and Congresspeople were defeated and the New Christian Right appeared as a political force to be reckoned with. How are Presbyterians who appeal to the same God to understand this new religious movement that opposes much of the social teaching of the Presbyterian Church?

There are two perspectives for understanding the fundamentalist contribution to these new right politics. The first perspective is that of seeing fundamentalism as a militant demand for a respected place in society by those whose values and views had been dismissed by the secularizing society. Fundamentalism was an irrational project of those whose America had changed from under them. The second approach is to see fundamentalism as an ideology with deep roots in the mainstream of Protestant evangelical theology. Marsden's essay synthesizes the two views. Yes, the fundamentalists who are now political activists are bitter that their country has become pluralistic, secularized and in their perspective internationally weaker and sexually depraved. However, fundamentalism is also a complex belief system, as coherent as many others, with its own distinctive traditions and deep roots.[7]

In the current scene, political fundamentalism is affirming the political activist side of their tradition, which is a modification of the Puritan perspective by their experience of the nineteenth and early twentieth century. This perspective sees an America turning away from its foundations of Christian principles. God's blessing on America varies with the degree to which it obeys God's laws. Of particular concern to the religious right are laws to protect the nuclear family. Abortion, pornography, and homosexuality are evidence of the flaunting of God's laws, and America is receiving God's anger in its decline. The Equal Rights Amendment was seen as an assault on God's law of how the family should be structured.

The demand to counter evolutionary teaching and for prayer in the public schools are both seen as restoring America to its more Christian roots. The practice of the new religious right is part of the democratic process, but its program is a return to a perception of a prior order. The myth of a righteous-Christian America is used to change governmental policy, in a time when the pluralistic-critical-liberal myth seems to be tottering.

Other elements of the purer America myth are a strong national defense and laisséz faire economics. More investment in defense is assumed to produce greater wealth. The myth then is of a religious America that will not demand sacrifice or tough decisions from anyone. Prosperity and security will flow with an opposition to the deviant sexual policies of others, the renewal of prayer in schools, the defense of creationism, and general moral revival.

The myth is not too strong, but in periods of great stress revolutionary myths may not need to be too credible to exert influence. Particularly if the public is willing to accept slogans as guides to politics, then oversimplified T.V. messages and mailings can undercut the information and debate needed to make a republican form of government function.

The commitment to political activism on the part of religious conservatives is to be welcomed. They certainly are correct that their faith impels them to participate in morally reforming America. Criticism that the new Christian right oversimplifies political issues must also be directed at many if not most of the politicians in the United States. The very reliance on T.V. for political information oversimplifies the choice before the body politic. The organization of the Moral Majority, the National Christian Action Coalition, the Christian Voice Moral Government Fund, Religious Roundtable and others is designed to avoid improper intrusion of the church into government.[8] They are skillfully using voluntary association models of organization to impact public policy and politics. The critique of their politics is best joined at the level that it is unbiblical and immoral to support policies which hurt the poor. It is a violation of shalom and Jesus' call for us to be peacemakers to support the increased building of nuclear weapons.[9] Policies and programs which encourage moral and political absolution are inherently detrimental to a political system that requires compromise. Laisséz faire economics, Victorian images of family, absolute support for Taiwan and South Korea are not Biblical imperatives. Prescriptions for and predictions of the future of the world are not available from *The Revelation of John* which was written in and for the Roman Empire. *Genesis* does not teach a theory of science about the origin of humanity or geology.

Voters will support right wing religious leaders naively. Many have also supported progressive religious leaders and their candidates naively. Both forms of political naivete are to be deplored. But the challenge to a more serious religious political engagement should be welcomed by Presbyterians.

Church-State

The history of the church's engagement with the state shows that no one pattern of church-state relationships is absolute. Our American pattern of maximum freedom for the church to worship, teach, proselytize, and act in society is still not the predominant pattern among most of the world's population. The combination of the freedom of religion clause and no establishment clause in our Bill of Rights was a bold act at the time of its promulgation. It defied the commonly accepted patterns of Europe. Gradually, freedom of religion has become an increasingly accepted norm of humanity, but in practice it is severely curtailed throughout much of the world.

The history of the relationship of church to state in this country even with the constitutional basis has been an evolving process which has still not reached a final form.[10] The churches in America have learned to be thankful for their freedom from the state. This freedom has encouraged the health and vitality of the churches themselves, prevented discrimination against particular expressions of religious conscience by other religious groups, and left religious groups free to witness to the society in terms of their religious convictions.

The people of the United States are a very religious people, as studies from de Tocqueville to the latest Gallup Poll have shown. It is inevitable that a civil religious spirit arises, and within limits it is appropriate for this common religious sense to be evoked at national ceremonies and in times of stress. The danger of civil religion inheres in its temptation to national idolatry. This danger is best avoided by the particular faiths criticizing civil religion if it becomes too nationalistic or too sentimental. Abraham Lincoln's skillful use of Biblical faith is a good example of the Biblical teachings of God's transcendence and justice correcting civil religion's tendency to become too provincial or partisan. The vitality of the churches' own teaching is the best protection against inherent dangers in civil religion.

The Supreme Court has only opened the door a crack to support for parochial education. The arguments of supporters of parochial education that in the name of fairness their schools deserve more public monies has some merit. However, the explosion of parochial education which could accompany any widespread system of supporting financially any education parents would choose would vitiate the public educational system. The religious education children need can be provided through church educational programs without entering into governmental support for church education. On both constitutional grounds and reasons of the public good, continued reluctance to open public monies to church education seems a wise policy. The Supreme Court's rigidity on non-support for parochial education may have saved the country from a deeper crisis with the current explosion of religious schools.

The abortion issue has traditionally raised questions about the church-state issue. The power of the Roman Catholic church to exercise political clout on this issue has been deeply resented by Protestants and secularists alike. It has seemed as if one church's theology has been overriding the theological positions of other churches. The emergence of the issue as the banner issue by the new religious right complicates the picture even more. After surveying the many denominations that oppose legislation outlawing all abortion, John Bennett warned: "An absolutistic law against abortion would force many people in these religious traditions to act against their consciences, but the absence of such a law does not force anyone to go against his or her conscience."[11] Still because some regard abortion as murder, the struggle will go on. The struggle over a constitutional amendment will be a political fight reflecting deeply held religious beliefs. Presbyterians who may generally deplore most abortions will not want to see overly restrictive laws infringe upon conscience. They have recognized that in some situations abortion can be responsibly chosen. To justify the demand for anti-abortion legislation or the withholding of public funds for abortions for the poor, the argument will have to be established that such acts will produce less social harm than the present national policy respecting the privacy of the woman's conscience.

Roman Catholics and Reformed Christians discussed the abortion issue during 1976-1979 in Round III of the Roman Catholic/Presbyterian-Reformed Consultation. The Reformed commentary on the joint statement on abortion is here affirmed:

The separation of church and state in the United States should not be so interpreted as to preclude the right of the church to influence civil policy. However, the very separation of church and state places certain limits upon the manner of the influence which the church exerts. No limit is placed upon the church's right to influence civil policy by educational methods.

Nor would we seek legislation which curtails the freedom of religious expression for others. Accordingly, no legislation should require abortion where forbidden for religious reasons, nor preclude abortion where it is desired for religious reasons. Thus attempts to influence policy in the United States should focus on the secular aims of the legislation rather than the religious beliefs of those who promote or those who oppose it.

Moreover, single-issue advocacy is of exceedingly high risk for Christian activists, both to the state and to the church. It harms the credibility of the church as a trans-political institution when the church appears to be no more than one more political pressure group, and it threatens the integrity of the state by weakening the broad base of political leadership.[12]

Voluntary prayer is an option in the public school system now. The issue is whether schools can recognize and encourage a form of prayer that does not move toward establishing a religion or that does not violate someone's freedom of religion. It is hard to conceive how a prayer can be addressed to God in particular words without choosing a particular form of prayer. If the Virgin Mary is addressed, or if the prayer is in the name of Jesus, it advocates a certain religious interpretation. A period of silence might be constitutionally acceptable, but then only minimal gains have been made for anyone's religious sensitivity. It is better for the sake of our pluralism and our freedom of religion not to coerce any youngster religiously in the schools. Parents and church can present teaching in prayer and the child will pray and be reverent in all of life as it is appropriate in our culture. The types of prayers that might be adopted by our school boards or our teachers are bound to be offensive to some and in many cases not very religiously profound. Prayer may be left to the individuals, the homes, the churches and keep it out of the public schools in any formal sense.

Prayer in the public schools, like required teaching of creationism, is an important symbolic issue for the new religious right in its campaign for American nostalgia. The establishment of either would not add to the education or piety of our children.

The New Testament teaching about church and state can be summarized as: "Civil authority is seen as part of God's plan and ruling, but it is not in itself divine. Only God is lord, never Caesar!"[13] Peter put it for himself and the Apostles: "We must obey God rather than men" (Acts 5:30). The church as God's gathered people listens to its own sources of truth and goes its own way. This will inevitably from time to time bring the church into conflict with the state. In our day the conflict in this country that may be the most significant is over issues of war and peace.

The churches listening to their members in all parts of the globe cannot bow before the ideology of a nation's security. The Confession of 1967 put this truth as follows:

> God's reconciliation in Jesus Christ is the ground of the peace, justice and freedom among nations which all powers of government are called to serve and defend. The church in its own life, is called to practice the forgiveness of enemies and to commend to the nations as practical policies the search for cooperation and peace. This requires the pursuit of fresh and responsible relations across every line of conflict, even at risk to national security to reduce areas of strife and to broaden international understanding.

As members of a universal community worshiping a God who has no favorites among the nations, Christians are not awed by claims of national interest or national security.

Confronted by ever-increasing expenditures and ever more fantastic planning for nuclear war, Christians are brought into tension with the state. As they choose to be faithful to Christ as peacemakers, the tension with existing national security policies increases. They are led to seek out new policies and to say no to militarism. Saying no to national policy may eventually change national policy, as it did in Vietnam. However, national policy may not change and it may cause suffering to faithful Christians. The gift of Christ's peace may require martyrdom.[14]

Biblical Resources

The Biblical messages inform our total lives and our whole perspective on the relationship of faith to politics. For us Christians, such messages function as internal guides for our thoughts and action. We have grown up on the history of Abraham, the migrant man of faith; Moses, the prophetic law giver; David, the righteous and troubled king; Amos, the critic of the kingdoms; Mary, who sang of God tearing imperial powers from their thrones; and Jesus, the proclaimer and martyr of the Kingdom of God. However, we must move beyond the general way the Bible has made us and informed the church to take our issue of faith and politics specifically to the Bible.

It is very difficult to relate the Bible to our politics. The Bible is so vast, encompassing wisdom about God and politics from a thousand-year period. Politics is such a broad abstraction, covering foreign policy issues between empires to conversations about street safety for our children. Our times are quite different from Biblical times. A focus primarily on the farewell passages (Chs. 13-17) in the Gospel of John, narrows down the problem. The ultimate issues are found where the commands of Jesus are most heatedly resisted. The issue was between Jesus as King of Israel and the rulers of the world. To follow Jesus is to follow his way and the readers of the Gospel could clearly hear this might mean martyrdom.

Expanding beyond John to other *New Testament* texts, three answers to the relationship of the Bible to politics are excluded: apathy, "single-issue" politics, and reduction of politics to voting. Faith calls for the total person's engagement with utmost seriousness in the arenas which resist Christ's peace. Certainly followers of Christ will not be able to rest in political apathy, or in self-seeking use of one-issue politics to gain power, or in thinking that Christian discipleship only means voting after a searching study of John 11-13.[15]

The 117th General Assembly of the Presbyterian Church in the U.S. adopted *A Declaration of Faith* which is cross indexed to scripture. The referenced scripture to the declaration below indicates the relevance of scripture to faith and politics.

> The church exists within political communities.
> Throughout its history the church has struggled
> to be faithful to God in political situations:
> under persecution,
> or as an established arm of the state,
> or in separation from it.
> God rules over both political and religious institutions.
> We must confuse neither with the kingdom of God.
> We must not equate the Christian faith
> with any nation's way of life
> or with opposition to the ideologies of other nations.
> We hold Christians are to be law-abiding citizens
> unless the state commands them to disobey God,
> or claims authority that belongs only to God.
> We must not allow governments
> to impose Christian faith by legislation,
> nor should we demand undue advantages for the church.
> The church must be free to speak to civil authorities,
> neither claiming expert knowledge it does not have,
> nor remaining silent when God's Word is clear.[16]

The scripture references are to: 1) 2 Samuel 12:1-15 describing the conflict between the prophet Nathan and the King David over David's unjust orders for Uriah's death; 2) I Kings 21 detailing Elijah's prophecy against Ahab for the death of Naboth and the expropriation of his vineyard; 3) Isaiah 37 recounting Isaiah's role in interpreting to Hezekiah the defeat of Sennacherib; 4) Romans 13:1-7 in which Paul expresses the authority of God recognized in secular rulers, even pagan Roman emperors; 5) I Peter 2:11-17 exhorting Christians to live as free people and as slaves to God, putting ignorance to silence by good conduct; and 6) Revelation 14:9-11 urging God's people to keep God's commands, remaining loyal to Jesus even in defiance of pagan political demands of worship of the state.

I Samuel 8 in which Samuel agrees reluctantly to end the period of charismatic-religious leadership in Israel and to give Israel a king underlies much of the political theology of this background paper. I Samuel 8 testifies that even kingship is given by God to humanity. Charismatic-religious leadership was preferable, but it failed in Samuel's sons who took bribes and perverted justice.

Kingship became necessary, but I Samuel 8 details the burdens of taxation, the taking of children for the military, the seizing of the land, and the pretensions of government. Religious leadership concedes reluctantly to government, as government is awkward, expensive, and usually unjust. Yet government is necessary, even God wills it. I Samuel 8 captures the sense of the ambiguity surrounding politics that this paper affirms. It recognizes the religiously sanctioned need for government. It points to the need for continued critique and participation in government as Samuel himself represented it. Historically we can see that here in scripture religious-political leadership is succeeded in history by a more secular-political leadership which is still under God. There is a provisional separation of religion and politics in Israel, but also a continuous engagement best represented in prophetic religion.

Our History

Presbyterian resistance to the church acting in society is rooted in ignorance of Presbyterian history. For the founder of the Presbyterian strand of the reformation was continually involved in reforming society through prayer, preaching, organizing, and political action. John Calvin (1509-1564) adopted the inward faith of Martin Luther, but he articulated its ethics in a world-transforming direction.

His understanding of Christian ethics relied on the whole Bible, honoring the role of the Old Testament in norms as well as the New Testament. The summary of Christian life was found in the Ten Commandments, the double love commandment of Jesus, and in natural law under the guidance of Christian love. The church's role was to advise the political rulers as well as to pray for them. The correctness of God's law expressed in natural law could be perceived by human conscience. Because of the fall away from original righteousness, the conscience had to be guided by Biblical law. The great strength of his developed social ethic was in its commitment to transform society; its weakness lay in a tendency toward legalism and severity of discipline when it was implemented.

The state had an honored place in the theology of John Calvin, who devoted the final chapter of his *Institutes of the Christian Religion* to explaining his theology of politics. The holders of public office were to be respected and honored, as their work was of God. Though Calvin knew of the foolishness of public office holders and joined in campaigns to remove politicians, he wrote:

Wherefore no doubt ought now to be entertained by any person that civil magistracy is a calling not only holy and legitimate, *but far the most sacred and honorable in human life.*[17]

Calvin worked for a moderate government of regulated liberty in which the most meritorious of the citizens would exercise power. Though no advocate of revolution in his day, he knew the need for civil disobedience against idolatrous demands, and he opened Christian political theory to the overthrow of unjust monarchs. The crack he opened to Christian revolution became a wide door in the development of his thought in the hands of French, Dutch, English and Scotch followers.

He taught that the state had to regulate life to protect the poor from the rich. He personally participated in starting industries for the unemployed, in regulating commerce to protect the weak, and in establishing relief services for refugees, free education, and city-run medical services.

The church, though having its primary role in the spiritual realm, had to serve the public realm. It prayed for the public holders of office. It lobbied the leaders of the body politic to establish justice, particularly for the poor. It warned rulers when their policies were unjust. Finally, and probably the only place where we would demur from Calvin's statecraft, was in the role he assigned the church to assist the state in promoting true religion and in enforcing church discipline. In this view he was typically of the sixteenth century and not of the New Testament. Four centuries of historical experience have led his followers in this country to hope that while the state will not do anything to suppress true religion, we do not need its assistance in enforcing one strand of religious persuasion. We now affirm the teaching of the early church that the state is incompetent in matters of religious life and we ask to be left free from state interference.

The contribution of Calvinism to religious liberty did not find sufficient expression in Calvin's Geneva. It remained for John Milton and other Calvinists in the Netherlands and England to work out Reformed grounds for religious freedom. However, James Madison, who learned his Christian social ethics at the feet of the Presbyterian minister John Witherspoon at Princeton, wrote: "Let not Geneva be forgotten or despised. Religious liberty owes it much respect, Servetus notwithstanding."

Though much has been written about the worldview of Calvinism supporting the development of science and technology, its contribution to the American system of politics is even more evident. Whether we locate the direct influences in James Madison drafting the Constitution, or in the New England heritage of Puritanism, or in the Calvinistic insights present within the vaguely Christian deism of the founding fathers, the affinity of Calvinist ideas and the American political system is striking. The contribution of the Calvinists can be seen in: 1) The separation of church and state and the high value attached to both; 2) the recognition of the continual struggle to reform the society through law for human good; 3) the need for voluntary associations of people covenanting together for the health of politics; 4) the utilization of broad traditions of human wisdom for political ethics; 5) the value of a system of social ethics which includes standards of justice and processes of application of justice to cases; 6) the need for political systems to be constitutionally regulated and under law; and 7) the need for checks and balances within political systems because of the reality of human sin.

In the American experience Presbyterians have participated actively in their church bodies and in their scattered ministries in the political process.[18] The history of the Presbyterian church involvement in the revolution, in the abolitionist movement, in sabbath and temperance campaigns, in issues of war and economy does not reveal unanimity on significant issues. It does make the social-political activism clear, especially where major moral issues are seen to be at stake.

Presbyterians as a distinct religious minority in a secularizing and pluralistic nation cannot pretend their understanding of Christian ethics will be acceptable to the whole nation. There is a role for a self-conscious, theologically informed minority to play in the continued reform of the United States. The history of Presbyterian involvement in politics is full of fanaticism, ignorance, and complicity with evil. It is also a history of well-informed, theologically literate, wise policies in the public realm for the public good. This part of the history, particularly, needs to be affirmed.

Christian Political Ethics

A central question of political ethics is: "Why ought one to obey the state?" A Christian political ethic puts a different question: "How can we love God in serving our neighbors through politics?" The purpose of humanity is to love God and to help the neighbor know the love of God. Therefore, Christian political ethics cannot be autonomous; that is, Christians cannot think of the state as an order independent of God which they are free either to remold or to rebel against apart from God. Christian political ethics are not heteronomous; that is, the laws of the state are not obligatory on Christians apart from God. Christian political ethics are theonomous; they are the ordering of government for the purposes of God.

There is of course a lot of human wisdom about political order founded in either autonomy, or heteronomy, or even in non-Christian religious traditions. But the Christian political ethic is seeking to understand the political dimensions in light of God's purposes for humanity. The human wisdom will be utilized, but it is to be evaluated in terms of the insights of Christian faith grounded in the revelation of God's nature in Jesus as the Christ.

All human wisdom about political order must for Christian political ethics be regarded from the perspective of how it serves the concrete good of the neighbor. God wills the freedom and peace of the world's people. The Bible provides us with testimony to the occasion of God's struggle to realize shalom and freedom for the people of Israel and the church. This testimony of God's love being expressed in rulers, in legislation, and in movements of liberation, both spiritual and political, is the guide for contemporary formulation of Christian political ethics.

John Calvin's *Institutes of the Christian Religion* distinguishes between the spiritual realm and the political realm. They are distinguished but related. Calvin writes more about the ordering of the spiritual realm, but the ordering of the political realm is a clear responsibility for the Christian. In fact no earthly vocation is of a higher calling than that to political responsibility. The ordering of the political realm is carried out by reference to the natural law. The natural law expresses the law of God in terms of justice which is the purpose and norm of all human laws. If laws express justice, it is not necessary in Calvin's political theory that they correspond to the particulars of Biblical law. Biblical legislation was detailed for its day; in our day the standard of justice will inform us as to the detailed laws for our time.

In Reformed thought, liberty can be obtained in the spiritual realm without

[18]

being realized in the political realm. Given the tyrannies most people have lived under, we are thankful that spiritual freedom can exist without social liberation. Freedom in the political realm cannot exist without freedom in the spiritual realm. Freedom, particularly Christian freedom, in the spiritual realm, drives for expression in the political realm. It is a great thing to know both spiritual and political freedom; God wills it.

To quote Max Weber: "Politics is the slow boring of hard boards." A political ethic to be Christian takes cognizance of the human refusal to love and fear God and of the inhumanity neighbors render to neighbors. It acknowledges that people will misuse political power when they achieve it. In short, it takes account of sin. Sin basically is the refusal to trust and love God and the resultant disarray in human relations. Racism, sexism, militarism, and economic exploitation all have their roots in the human refusal to trust God. Humans violate the freedom of other humans and organize their political world in rebellion against God. Still God works through the political world to protect humanity and to counter the results of human sin. Therefore politics remains ambiguous. It is both God's working to liberate humanity from human evil and an expression of human evil. The reduction of the human evil to manageable proportions is the never-ending task of anyone who, inspired by God's love, takes up the task of political responsibility.

The Biblical term for the goal of the political life is justice (Amos 5:21-24, Micah 6:8, Jeremiah 22:15-16, Isaiah 1:14-17, Deuteronomy 16:18-20, Psalm 33:5, Proverbs 21:3, Luke 4:18, Romans 14:17). A just order presupposes the denial of oppression and liberation from the oppressor. It involves the overthrowing of human evil. It is fair distribution of the earth's resources so that all have opportunity to flourish. It is the recognition of each person's right to be a free human being. Justice is the expression under conditions of human sin of the imperative of God to love one another. The Christian sense of justice is more than Aristotle's "To each his due"; it is to each his due as a loved child of God.

Many institutions of life contribute toward justice. The political order, though, as the central coordinating order of society, has particularly awesome responsibilities in securing a reasonable approximation of justice. Pure justice in either its philosophical expression or in terms of total equity is unattainable in history. God's love, however, requires the constant struggle for justice and the removal of those who in their roles as public servants impede justice. John Calvin wrote of God's overthrow of intolerable governments and said: "Let the princes hear and be afraid" (*Institutes*, IV.20.31).

The history of Western society since the Reformation has been a long, bloody struggle to achieve a tolerably just order. Reformed political thought, while seeking to realize justice as the social realization of love, has learned from this history. The Reformed churches were not in their origins tolerant; revolutionary movements never are. The failure of any one form of Reformed thought to carry the day within the sectarian controversies led it finally in John Locke, John Milton and others to recognize that toleration was a principle of justice. God tolerates many errors and political society can tolerate error, encourage pluralism, and survive when people covenant together to respect diversity. The U.S. Constitution, in forbidding the establishment of religion, encouraging freedom in speech, assembly, and press, recognized the need for toleration. The Constitution also recognized that legislation had to be adequate to the social dynamics of a society. So while ignoring Thomas Jefferson's recommendation of frequent revolutions, it provided for the reform of constitutional order. The Reformed concern for proper polity and democratic procedures in church government reinforced the movement of government of the society according to democratic and predictable rules of behavior.

The distribution of the powers of government among different centers both protected liberty from tyrannical usurpation and forced governmental decisions to be acceptable to major interests within the society. It also slowed down the speed with which governmental decisions could be made and allowed considerations of prudence to exert weight on decisions. Though the distribution of powers was probably to avoid the perceived dangers of either mob rule or tyranny, it also reflects Madison's realism about the human beings who would actually administer the government.

The movement of large segments of the population into the political process of the country has increased the pressures for equality and liberty. Equality means the elimination of arbitrary distinctions in society. The basic recognition that people are equal in their rights and that each person is to be treated equally with one's self pushes the reforming agenda in society. The present degree to which one's opportunities are determined by the social stratum into which one is born is revolting even if less obnoxious than at some previous periods. Given the recognition of equality in the 1776 Declaration of Independence, the 1789 Declaration of the Rights of Man, the 1948 Universal Declaration of Human Rights, the continued existence of oligarchic privileges on the basis of birth in Western society is a measure of the gap between ideals and reality. The resistance to the straightforward Equal Rights Amendment also bears stark evidence of the ancient and persistent privileges claimed by males over females.

Martin Luther King, Jr.'s, use of the text from Amos 5:24, "Let justice roll down like waters" was an appeal to liberty as well as equality. Liberation from the oppressive terror of the white population was the goal as well as social and economic equality. Wherever oppression exists, liberty is to be struggled for and God, according to the Bible and Reformed political thought, does not use only the means of the ballot box or nonviolent resistance to change the mind of the oppressor. In America, the ballot box and nonviolent tactics of coercion may be the best tools and God may move people to their use, but they are not the tools of God for many other situations. Liberation is a principle of justice, as is equalization. But it is not a self-sufficient definition of the goals of Reformed political thought. Reformed political ethics are complex, requiring the ongoing struggle for justice as an expression of God's love. In the Western world equality and liberty are mediating principles of justice. They are guided by actions which will order a society toward justice through: toleration, predictable rules, prudence, and personality.

To recognize personality as part of the meaning of justice is to honor the wisdom in all of the declarations of the rights of humanity, and to resist tendencies to reduce personality to a thing. Basic to the meaning of justice is personhood and any movement that reduces people to less than persons is to be resisted. There is a spiritual freedom of the person even in situations of oppression, but that freedom is not justice. It is unjust to treat people with less respect than they have as images of God on which their personhood depends.

A Reformed goal is the maximum human liberty tolerable without harm to others. Calvin argued for liberty without licentiousness. Law is a bulwark against disorder. However as law relies on sanctions it can become oppressive. As the state legislates morality for the common good, it must exercise caution that it is protecting liberty while legislating against truly harmful acts.[19] Arguments for particular legislation must be grounded in the moral consensus of the nation and correspond to standards of natural law summarized as justice.

So Reformed Christians are called out of a love for God to be politically active. They are expected to recognize the political order as an ambiguous arena in which they work with God. Freedom in Christ is not dependent on political freedom but it contributes to political freedom. Longing for the Kingdom of God, the Reformed Christian does not expect worldly utopias but knows that God seeks just order for the children of God. A just order will practice toleration, government by rules, prudent politics, and the protection of personality. Liberty and equality are expressions of love to be striven for in societies which will realize them according to their own history. God will in God's own way, beyond our knowing, bring fulfillment in the Community of God.

Endnotes

1. Professor Anne Murphy analyzes the current problems in the American political system in her essay commissioned for the study volume, *Reformed Faith and Politics*, Chp. 14.
2. Professor Dorothy Dodge sketched the changes in the political system of the USA in the last decade and argued that far-reaching changes are possible in the 1980s in her essay for *Reformed Faith and Politics*, Chp. 10.
3. See: Paul Minear in *Reformed Faith and Politics*, Chp. 3.
4. The Reverend Albert C. Winn exposited liberation theology for the volume, *Reformed Faith and Politics*, and the comments in the background paper reflect his work, Chp. 6.
5. Ibid.
6. Ibid.
7. The discussion of the fundamentalist approach to politics is dependent upon Professor George Marsden's research. See: His essay in *Reformed Faith and Politics*, Chp. 5.
8. See: Peggy L. Shriver's descriptive essay on the new Christian right commissioned for *Reformed Faith and Politics*, Chp. 4.
9. The exegesis of Professor Paul Minear's essay on the farewell discourses of Jesus in *Reformed Faith and Politics* supports this argument as does the repeated positions of the PCUS and UPCUSA in their endorsement of nuclear freeze campaign and in their policy statement, *Peacemaking: The Believer's Calling*.
10. The papers by Professors John C. Bennett and Jane Dempsey Douglas in *Reformed Faith and Politics* and the unpublished address at the Purdue meeting of the United

Presbyterian Women, July, 1982, by William P. Thompson, Stated Clerk of the UP-CUSA are drawn upon in formulating the church-state discussion, Chps. 7, 9.
11. Ibid.
12. *Ethics and the Search for Christian Unity* (Washington: United States Catholic Conference, 1981), pp. 27-28.
13. Jane Dempsey Douglas in *Reformed Faith and Politics,* Chp. 7.
14. Paul Minear in *Reformed Faith and Politics*, Chp. 3.
15. Ibid.
16. *A Declaration of Faith* (Atlanta: General Assembly PCUS, 1977), pp. 16-17.
17. *Institutes of the Christian Religion*, (Philadelphia: The Westminster Press, 1960) IV.20.4, underlining added.
18. Professor Louis Week's research on Presbyterians in American politics forms the basis for the discussion of the background paper. See: His essay in *Reformed Faith and Politics*, Chp. 8.
19. David Little, "Legislating Morality: The Role of Religion," *Christianity and Politics: Catholic and Protestant Perspectives* (Washington: Ethics and Public Policy Center, 1981).

FAITH AND POLITICS: THE DIFFERENCES

George A. Chauncey

What differences can and ought our faith make in our politics? I want to suggest three differences that faith does not make and cannot make, and for which, therefore, no claims for faith ought to be made. Then I want to identify five differences that faith can, ought to, and sometimes does make in the political life of the faithful.

Differences faith does not and cannot make

First, *faith does not and cannot give us certainty about God's will on particular political or economic issues.* Faith does not enable us to claim God's endorsement for any particular political platform, economic policy, or political economic system. On the contrary, faith forbids our absolutizing anything that is relative.

This is not to say that we can know nothing of God's will and intention for humankind, or that no illumination at all is provided by faith and beliefs about God as we make difficult political and economic choices.

The God of Biblical faith clearly delights in justice and despises injustice. The Holy One of Israel clearly shows particular concern for the poor and the oppressed and holds the rich and powerful accountable for their dealings with the needy and powerless. The Lord of the universe clearly demands care of the created order and holds us responsible for our stewardship of what has been entrusted to us. The case is not that God has given us no clues whatsoever about how we are to govern ourselves, organize our economy, or stand on particular issues. On the contrary, the Biblical revelation provides much more specificity than most of us care for!

Yet, despite the clarity of the revelation of God's good intentions for and claims on the human family, faith never provides us absolute certainty about the rightness—not to mention the righteousness—of our stance on particular political and economic issues. This is because political judgments are always human judgments; and human judgments are always made, alas, by human beings who are finite, fallible, and flawed. Thus, while we always have the obligation to

[23]

REFORMED FAITH AND POLITICS

make our political judgments in light of our deepest beliefs about God, we never have the right to claim God's authorization for the judgments we make. Reinhold Niebuhr has reminded us of the danger of assuming otherwise:

> The sorry annals of Christian fanaticism, of unholy religious hatreds, of sinful ambitions hiding behind the cloak of religious sanctity, of political power impulses compounded with pretensions of devotion to God, offer the most irrefutable proof of the error in every Christian doctrine and every interpretation of the Christian experience which claim that grace can remove the final contradiction between (human beings) and God. The sad experiences of Christian history show how human pride and spiritual arrogance rise to new heights precisely at the point where the claims of sanctity are made without due qualification.[1]

In the second place, *faith does not produce instant consensus in the Christian community.* It does not engender unanimity of judgment. It does not prompt total agreement on political and economic matters. Not all true believers are automatically Democrats! (I must confess that that latter truth was one of the most difficult for me to learn. I grew up during the Depression in the Deep South where, as a matter of fact, all true believers *were* Democrats. I was a grown man before I met my first Christian who was a Republican.)

Christians differ in their views because political and economic judgments are always compound of both faith and facts. Even those who share the same faith can and often do read the facts in different ways—and thus arrive at different political judgments.

The fact that we differ in our political and economic judgments is not a reality to be accepted with regret but one to be affirmed in joy. Debate in the Christian community on critical issues is a sign of vitality, evidence that people care. Besides, opposing views always keep all of us more honest. John Oldham offered half a century ago this vision of the church as a community of moral discourse on divisive issues:

> The church should be the place where barriers of race, nationality, class, sex and education are done away with . . .; a meeting ground where those who are divided in questions of politics and economics can realize afresh their unity in loyalty to a common Lord, can discuss their differences in the reality of this fellowship and learn to understand each other. In the modern disintegration of social life the church ought to provide centers in which (people) can find protection, shelter and security in the care and love of their (neighbors), and rediscover the meaning of community in the support and comradeship of a society the members of which bear one another's burdens and seek the good of all.[2]

Finally, *faith does not provide us that social analysis, economic understanding, and political savvy that is essential for effective political action.* Faith is no substitute for the facts. Good intentions don't take the place of political skills. Just because our hearts are wholesome and our motives pure, we are not relieved of the obligation to do our homework in political analysis and our legwork in organizing for action. William Lee Miller pointed to that truth when he observed that, "The trouble with the politics of many Christians is not that they aren't Christian enough; it's that they aren't political enough."[3] Winston Niles Rumfoord, Kurt Vonnegut's great historian of the war between Earth and Mars, put it like this:

> There is no reason why good cannot triumph as often as evil. The triumph of anything is a matter of organization. If there are such things as angels, I hope they are organized along the lines of the Mafia.[4]

If our faith does not give us certainty about God's will in particular situations, does not create instant consensus in the Christian community, and does not relieve us of our obligation to do our political homework, what does and can and ought it do? Five suggestions:

Some differences that faith can and ought to make

First, *faith—along with a sensitivity to the power and promise of politics— can and ought to provide us a strong motive for engaging in political action.* Our commitment to God and God's cause—along with an appreciation of politics as an arena for the service of God—can and ought to provide a powerful compulsion for us to get involved.

To express it like this is to acknowledge that there are two grounds for political engagement by believers—theological grounds, i.e., grounds growing out of our deepest convictions about God, and social analytical grounds, i.e., grounds growing out of our reading of politics.

What, then, are some of those convictions about God that can and ought to drive us into involvement? Here are a few:

God is sovereign. God is Lord. God is Lord not just of some people but of all people, not just of the church but of the world, not just of individuals and their inner dispositions but of institutions and their interactions, not just of some little sphere called the spiritual but of the whole complexity of human and natural existence.

This sovereign Lord loves and works in history for the well-being of all—all people, all nations, all classes, all races. God loves not just the church but the world, not just the chosen people but the whole human race they are chosen to serve. There is no person, no group whom God does not love and whose good God does not actively seek. God's good and gracious intention for the whole human community is *shalom*—peace, health, wholeness, harmony, security, well-being, joy.

This sovereign Lord who loves and works for the shalom of all has a particular concern for the poor, the needy, the helpless, the oppressed. God is partisan to such folk. God makes what John Bennett calls a "strategic concentration" of love on them. God sees their affliction, hears their cry, knows their suffering, and acts in history to liberate them. God demonstrates the character of the justice God demands by feeding the hungry, clothing the naked, empowering the powerless, and securing the rights of the poor.

Finally, because God has a passion for peace and justice, we are to have a passion for peace and justice. Because God shows partiality with and for the poor, we are to be partisans with and for the poor. Because God's cause is the cause of liberating the oppressed and empowering the weak and establishing shalom in the land, we are to make this cause our own. Such is our calling. As John Calvin put it:

> We are not our own; therefore, neither our reason nor our will should predominate in our deliberations and actions. We are not our own; therefore, let us not propose it as our end, to seek what may be expedient for us according to the flesh. We are not our own; therefore, as far as possible, let us forget ourselves and the things that are ours. On the contrary, we are God's; to (God), therefore let us live and die. We are God's; therefore let (God's) wisdom and will preside in all our actions. We are God's; toward (God), therefore, as our only legitimate end, let every part of our lives be directed.[5]

Is the political arena, then, an arena in which we are to serve God's cause? Two realities make the answer an overwhelming "Yes." One is that public policy decisions affect—for good or ill—millions and millions of God's loved ones. Through decisions made in Washington, Moscow or Tehran, people—God's people—are either hurt or helped; and peace and justice—God's intent for God's people—are either served or betrayed. Not everything in the world happens in Washington; but what happens in Washington affects practically everything in the world. Political decisions are important!

The other reality is that none of us can avoid making some sort of political witness—even if it is the negative one of silence and withdrawal. Politics is—among other things—a power struggle, a contest for the power to make decisions that affect the whole. In this struggle, neutrality is impossible because silence always implies consent to the stronger party in the struggle. For his purpose, Hitler did not need the praise of the church in Germany; he needed only its silence. For their purposes, militarists, racists, and sexists in this country don't need the church's active endorsement; they need only our passive consent.

Sensitivity to these two political realities, along with a devotion to God and God's cause, can and ought and sometimes does provide the faithful a powerful motive for getting involved.

In the second place, *faith can and ought to provide us a mission or purpose in involvement.* We ought to get actively involved for the purpose of securing peace and justice for the whole human family, with particular concern for securing the rights of the poor.

One of the strange developments in church history is that only a handful of relatively small church groups in this country—the Society of Friends, the Mennonites, the Church of the Brethren—are called "peace churches." What does that say—for pity's sake—about the Presbyterian, Methodist, and Baptist churches? What's the opposite of a "peace church" anyway?

I wish that I could believe that we mainline Christians were victims of some horrible misunderstanding. I wish that I could believe that we really were peace churches—a people consumed with a passion for peace and justice—and that we were simply misunderstood. But all of us know that the reason nobody considers the Presbyterian Church a "peace church" is that we Presbyterians have managed to keep our passion for peace and justice under strict control!

But are not making peace and seeking justice at the very heart of our calling as a Christian community? Did not Jesus say, "Blessed are the peacemakers . . ." (Matthew 5:9) and "Set your minds on God's kingdom and (God's) justice before everything else . . ." (Matthew 6:33, New English Bible)? Did not Paul remind us, "God has called us to peace" (I Corinthians 7:15)? Did not the prophet report this Word: "I, Yahweh, have called you to serve the cause of justice" (Isaiah 42:6, tr. by José Miranda)? Our mission is clear: We are to engage in politics for the sake of peace and justice.

In the third place, *faith can and ought to provide us moral standards for evaluating policy options before us.*

We human beings are incurably valuing animals. We constantly make value judgments about our jobs, our salaries, the economic situation, the policies of our government. We like some things and do not like others. We call some situations good and others bad.

We always make our value judgments in light of some standard, some cluster of beliefs, values, interests, concerns. When we call something good we do so because it conforms to the standard by which we are evaluating it. When we call something bad, it is because it violates or falls short of that standard.

Quite often we use a variety of standards for evaluating the same situation. That makes sense. Most things need to be looked at from a variety of angles. Will this thing work? What are the financial costs? the social costs? the political prospects?

What fidelity to God requires is that the *ultimate* question we ask of any political proposal be this: Is this consistent with what we know of God's intention for shalom, God's demand for justice, God's special concern for the poor? Ultimate here means determinative, governing, overriding. Thus, if a conflict arises between our economic self-interest and our ethical obligations to the poor, the former must yield to the latter. If we find that we cannot make as much money as possible and love and serve our neighbors, we must choose the way of love. If we discover that our nation's vital interests are in conflict with the moral right of another people to self-determination, our nation's interests, no matter how vital, must yield. Our ultimate standard for valuing policy proposals and political options must be the intent and claim of God. Beverly Harrison summarizes the Biblical perspective in this way:

> The people of God live under a stringent expectation of communal right relationships in which the meaning of justice is discerned particularly by the way the community deals with those who are most marginated, or are not well-placed to defend their own needs and interests. In biblical terms, the righteous community—the one rightly related to God—is the community

which expresses its fidelity to God through concern for the least well-off persons and groups. Jesus radicalized and deepened this prophetic theme of justice in praxis and teaching by identifying *his* continuing presence with the presence of those who were especially victimized by society's existing arrangements. A theologically based ethic . . . cannot aim at anything less than a social policy which takes special account of the effects of that policy on those already most disadvantaged in society.[6]

In the fourth place, *faith can and ought to produce a distinctive manner or style of political action.* Our trust in God should affect not only why we get involved and what we get involved for, but also the way in which we engage in political activity. "Let your manner of life," says Paul—and this includes political life—"be worthy of the gospel" (Philippians 1:27).

What manner of political life would be worthy of the gospel? I have already suggested some things that I think ought to characterize our political action: a passion for peace and justice that reflects God's passion for peace and justice; a partisanship with and for the poor that mirrors God's special concern; a sense of stewardship that compels us to do both homework and legwork; and a humility that grows out of an acute awareness that on any particular issue we may well be dead wrong. Another dimension of a Christian manner of political life is freedom. Confidence in God—in God's lordship, God's love, God's faithfulness— ought to set us free for creative political activity.

Confidence in God's lordship, for example—the firm awareness that God alone is Lord, that God alone is absolute, that everything else is relative—ought to free us to raise all sorts of questions about our society and its assumptions. Because we know that God alone is ruler, we ought to feel free to inquire about the emperor's clothes. Because we know that God alone is holy, we should not hesitate to ask questions about society's sacred cows. Louis Wirth once observed that:

> The most important thing . . . that we can know about a (person) is what (that person) takes for granted, and the most elemental and important facts about a society are those that are seldom debated and generally regarded as settled.[7]

Lots of things about our society that are seldom debated ought to be debated. Lots of things that are generally regarded as settled ought to be questioned. Christians ought to be in the vanguard of those asking the hard questions.

Confidence in God's love and grace—the firm conviction that God loves us not because we are good but because God is good, and that nothing can ever separate us from the love of God—should free us to take risks, to support hopeless causes, even to fail. Some people are compulsively careful in their politics. They shrewdly calculate every possibility and back only sure winners. Their main pre-occupation is with what is "politically feasible." They would rather stay out of the fight than lose. I have absolutely no objection to winning. As a matter of fact, I'd rather win than lose. And I fully appreciate the value of counting the votes before they are taken and of calculating the costs of any political move. But surely, faithfulness to the cause of peace and justice rather than the feasibility of political proposals ought to be the primary concern of believers; and at least once in a while, confidence in God's grace ought to liberate us to take risks. And perhaps, by taking some risks, we can from time to time open up new possibilities. "High politics," says William Lee Miller, "is not the art of the possible; it is the art of enlarging what is possible and of making what has hereto been impossible come in the range of what can be considered."[8] Confidence in God's love should free us to engage in "high politics."

Finally, confidence in God's power and trust in God's promises should free us to hope. Christian hope is not to be confused with any easy optimism. It is not a matter of "wishing makes it so." Christian hope is simply the quiet confidence that God will eventually win the victory. It is the assurance that we can count on the promises of God. Christian hope is singing with Martin Luther:

> Let goods and kindred go,
> This mortal life also;
> The body they may kill:
> God's truth abideth still;
> God's kingdom is forever.

That's the hymn of a liberated community. And we are all invited to sing it.

Faith provides a motive, a mission, and some moral standards for evaluating policies; and faith results in a faithful manner of political life. Finally, *faith can and ought and often does provide believers "manna in the wilderness"—the means and strength to hang in there.*

To the degree that we envision a new society, we are going to be distressed by the way things are in this world. To the degree that we hunger and thirst after righteousness, we are going to be depressed by the power of injustice. To the degree that we pour our hearts and souls into the struggle for peace and justice, we are going to be dismayed over our apparent powerlessness. And we are going to be tempted to quit, to give up, to say that nothing can be done.

In such situations, faith enables us to hang on. How so? What are the ingredients in faith's survival kit? Surely, many things enable Christians to keep going: the magnitude of human need; the clarity of God's imperative; the greatness of the cause of peace and justice; the companionship and support and encouragement of one another. But the key reality for the community of faith is the presence of God in the midst of the struggle.

The account of the call of Moses in the third chapter of Exodus is one of the great passages of Scripture. We all know the story. The Lord said, "Whom shall I send, and who will go for me?" and Moses replied, "Here am I, Lord; send somebody else." God wanted Moses to go lobby the Pharaoh for the release of the Hebrew slaves, and Moses didn't want to go! The narrative recounts that marvelous dialogue in which Moses raises all his objections, and God tears them down, one by one. At the end, Moses agrees to go. What changed his mind? Two things. One was the assurance that the cause for which he was being drafted was God's cause, a cause in which God was actively involved. "I have seen the affliction of my people who are in Egypt; I have heard their cry; . . . I know their suffering, and I have come down to deliver them . . ." (Exodus 3:7-8). The other was the promise of God's presence: "I will be with you" (Exodus 3:12).

God was as good as God's Word with Moses. God was with him in the midst of the struggle. God offers the same promise to us: "Get involved. Seek justice. Make peace. Fulfill your calling. And I will be with you. You can count on that."

ENDNOTES

1. Reinhold Niebuhr, *The Nature and Destiny of Man* (New York: Charles Scribner's Sons, 1949), Vol. II, p. 122.
2. W.A. Visser 't Hooft and J.H. Oldham, *The Church and Its Function in Society* (New York: Willett, Clark and Co., 1937), p. 148.
3. William Lee Miller, *The Protestant and Politics* (Philadelphia: Westminster Press, 1958), p. 90.
4. Cited by Jeffrey K. Hadden, "The Gathering Storm Revisited: Religious Institutions in the Immediate Decades Ahead," *Journal of Current Social Issues,* Vol. 10, No. 2 (Spring 1972), p. 9.
5. John Calvin, *Institutes of the Christian Religion*, translated by John Allen (Philadelphia: Presbyterian Board of Christian Education, n.d.), Book III, Chapter VII, Para. 1.
6. Beverly Harrison, "The Politics of Energy Policy," in Dieter T. Hessel (ed), *Energy Ethics: A Christian Response* (New York: Friendship Press, 1979), p. 59.
7. From the Preface to the English Edition of Karl Mannheim, *Ideology and Utopia* (New York: Harcourt, Brace & World, 1962, 1936); cited in J. Philip Wogaman, *The Great Economic Debate* (Philadelphia: Westminster Press, 1977), p. 29.
8. William Lee Miller, *Of Thee, Nevertheless, I Sing* (New York: Harcourt, Brace Jovanovich, 1975), p. 38.

MY PEACE I GIVE TO YOU: TOWARD AN UNDERSTANDING OF THIS GIFT

Paul S. Minear

By way of orientation:

How strongly are political actions now shaped by faith? How strongly is faith shaped by the Bible? It is easy for skeptics to underestimate that degree, as it is easy for believers to exaggerate it. Whether we are skeptics or believers, it is easy to deceive ourselves. Without attempting to calculate the precise degree of such influence, we will concentrate on exploring the potential force of the first item—the Bible. What role does it, or should it, play in shaping faith as that faith, in turn, shapes the practice of politics?

The bearing of faith in Christ (f) on the practice of politics (p) in America is a question frequently raised today. For brevity's sake, we will think of this as the f/p connection. The exploration of this relationship in a reformed context presupposes the conviction that the Bible should provide basic guidance in this investigation. Thus a third letter is added to the formula, B/f/p. The implication is obvious: for Christians the Bible in some sense shapes faith, as faith in some sense shapes political action. Or, reversing the sequence, to some degree political action is a response to faith, as faith to some degree is a response to the Bible. This essay, then, deals with the role of the Bible, whether potential or actual, in that B/f/p connection.

But when this question is raised, it immediately poses a major difficulty: that of handling three such abstract and such massive generalizations. Each of the three nouns (B/f/p) points to a realm of human experience that is far too volatile and far too gigantic to measure or to map. Take the third letter for example. P stands for politics in American life, stands for the sum total of citizens' activity in governmental agencies, local, regional and national, stands for the kaleidoscope of attitudes and actions evoked by legislative issues that range from real estate zoning to abortion to atomic warfare, stands for every degree of participation in government, from refusing to do anything to obsession with solving each successive domestic or foreign crisis. What soaring satellite can photograph such a vast expanse?

The letter F calls to mind a universe that is no smaller. F stands for the faith of millions of Americans who are members of more than two hundred denominations, stands for their diverse and deeply-rooted traditions of doctrine and customs, of sanctities and hierarchies, stands for their subconscious as well as conscious loyalties. Some of those members belong to impoverished minorities, some to affluent majorities; some are martyrs on the left, some wield great power on the right. Faith stands for whatever it is that impels all those folk to think of themselves as Christian. Who can speak with precision and confidence of that vast constellation?

The letter B confronts us with difficulties no less gargantuan. Though it seems to refer to a single book, that book contains a library of traditions that emerged over a span of a thousand years. Those who produced and used that library experienced fantastic extremes of poverty and wealth, slavery and independence, exile and return. During that millenium there were so many deaths and so many rebirths that one may well question whether at the end we are dealing with the same people as at the beginning. The range of ideas to be encountered within the library is so vast that it is quite impossible to sift out any uniform deposit of beliefs or political practices. Moreover this library was not altogether complete when its latest document was added, for each book within the collection has been transmitted to us through centuries of retranslation and reinterpretation. The text of scripture may not change overmuch, but understandings of the text do. How, then, can we establish the boundaries of the Bible in such a way that we can use it in discussing the B/f/p connection?

Let us suppose, however, that we succeed in defining that connection within a given century, the period of the New Testament, for example. At once we confront another problem. Can we assume that there are enough similarities between those ancient churches and our modern churches to justify linking the ancient B/f/p to the modern? Surely the visible contours of church life in Richmond, Virginia, are so different from the church in Paul's Corinth that we may well doubt whether the two branches belong on the same family tree. What firm bonds connect the working faith of Christians in Paul's Rome to the operative beliefs of American Protestants? When Romans 6 is read next Sunday in almost any American church, a legitimate response might be derisive laughter. Does this congregation actually think of itself as "dying with Christ" in the same sense as Paul's Roman readers?

But even if we assume that a modern congregation is a lineal descendant of early Christian congregations, can anything be done to overcome the radical disparities in political situations? The organization of power in Washington, D.C. is so remote from the government in Judea in Jesus' day that nothing he said about Caesar is readily transferable to the U.S. When B/f/p 30 A.D. (is so wholly different from) B/f/p 1982, why should the former be consulted in shaping the latter? Perhaps there is wisdom on the part of those who have altogether ceased to consult the Bible on political matters. Perhaps Christians who insist on preserving a role for the Bible may be deluding themselves; they may be using the Bible as ventriloquists use their dummy rather than as loyal believers who listen for divine guidance. Readers of this volume must reckon constantly with these difficulties, and especially with this last.

To circumvent some of these difficulties we have severely limited the scope of this essay. We will deal not with the whole Bible, or with either Testament as a whole, but focus on a single book, the Gospel of John, and in fact, a segment of that book (Chapters 13-17). We will not ask that ancient writer to speak to our own B/f/p connection, but only to the f/p connection as it emerged within the dialogue which that author initiated with his initial readers. If we can penetrate that original dialogue and recover his sense of the situation, who those believers were and what their essential mission was, he may also give us a different sense of our own situation as we face problems that seem to be so completely different.

Establishing contact with John

A first step is to establish contact with the anonymous author whom we call John. In these chapters John is telling a story for a circle of readers in his own churches. That story tells of Jesus' final conversations with his disciples on the evening before his arrest. It is Jesus' farewell to them.

This farewell address is told in such a way that readers take their stand with Jesus on that evening when Judas left the supper table (13:31). They are encouraged to look backward with Jesus, recalling all that had happened earlier. He had glorified God on earth and had finished the work assigned to him (17:4). He had called the disciples whom God had given him, and he had loved them to the end (13:1). He had taught them his new commandment (13:34). The remembrance of things past reached back even further—to the glory God had given Jesus "from the foundation of the world" (17:24).

The address, however, concentrates on Jesus' forward look from that same supper. It speaks of that future in several ways. For example, it clearly anticipates "the hour" when Jesus would "depart out of this world to the Father" (13:1), that is, the "end" to which he had loved "his own." As John tells the story, Jesus knew where he was going and knew, as well, that no disciple was ready as yet to follow him (13:36f.).

The address also pictures Jesus as knowing in advance what lay ahead for the disciples. His arrest and death would uncover their misunderstandings, denials and betrayals. He shaped his farewell message so as to reach them on the other side of those betrayals: "I tell you this now, before it takes place, so that when it does take place, you may believe that I am he" (13:19). He anticipated the time when their illusions would give way to knowledge and their fears to courage.

Nor was this the limit of vision. After their courage had been restored, Jesus would send them out on assignments like his own, where they would be greeted in similar ways. "Whoever will receive you will receive me" (13:20). "If they persecuted me, they will persecute you" (15:20). Their passion would follow his. The message even looks forward to the time when the last of those first messengers would have died; Jesus prayed also for the generation of believers who would follow in their steps (17:20-26; 21:20-23).

It is this forward look that dominates the conversations. When as readers we imagine ourselves as present with Jesus on that very evening, we realize how fully John thought of Jesus as a prophet who could read his disciples' souls and read the course of their lives. In fact, the very telling of the story may illustrate the gift of the Spirit to John: "he will teach you all things, and bring to your remembrance all that I have said to you" (14:26). So much for the story as seen from Jesus' angle.

We can establish a still closer contact with John, for we can take our stand with him at that later time when he was writing the Gospel. He conveyed his own remembrance of things past by telling the story as a whole. He looked back not only to the death of Jesus but to the deaths of the disciples (21:18-23), not only to Jesus' promises but to their fulfillment as well. And to what did he look forward? To his own and his readers' continuation of the same mission, under the same hazards. The deaths of their predecessors were no doubt inspiring, but they were daunting as well. These believers, both John and his readers, faced the same hostility and the same fate. They did not know how they would behave in the crisis, whether like Judas or Peter or Thomas or Philip. But they were called to carry on the same mission as their predecessors. It is probable that neither John nor his readers had known Jesus before the first Easter. Yet they found in his Farewell Address words and actions that would help them cope with their own precarious positions. This is the point where we can best make contact with John, the point where he was telling this story for those readers as they faced outer dangers and inner dreads.

Establishing contact with John's readers

What, then, can we know about them? Living in a hostile world, any minority religious community is subject to severe internal strains. Members need a strong sense of cohesion, of mutual support, of ties that bind them closely to their coworkers. Jesus' prayer spoke directly to this need. Readers had available a unique kind of solidarity, oneness with all other believers who had never seen Jesus and who were therefore dependent upon the word they had heard (17:20-26). Jesus' prayer also spoke of their oneness with the earlier generation of disciples, the original band of witnesses and martyrs whom Jesus had trained. (17:9-15). The prayer emphasized an even more basic solidarity with the Father and the Son, and with the Spirit which the Son had promised. For many minds, such language is so "doctrinal" that it has lost its saltiness; yet it covers many quite ordinary and everyday bonds—in asking and receiving, in eating at a common table, in washing and being washed, in loving and being loved. John wanted his readers to become aware of these bonds, for such awareness could strengthen their hearts as together they faced treachery and danger on all sides.

Those dangers were by no means minor nuisances. Why was the story of Jesus' martyrdom so important? Why, too, the accounts of the beloved disciple and Peter? Only because John and his readers were themselves potential martyrs. It was the sharing of danger that united every servant to all the other servants and to their common master. All this is expressed in the simple axiom: "a servant is not above his master" (13:16). The Farewell Address makes sense only if this prospect of martyrdom bound John's readers to the love that had been at work in

Jesus' death and to the love that had finally been vindicated in Peter's death (21:18, 19). John had in mind Christians who faced dangers as great as any faced by their heroes of the past.

On thinking in terms of "we" and "they"

A religious community instinctively develops the habit of separating itself from the surrounding society and of indicating this separation by its use of the plural personal pronouns. That the Johannine churches were no exception is evident as one reads the Farewell Address.

> "If they persecuted me, they will persecute you;
> if they kept my word, they will keep yours also" (15:20).

Here the *you* is defined by identity with *me* and *my* word. And persecution marks the boundary between *us* and *them*. That persecution, in turn, is defined by Jesus' crucifixion, which is now spoken of as a model of persecutions to follow. *We* are the martyrs, *they* the murderers. Who, then, are those murderers? The text leaves little doubt.

> "They will put you out of the synagogues; indeed, the hour is coming when whoever kills you will think he is offering service to God. And they will do this because they have not known the Father, nor me." (16:2, 3).

We may safely draw a cluster of inferences from this prediction. The pronoun *you* refers to followers of Jesus who have earlier been members of the synagogues. They have been, or are being, evicted by other Jews who have the needed authority and power, i.e., the synagogue heads. Those expelled have not welcomed that eviction, presumably because they consider loyalty to Jesus to be in line with life within the synagogue. Their adversaries reject that conviction and base their violence upon an opposite conviction. In intention, both groups are convinced that they are "offering service to God," but the action by the evicters proves that they do not recognize either Jesus as Son or God as his Father. The collision within the synagogues discloses the fact that two quite different gods are being obeyed, the measure of violence being the measure of sincerity and devotion on both sides. As Jesus' hour had marked the climax of his work, a similar hour would come for his followers. Then they would share his victory and announce the judgment of God upon their murderers. Then the two generations of martyrs would become one, as also the two generations of murderers.

The Gospel of John was aimed at a situation of bitter conflict in which *we* and *they* had quite specific meanings. *We* were the followers of Jesus, including both the charismatic leaders (17:6-19) and those who believed because of their word (17:20-26). *They* were the world, the Jews, the Pharisees, chief priests and rulers, who in evicting Jesus' followers from the synagogues and in killing them were disclosing their ignorance of this Son and his Father.

But in making this identification of *us* and *them* we must not make a mistake by treating this boundary as a wall. Such an identification was quite temporary.

In the prologue, three clauses were linked together: he came to his own (the Jews). . . . his own rejected him (the Cross) . . . those who received him became children of God. The second of these clauses (the rejection) should not cancel out the first clause (his coming to them) or the third (their birth as children). One of the first disciples was described as an Israelite, free of guile, whom Jesus saw sitting under the fig tree, and who recognized in him the king of Israel (1:47-49). The first "ruler of the Jews" to encounter this king of Israel rejected him at the outset but in the end demonstrated his support (19:39). On Jesus' final approach to Jerusalem, the daughter of Zion hailed him as king (12:12-14). With the possible exception of the Samaritan "believers," all of the disciples in the Gospel were Jews "to whom the arm of the Lord has been revealed" (12:38). As true sons of Abraham and disciples of Moses they had been drawn out of the "world" by a love that loved them to the end. Unlike "the Jews," these Jews had come to know both the Father and the Son,—in John's time no less than in Jesus'.

It was these Jews whom Jesus sent to "the Jews," anticipating for them the same rejection he had received. He ordered them to bear fruit under the same conditions and thus he expected positive results from their work. Their success, in fact, required a collision between the two communities, each using a different strategy and relying on a different kind of power. In the final showdown in Jerusalem a final judgment had taken place which had disclosed the line between the two communities. There everything had depended upon how the various participants defined two terms which were inherently political: the king, the Jews. When Pilate affixed those two words to the Cross, he forced all who believed in Jesus to redefine both terms. The Evangelist spelled out that redefinition:

My kingship is not of this world;
if my kingship were of this world,
   my servants would fight
   that I might not be handed over to the Jews,
but my kingship is not from the world. (18:36).

In short, the line between *us* and *them* follows the line between incompatible kingships, strategies and powers.

On discerning the spirits

We now turn to explore another boundary line that was important to John, a line within his own community which separated one group of charismatic leaders from another. The category "the Jews" was not the only flexible category in his lexicon; the same flexibility applied to the category of disciple, as shown by the actions of Judas, Peter, Philip, Thomas and the beloved but anonymous disciple. Though each of these was a person in his own right, by the time the Gospel was written each had become a symbol of weaknesses and strengths among church leaders. Their role as leaders was traced directly to their receiving from Jesus the gift of the Holy Spirit.

According to Luke's account of Pentecost, the church was from the beginning the scene of a veritable explosion of prophetic gifts (Acts 2:1-36). So, too, Paul's letters to Corinth reflect the presence in that church of problems created by the profusion of charismatic gifts—problems which Paul tried to solve by stressing the priority to be given to the gift of prophecy and to the demands of love (1 Cor. 12-14). A third instance of those same problems was reflected in the Gospel of Matthew, whose edition of the Sermon on the Mount reached a climax in Jesus' warning against false prophets. These leaders were hungry wolves that wore the clothing of sheep. They were credited with power to cast out demons and to do many mighty works in Jesus' name, but they refused to obey his commands, those very demands that Jesus had spelled out in the sermon (Mt. 7:15-27). With such deception the risen Lord would have nothing to do (v. 23). Texts like these make it clear that conflicts among groups of charismatic leaders broke out in many churches. In fact, those conflicts probably had much to do with the writing of all four Gospels. If the commands of Jesus, as illustrated by his actions, were to serve as a standard by which charismatic gifts were to be measured, churches needed trustworthy records of those commands and actions, such records as the Gospels provided.

It is this very struggle among charismatic leaders which we can discern between the lines of Chapter 14. In this chapter Jesus repeated a promise no less than four times, a sure sign of its importance:

"If you love me, you will obey my commandments, and I will pray the Father, and he will give you another Counselor, to be with you forever, even the Spirit of Truth, whom the world cannot receive, because it neither sees him nor knows him . . ." (14:15-17, 21, 23, 24, 28).

From this promise we may safely draw a cluster of inferences concerning the conflict among the prophets in John's churches. "If you *love* me . . ." From this we infer that all these leaders, like Peter in Chapters 13 and 21, affirmed their love for Jesus. "*If* you love me . . ." From this we infer that Jesus questioned the truth of their love and insisted on testing its genuineness. How? In the same way as in Matthew's sermon: "you will obey my commandments." We infer that some charismatics failed this test and that one purpose of Jesus (and John) was to induce them to correct this failure.

To those who vindicated their love by obeying those orders, Jesus gave this promise: "I will pray the Father and he will give . . ." The sequence is important. The only Spirit that is authorized to serve as "another Counselor" will be the Spirit which the Father has given in response to Jesus' prayer. Yet that is a spirit which "the world cannot receive." In churches where many leaders were claiming the spirit, the churches must learn to distinguish one spirit from another. As shown by its hostility to Jesus' example and demands, "the world" (in the sense of 15:18 and 16:11) was incapable of seeing or knowing the Spirit of truth. By contrast, Jesus promised his disciples that his Spirit would "be with you forever."

We note two further things about the promise. First, the *you* of the promise is plural. John's concern is not alone with individual leaders but with the entire leadership. "The Paraclete is not the individualistic teacher within the heart of every Christian but a fundamental ministry within the Johannine community".[2] Second, the Spirit had a very definite contribution to make to that ministry: "he will teach you all things and will bring to your remembrance all that I have said to you" (14:26). How could they obey his commands if they did not know what they were? After Jesus' death, when these disciples and their successors would continue his work, the Spirit would convey those orders afresh. Which ones did Jesus have in mind specifically? Those on washing one another's feet? On feeding his sheep? On asking? On loving one another? On overcoming their fears? On walking the same road he had taken? The commands varied, but one thing is clear. For this Gospel, obedience to such orders marked out the boundary between two groups of charismatic leaders. In the situations they faced, these commands were no vague sentiments intended for a nebulous audience, but very specific controls to be respected by leaders who were inclined to alibi their disobedience by an appeal to their possession of impressive spiritual gifts.

So this Chapter locked together three things: love for Jesus, possession of the Spirit, obedience to his commands. Christian leaders who claimed the first two but ignored the third were self-condemned. Without obedience, the claim of love was self-deception. Without obedience, the claim of the Spirit marked a victory by the world. Why was this obedience so important? Because "the word which you hear is not mine, but the Father's who sent me" (14:24).

If this reading of the text is sound, the Evangelist was carrying on a battle on two fronts. One we-they conflict was located between true and false prophets within the churches; the other we-they line separated Christian leaders from the authorities in the synagogues. In some ways these two boundaries were quite distinct. Yet they came together at the point where persecution from outside induced such panic among the disciples that they renounced their faith. Judas had his successors among John's readers, who after eating the bread of Jesus "lifted up their heels" against him (13:18). The whole of the Farewell, if not the whole of the Gospel, was designed "to keep you from falling away" (16:1). Only when we recognize the power of that panic can we recognize the greater power of the peace which at least some of Jesus' disciples received from him.

On the gift of peace to the disciples

One of the dominant accents in the Farewell is the promise of this peace. It should already be clear that this gift was directly adapted to the battle needs of the disciples, for they were engaged in a war between two gods, as soldiers enlisted by the king of Israel in his struggle with "the Jews." That king had been a martyr and, as such, a model for them to emulate. In such a context, we must view his peace as something very different from most literal conceptions of peace. Most dictionaries define peace as the cessation of hostilities or as a treaty marking the end of a war. Not so, John. Jesus was in fact preparing his intern prophets for a period of continuous persecution and even an intensification of hatred. For that period, the same Spirit that would remind them of Jesus' commands would also convey to them his peace:

> "Peace I leave with you;
> My peace I give to you;
> not as the world gives
> do I give to you.
> Let not your hearts be troubled,
> neither let them be afraid." (14:27).

In those days the word for peace was a simple word of greeting and goodbye. That ordinary meaning is present in John; yet John invested that simple greeting with profound overtones. This peace is Jesus' gift of his peace. The accent on the personal pronoun is the same as in 18:36: *my* peace . . . *my* kingship. This king has the power to grant this royal peace. Its recipients are soldiers who have obeyed his commands and have allowed his Spirit to "teach" them "all things." "Not as the world gives . . ." There are two gifts available and choice must be made between them. And this choice of gifts is simultaneously a choice of power: "The ruler of this world is coming. He has no power over me" (14:30). By implication, this verse invited John's readers to ask which power was greater, Jesus' power over the world, or the world's power over Jesus. Peace and power were twins.

The text suggests other inferences. Parallel to the giving of peace was the command: "Let not your hearts be troubled, neither let them be afraid." Peace is fearlessness. Here, as elsewhere in John, fear is a response to danger from "the Jews." The untroubled heart is a heart immune to panic (the verb here is the same as in 12:27). The disciple who is unfazed by the prospect of death has destroyed the devil's power (as in Heb. 2:10-18). Another equivalent for peace is joy: "If you loved me, you would have rejoiced . . ." (v. 28). Presumably, each instance of going to the Father should be an occasion not for sorrow, but for rejoicing. Another corollary is obedience, or doing as the Father commanded. This obedience, in turn, is unmistakable evidence of love for the Father. Thus a single paragraph in John contains no fewer than six components in Jesus' gift of peace: the Spirit, power, courage, joy, obedience, love.

It is perhaps not unintentional that the promise of peace should be immediately followed by an apparent *non sequitur*: "Rise. Let us go hence" (v. 31). Jesus' journey to the garden was a symbol of his power over the world and of his love for the Father, and therefore an embodiment of his peace, courage and joy. He viewed that journey as a conclusion of his own assignment: "that the world may know." In his going, he invited his disciples to go with him to the same garden, as if to say, "If you love me and my Father, and if you want the world to know, join me on this road". In one sense they did accompany him (18:1), but in another sense, first Peter (13:36-38) then Thomas (14:1-7) and then Philip (14:8-11) failed utterly to comprehend where he was going, failed to understand his strategy. Jesus' promise of peace would come into effect only when, later on, in looking back to the same garden, the Spirit would remind them of his promise (14:26). So, too, in reading John's Gospel, the charismatic leaders in the church would find in this Farewell a comparable riddle, warning, invitation and promise. Here John provided them with a picture of the connections between Jesus' faith and his political strategy (f/p).

On the gift of peace to the world

If the first pledge of peace was designed to overcome divisions within the church among competing groups of charismatic leaders, a second pledge dealt more directly with overcoming the obstacles provided by the world's rejection of the Gospel. This second pledge comes at the end of Chapter 16, a fitting conclusion to the dialogue of the two chapters and an equally fitting prelude to the prayer of Chapter 7. Here is Jesus' final word to his disciples:

"I have said this to you, that in me you may have peace. In the world you have tribulation; but be of good cheer, I have overcome the world" (16:33).

We will not understand this declaration without recalling several basic accents in the Farewell Address. (1) The disciples had been called to share the same mission as Jesus: "that the world may know." A change in the world was a central goal. (2) The disciples had been called to share the same rejection by the world: "you will have tribulation." "If they hated me they will hate you." (3) Such a collision was inevitable, given the incompatible strategies used by the world and by Jesus. (4) The victory of Jesus over the world was a victory of his strategy, and disciples could share in that victory by adopting the same strategy. Their shared victory over the world would enable the world to know both the Son and the Father, and thus to change such policies as had earlier been followed (16:2).

In this context, let us not forget, the term *world* carried a very concrete force: the Jews, and mainly the Pharisees, chief priests and rulers. The Gospel pointed out three features in the world's strategy. First was the element of self-deception, a blindness rooted in holding position as accepted religious leaders and as authorized interpreters of scripture. Second was a blend of fears and animosities that was rooted in their desire to protect themselves from treason, to safeguard the sanctity of the religious institutions of which they were guardians, and to offer devoted service to God. Third was the use of violence as a means to eliminate this threat to everything they held precious. It was the coincidence of these three features that, for John, made the world the world, a realm governed by its own invisible ruler.

At each point John pictures Jesus as following an opposite strategy. He relied upon the Spirit of truth as being able to penetrate illusions and to heal blindnesses by overcoming that poison of self-righteousness which is endemic in every religious profession. He exemplified a love for the world, embodying God's love for that world aimed at its salvation. He refused to use violence in self-defence or to tolerate his disciple's resort to violence (18:11, 36). As John tells the story, the collision between these two strategies reached its maximum force in the "lifting up" of the Son of man. Here the opposing strategies of the two rulers clarified the identity of their servants, along with the kind of ignorance or knowledge that characterized those servants. To those on one side, this was the hour of greatest shame; to those on the other, the hour of greatest glory. To the world it was quite impossible to discern in this event the Son and the Father (16:2). To Jesus' prophetic witnesses this event marked a final victory over the world.

But what strategy should guide their efforts "that the world may know?" How could they convert their persecutors, not only to a belief in Jesus but to a trust in his strategy? The Gospel answers such questions by appeal to the coming of the Counselor: "If I go I will send him to you" (16:7). In Chapter 14 John had described the work of this Spirit in terms of contributions to the internal life of the churches. Now John turns to the contributions of the Counselor to the church's work in the world.

> When he comes, he will convince the world concerning sin
> and righteousness and judgment:
>> concerning sin, because they do not believe in me;
>> concerning righteousness because I go to the Father
>>> and you will see me no more;
>> concerning judgment because the ruler of this world
>>> is judged. (16:8-11).

John indicated that this prediction applied to the period after Jesus' death and after his return to the Father. It was directly relevant to the success of their mission to the world that hated and persecuted them. In effect, the presence of the Counselor would work a triple miracle.

"Convince the world . . . concerning sin?" The Counselor would convince some residents of the world that their hatred of Jesus' disciples, which they had believed to be prime examples of devotion to God and his law, had in fact been examples of sin. "Concerning righteousness?" The world had been sure that Jesus had been worthy of death. "They have not known the Father, nor me" (16:2). The Counselor could convince the world that in Jesus' death he had gone to the Father, that his death had vindicated his sonship, and that though his disciples could see him no longer they now embodied the same righteousness. "Convince the world . . . concerning judgment?" With this double reversal in the world's attitude toward Jesus, the world would come to recognize who had in fact been its ruler; it would come to acknowledge God's final condemnation of that ruler. In hearing Jesus' manifesto, "I have overcome the world," one-time residents of the world would receive the gift of peace (16:33).

But such a change would be nothing short of a miracle which only the presence of the Counselor could explain. Only by following the strategy of their ruler could they convince the world of his victory. Fear of "the Jews" would vitiate their ministry, as would any recourse to violence. They could only witness to his kingship by obeying his commands and by loving the world as he had loved it. What was at stake was nothing less than the final judgment of the *ruler* of this world. Jesus gave a twofold assignment to the Counselor: to guide the disciples into this truth (v. 12) and to convince the world of it.

The prayer of Chapter 17 is a fitting climax to the farewell. It welds together petitions for Jesus (vv. 1-5), for the disciples (vv. 6-19), and for the believers (vv. 20-26)—those three essential "members" of the Johannine churches. Concern for these three, however reaches beyond them to the world. Though the world hates all three (v. 15), their shared objective is that this same world may come to believe and to know (vv. 21, 23). In this work, the only real enemy is "the evil one" whose deceptions can only be defeated by the truth, by God's word (vv. 15, 16). Jesus had fulfilled his work in the hour when he had glorified God and been glorified by God (v. 1). The work of the disciples and the believers involved sharing the same hour and the same glory, the royal glory of their king. This glory was a bond that united them to the glory "before the world was made" (v. 5) and to the glory that would come when both the disciples and the believers would be "with me where I am" (v. 24).

We are now ready to summarize John's view of the f/p connection as expressed in Chapters 13-17. F is the action of believing and knowing both the Son and the Father, the action of accepting from them the gift of peace and the gift of glory. P is the action of the Son, described by him as a grain of wheat falling into the earth and dying (12:24), an action being continued by disciples and believers.

Is John's view typical of the New Testament?

In our opening paragraphs we announced our decision to focus the target to a segment of one Gospel rather than attempting a broader study of the whole Bible or a treatment of contemporary implications. The question remains, however, was John's presentation of the faith-politics question a solitary witness or a voice representative of the New Testament? In answering this question, four extensive passages from four different writers should prove to be sufficient.

In the Gospel of Matthew we turn to the longest single compendium of Jesus' teachings, the Sermon on the Mount (Mt. 5-7). Some readers may think we should turn instead to the jousting between Jesus and the Pharisees as to whether taxes should be paid to Caesar (22:17-22). But in that story Jesus was not speaking to his disciples but to enemies who had laid a booby-trap for him. His answer was designed to put those enemies on the defensive rather than to provide a policy statement that would be binding either for followers or for a general audience. Moreover, this story has proved to be a ball of silly putty in every reader's hands, its *moral* twisted to fit any passing whim. Its usefulness is minimal in contrast to the famous Sermon.

In the background of the Sermon is a struggle, similar to that in John, between the church and the synagogue and between the disciples and the Pharisees (hypocrites). But the ultimate enemy is identified not with those human adversaries but with the "evil one" whom they serve. Jesus' disciples must make an absolute choice of one master to serve; the choice of one leads to persecution, of the other to affluence. To serve "the Father" entails persecution, in which sons must share the Father's love for his enemies. Because of the will and character of this Father, the command to refuse to use violence becomes unconditional. The promises of blessedness in the beatitudes are Matthew's edition of John's gift of peace, with its corollaries of courage, comfort, power and joy. Matthew's emphasis on inheriting the kingdom of God is comparable to John's emphasis on sharing the regal glory of King Jesus. There are important links between the Lord's prayer in John 17 and the disciples' prayer in Matthew 6, links, as well, between the assurances of answers to prayer in Matthew 7 and John 14. Matthew's gate is neither more narrow nor more broad than John's. In both Gospels, disciples are commanded to love one another; in both, prophets are warned against arrogance and self-deception. Both Evangelists were convinced that Jesus was a true successor to Moses and that he had initiated a genuine fulfillment of "the law and the prophets." Without ignoring or belittling the contrasts between these two Christian authors, we can conclude that Matthew, no less than John, could define f as believing, knowing and trusting the Father of Jesus; he could also define p as sharing the *way* that Jesus had taken to life.

We may take a second sounding in Ephesians 5:21-6:20. This epistle provides us with a long section of advices concerning areas of p not touched by John. These deal with the mutual obligations of husbands and wives, parents and children, masters and slaves (5:21-6:9). By almost universal consent, modern readers rate these specific teachings as objectionable and unacceptable. Since the first century there have been such far-reaching changes in social institutions as to make these rules too obsolete to be taken seriously: (e.g., "Slaves, be obedient to . . . your earthly masters"). So strong is this revulsion that we ignore two very important factors.

In the first place, if we were as eager to transport ourselves back into the environment of Paul as we are eager to measure him by modern sensibilities, we would realize that in his day his policies were far less archaic and far less conservative than we had supposed. Many of his Christian fellows were appalled by his radicalism and by his liberation from many moral conventions. We should judge his political stance by such alternatives as were available to his initial readers.

A second consideration is more important. In the passage at hand we are prone to focus attention upon the specific actions he ordered; at every point he seems to be on the side of superior authority: husbands, parents, masters. We single out the p and overlook the f/p axis. But it is the linkage that is of prime importance; the following typical phrases show that we will not grasp the p aright until we understand its grounding in f:

> out of reverence for Christ . . . as to the Lord . . . Christ the head . . . subject to Christ . . . Christ loved . . . gave himself . . . members of his body . . . the instruction of the Lord . . . in the Lord . . . singleness of heart, as to Christ . . . doing the will of God from the heart . . . rendering service to the Lord and not to men . . . their Master and yours . . . no partiality with him.

These jagged phrases remind us that every specific advice emerged from the bond between this body and its head. That bond was, in fact, a slavery that was ultimately more significant than any action resulting from it and viewed in separation from it. The author was trying to cope with a profound mystery (5:32), in

which a believer's obedience to an invisible master was given priority over all
human affiliations, shaping those affiliations in patterns both new and old. If,
then, we look in John for comparable definitions of *p* we will look in vain; but if
we look for comparable appreciations of the f/p axis, the result will be far different. The two writings, while different in many ways, belong within the same
family.

This will become clearer if we itemize points in Ephesians 6:10-20 which
are reminiscent of similar points in John.

an ambassador in chains	a king facing arrest
God vs. the devil	the Father vs. the evil one
truth vs. the devil's wiles	the Spirit of truth
the gospel of peace	My peace I give to you
to withstand in the evil day	the hour is coming
the sword of the Spirit	the Spirit will guide you
which is the word of God	into all truth
supplications for the saints	love one another
put on the whole armor of God	I have overcome the world
the flaming darts of the evil one	keep them from the evil one
pray at all times	ask anything of the Father

If each of those points of convergence were fleshed out fully, there would be no
doubt about the result. Both writers appraised each current situation in the light
of the revelation of the will of God in the death and life-beyond-death of Jesus;
this revelation enabled both writers to discern the current battle-line between the
Father and the evil one, to decide on the best available armor, and to wage the
battle with courage and joy.

For a very different kind of document we turn to the Epistle to the Hebrews,
10:32-12:14. This text is long enough to provide an adequate sample, though
altogether too long to permit adequate comment here. We mention a few salient
features. As in John, the center of the stage is held by Jesus, "the pioneer and
perfecter of our faith, who for the joy set before him endured the cross . . ."
(12:2). As in John the example of Jesus serves to clarify the meaning of the
fatherhood of God and the sonship of his followers (12:5-8). Any act of disobedience, such as resisting discipline, transforms one-time children into orphans; by
contrast the acceptance of martyrdom gives evidence of both holiness and righteousness (12:10, 11). Fears and faint hearts are signs of the betrayal of Christ.
The author reminds his readers of former "abuse and affliction" (10:32-39) and
warns them of a coming recurrence, which they must accept as an expression of
their confidence in "the coming one" (12:37).

If one seeks in this text to separate *f* from *p* he is bound to fail; all actions are
bound too closely to faith to permit that. The examples of faith in the famous
honor-roll (Chapter 11) are simultaneously examples of actions, many of which
must be termed political. Faith and action are embraced within the same sentence, with only a grammatical distinction between the prepositional phrase and
the verb: By faith Abel offered . . . by faith Abraham obeyed . . . by faith Sarah

received power . . . by faith Moses left Egypt . . . by faith Rahab gave friendly welcome. In obeying Jesus, his followers joined this long line of witnesses and prophets who had "won strength out of weakness." Jesus had been the *way* for his predecessors as well as for them. This preacher viewed the saga of Israel through the lens of the Passion Story. That same story gave a sharp definition to the otherwise platitudinous injunction: "Strive for peace with all men and for the holiness without which no one will see the Lord ' (12:14). That such peace and such holiness had immediate political ramifications was made entirely clear by the commands of Chapter 13.

Our fourth sounding may be taken from one of the most representative documents in the New Testament, First Peter 2:11-3:22. This letter had a very wide address: Gentile Christians in five different provinces of Roman Asia, who had been undergoing severe persecution from both political and religious authorities. It provided a succinct and clear epitome of faith, of action within various human institutions, and of the interrelationship of faith and action.

Here we may find a most explicit set of instructions regarding one of those institutions: "Be subject for the Lord's sake to every human institution, whether it be to the emperor as supreme, or to governors as sent by him . . ." (This instruction is entirely comparable to that of Paul in Romans 13:1-7 which is more frequently consulted on this matter, but which contains so many obscure references as to invite divergent interpretations). Peter treats civil government on a par with such other established social structures as slavery and the family, so that the rationale for behavior in one realm holds for the other realms as well. He is more concerned with the evil to be done by Christians as "servants of God" than with the evil done by emperors or governors; he is writing to the former group and expects them to respect different standards, among which is this very brief but comprehensive summary: "Honor all men. Love the brotherhood. Fear God. Honor the emperor." This is as clear a statement of *p* as can be found in the New Testament.

We also may find extremely clear statements of *f*. Primacy is given to the story of Christ as a story through which these "servants" have been forgiven, have been healed, and have received their freedom. Every action now becomes dictated by their vocation: "To this you have been called, because Christ also suffered for you, leaving you an example, that you should follow in his steps" (2:21-25). They have been brought to God only through the fact that "Christ also died for sins once for all, the righteous for the unrighteous" (3:18-22). Whenever they do right and suffer, whether as subjects of the governor, as slaves of a master, or as wives of husbands, they have "God's approval." Moreover, the goal is not simply to preserve their own freedom or righteousness but to make a statement to those who inflict the injustice. The day of visitation (like John's hour and "the evil day" of Ephesians) will enable the unjust "to see your good deeds and glorify God" (2:12).

This text offers several excellent definitions not only of *p* or of *f* but of the f/ p axis: good conduct as the way to win the "war against your soul," as the way by which to "live as free men," by which to "silence the ignorance of foolish

[45]

men," by which to win over their adversaries "without a word" (3:1), and to prove themselves "heirs of the grace of life." The more closely a reader focuses his attention on these condensations of the f/p axis, the more he will appreciate the climax of the argument:

"Finally, all of you, have unity of spirit, sympathy, love of the brethren, a tender heart and a humble mind. Do not return evil for evil or reviling for reviling; but on the contrary bless, for to this you have been called . . ." (3:8,9) In this context Peter's injunction of peace is entirely consistent with Matthew's and with John's promise:

Seek peace and pursue it" (I Peter 3:11)
I have not come to bring peace, but a sword" (Mt. 10:34)
My peace I give to you (John 14:27)

Against the background of these four soundings, we leave it to readers to decide whether or not John is typical of the New Testament as a whole. Whatever may be the decision on that point, we return now to the Farewell Address in John and raise the second and final question.

Is an update possible?

By now, perhaps, the difficulties mentioned in the opening paragraphs may have become clearer. The more fully we penetrate the dialogue between John and his first audience the farther we seem to move from the actual political choices facing churches in the United States. Several rhetorical questions may suggest that distance. Are churches today really listening to the Farewell Address and to the Passion Story? Does the revelation of God's glory in the lifting up of Jesus still exercise genuine authority as scripture? Do we use the same boundary markers in separating the church from the world and in separating true from false prophets? Can we honestly claim to have received the gift of peace, of courage and of joy that Jesus promised? Do Christians as a community understand and follow the same road that Jesus took "to the Father?" To such questions candor requires a negative reply. That being so, it is not surprising that the Counselor is unable to "convince the world concerning sin and righteousness and judgment" (John 16:8). In reminding us of the blind self-confidence of the synagogue authorities and the anxious compromises of the charismatic disciples, John echoes the warning of e. e. cummings: "Many an honest man believes a lie. Tho' you are as honest as the day, fear and hate the liar. Fear and hate him when he should be hated: now. Fear and hate him where he should be feared and hated: in yourselves."[3]

Even though the study of John obliges us to recognize our enormous distance from the first century church, the Gospel opens to us various possibilities. The Gospel helps us to locate the ultimate battle-ground not on contemporary sociological, geopolitical or ecclesiastical maps, but on such a map as John used. Accepting this would deliver us from the confusions that stem from thinking in terms of the boundary between Christian and non-Christian segments of the population. It would eliminate modern Jews from the roster of enemies for they no longer hold the position of majority power and authority and no longer persecute. The Gospel suggests that we locate the ultimate battle-line wherever obedience to the commands of Jesus arouses the most violent hostilities. Few of those commands, in fact, fail to do that. Consider these, for example: the devaluation of wealth, the liberation of the helpless, the scorn of national security, the reliance on absolute honesty, the love for enemies, the repudiation of violence, fearless facing of death, unwavering trust in God. Where do such commands release hostilities? Where they are being heard and obeyed. Within the bodies called churches and among the leaders of those churches. Actually, the battle-line remains amazingly in the same location, even though always hidden, and the scripture can help us discern its presence inside our hearts as well as in the place where we live.

In such discernment, the Gospel makes it possible to rediscover in the story of Jesus' Passion the climactic battle between the king of Israel and the "ruler of this world." That story retains the power to compel a redefinition of the basic categories of thought: shame and glory, weakness and power, suffering and joy, defeat and victory, death and life, the devil and God. It was that story that enabled John and his prophetic colleagues to comprehend the only political strategy that was consistent with this way, this truth, this life. Accordingly, John makes it possible for us to think and to rethink various strategies that we may follow today. John's testimony to Jesus as king excludes at least three popular options.

First of all, it excludes the path of political apathy and passivity. There is a bit of gentle irony that tells of a person who discovered an absolutely sure cure for apathy; he found that no one was interested! That was not true of Jesus in the first century. People whom he met could not avoid taking sides: either overwhelming enthusiasm or violent resistance. In John's day those same reactions greeted Jesus' delegates. Yet that irony does seem to be true in responses to Jesus today. As an inventor of a cure for apathy he is greeted everywhere by yawns. At a minimum, then, the Gospel should make us realize how false the following formula would be: B/f/apathy.

Second, a study of scripture excludes "single-issue politics." By this I mean the inclination on the part of Christians to claim the whole weight of the Bible for a single, short-term campaign to gain governmental support for a selected issue, however that issue be defined. Within the perspective of the Gospel of John there is no room for a power-seeking religious majority, except among opponents of the demands of Jesus. That kind of p presupposes a different way of locating the battle-line between God and Satan, a different way of perceiving the mission of Jesus to his enemies, and a different way of calculating the peace, courage and joy that he promised those who share that mission. It is rare indeed that such a strategy serves to "bring to your remembrance all that I have said to you" (14:25); that makes it doubtful whether those campaigns can claim the authority of the Holy Spirit. They represent a non-scriptural definition of B/f/p.

A third way to update scripture is to suppose that participation in national elections is all that faith demands by way of action in public affairs. To think this would be to claim scriptural authority for a position described by Aristophanes some five centuries before Christ. In his play *The Frogs* this playright constructed an imaginary dialogue between Bacchus and Euripides:

> Euripides: If we withdraw the confidence we placed
> In these our present statesmen, and transfer it
> To those whom we mistrusted heretofore,
> This seems I think our fairest chance for safety.
> If with our present counselors we fail,
> Then with their opposites we might succeed.
> Bacchus: That's capitally said
> My politician . . .
> Was it all your own?
> Your own invention?[4]

To adopt such a definition of *p* is to beggar the original Christian force of *B* and *f* in the formula B/f/p.

We must leave to later essays in this symposium more detailed discussions of the positive relevance of Scripture to political strategies. We are not content, however, to halt our argument with the rejection of these three options. These negations are altogether too innocuous and too obvious to do justice to the disturbing and mysterious power of the peace conveyed by the crucified Lord to his disciples. The martyrs of the Gospel of John, those grains of wheat that fell into the ground and died, would surely spurn such caution and such prudence. John's definition of peace impels an exegete to say something more. Interpreted in the light of a continuing Passion Story, the Farewell Address calls, at the minimum, for a forthright attack on a Christendom that has ceased to test its love for Jesus by obedience to his commands, a Christendom that has ceased to measure the presence of the Spirit by its power to condemn "the ruler of this world," a Christendom that no longer vindicates Christ's victory over that ruler because it knows so little of his courage, his joy and his peace.

Endnotes

1. G.B. Caird, *The Language and Imagery of the Bible* (Philadelphia: Westminster Press, 1980), p. 51.
2. M.E. Boring, *Christian Prophecy in the Synoptic Tradition* (Cambridge: Cambridge University Press, 1982), p. 70.
3. e.e. cummings, *Six Non-lectures* (Cambridge: Harvard University Press, 1962), p. 70.
4. Aristophanes, *The Frogs*, Translated by J.H. Frere, in *Four Famous Greek Plays*, ed. B. Landis (N.Y. Modern Library, 1929), p. 280.

PIETY, PLURALISM, AND POLITICS

Peggy L. Shriver

Persons who are tired of change, who would like to have a society where people agree on what is morally wrong and punish transgressors, and who blame our country's economic and military vulnerability upon a dangerous moral decay are candidates for membership in Moral Majority. Many feel that we must take whatever steps are necessary to make us number one militarily and morally again, for we are God's chosen nation for bringing the world into righteousness and belief. Despite past reluctance to be politically active, such people are now feeling that it is up to them to set our nation back on course, to rid it of immoral and ungodly leadership and influences.

One may, however, share many of the frustrations of change, of shifting values, of a loss of national purpose and still find the answers of Moral Majoritarians abhorrent. One may wish for less change, for an absolute sense of values, preeminence for our country, an exclusive blessing from God, but know "deep in one's heart" that we can't go back to the Good Old Days of a Christian America that seeks to make the rest of the world in its own clear-cut image. One may discover one is more a citizen of the world, more cosmopolitan, less authoritarian and imperialistic than one suspected. Does that make one also less religious? That may become a point of considerable disagreement with subscribers to Moral Majority views.

The issues that these attitudes represent lie deep within American culture, and a political outcropping of some of them has occurred repeatedly in our two hundred year history. Battles over Sabbath observance, slavery, and temperance have evolved the politically active religious coalition, single issue politics, and groups vigilant to protect the separation of church and state. For example, the Anti-Saloon League is an early prototype for Moral Majority, not claiming itself to be a religious group but receiving major support from churches throughout the country in its abolitionist lobbying for a "single issue." The extremist political right has also had its share of extremist fundamentalist Christians, more recently the Billy James Hargis' Christian Crusade, Carl McIntire's Bible Presbyterians, Fred Schwarz's Christian Anti-Communism Crusade, and Edgar C. Bundy's

REFORMED FAITH AND POLITICS

Church League of America, inheritors of an intolerant mix of religion and politics from the Know Nothing era. These are aging warriors, however, and the New Right secular political movement has turned to fresh organizations and novice leadership. The religious mainstream and liberal Christians have formed coalitions and established single issue groups with considerable effectiveness throughout the Civil Rights and Vietnam era and in the rise of concern for women's issues. The New Right has taken cues from these tactics in the formation of its own single issue and coalition style. Although there is no space to be comprehensive, it is helpful to look at a few in some detail.

Organizations and Organizers

The organization which calls itself Moral Majority was founded by Protestant pastor Jerry Falwell, Roman Catholic Paul Weyrich of the Committee for the Survival of a Free Congress, Howard Phillips, a Jew, who dismantled the OEO program for Richard Nixon and subsequently founded Conservative Caucus, and Robert J. Billings of the right-wing National Christian Action Coalition, with able assistance from Richard Viguerie, the direct mail fund-raiser for conservative groups. Although Rev. Jerry Falwell's name has been most closely associated with it through his numerous public appearances, it is not a religious organization but a political one. It attempts to reach Jews, Mormons, Roman Catholics, Protestants, and the morally indignant. It has been most successful in reaching fundamentalists. Although figures are often not too meaningful, Falwell claims some 72,000 ministers, priests, and rabbis as a part of the four million he counts within the movement. There are organizations in nearly all states calling themselves Moral Majority, with a state chair and executive committees, but they are not controlled by the national headquarters. Although it claims to be a nonpartisan political group, its orientation is toward the extremely conservative right. It has no theological dogma.

Concentration upon Jerry Falwell as spokesperson for Moral Majority, and indeed for the religious right in general, inevitably leads to misunderstanding and confusion about both Moral Majority and the religious right. He is a firm fundamentalist pastor, with his own congregation of Baptists in Lynchburg, VA, and sponsors the Old Time Gospel Hour, which gives him national visibility. Falwell has built Liberty Baptist College as part of an elaborate educational, television, and church network. All of these are quite separate from Moral Majority.[1] He usually speaks without making clear differentiation between his various roles— which seem, however, quite clear and separate to him. To make matters even more complicated, he has published several books that claim no relation to Moral Majority, such as *Listen, America!* and a co-edited book, *The Fundamentalist Phenomenon.* He is quite articulate and speaks publicly in a much more modulated tone than the fund-raising letters he sends to raise money for the Old Time Gospel Hour, which sometimes sound a bit hysterical and silly. Also, his position is constantly undergoing change, modification, and revision to meet the charges of his critics. He has seemingly learned from his critics, too, which is commendable. Sometimes it is difficult to put together what he has learned through his critics and what he continues to say when he speaks his mind passionately. For example, in the same interview with *Christianity Today*, he says:

> God has raised up America in these last days for the cause of world evangelization and for the protection of his people, the Jews. I don't think America has any other right or reason for existence other than those two purposes.
> . . . I think America is great, but not because it is a Christian nation: it is *not* a Christian nation, it has never been a Christian nation, it is never going to be a Christian nation. It is not a Jewish nation. It is a nation *under God,* and a nation in which for 200 years there has been absolute freedom to preach whatever religious conviction one might have, without ever impinging the liberties and freedom of others.

But he *does* attempt to put them together, as he continues:

> In order for the churches in America to evangelize the world, we need the environment of freedom of America that will permit us to do it. If we, through Moral Majority and other such organizations, protect and preserve those principles, America will stay free, so that the ultimate goal of the gospel—world evangelization—can be pursued by the churches.[2]

But the person who received his letter of October 2, 1980, draped in stars and stripes, was probably unaware of these subtleties while reading:

> I'm looking for flag-waving Americans! I am urgently searching for one million Flag-Waving Americans! And I want them to fly the American Flag in front of their homes or offices on Election Day—November 4th. Why? Because regardless of who you vote for, I want this nation to know that Christians are proud of their flag! Will you join me as a Flag-Waving American?
> "You see, what this country needs is Christians like you, who will get tears in their eyes when they see 'Old Glory' unfurled. We've had enough anti-God, anti-American flag burning Americans who are disgracing our stars and stripes . . . May I send you a Flag Kit?" ($50 to the Old Time Gospel Hour . . .)

In some ways, Jerry Falwell represents a subtler, warmer, more flexible and open style of leadership than many others in the religious right, including others who remain more quietly in the background of Moral Majority. One should become immersed in *Moral Majority Report* to get a sharper sense of its goals and ideology, apart from its rather smug, sometimes winsome advocate. A 1980 promotional brochure for Moral Majority calls for mobilizing the grass roots of moral Americans: "to lobby intensively in Congress to defeat leftwing, social welfare bills that would further erode our precious freedoms," to "push for positive legislation which will insure a strong, enduring and free America," to help local communities to "fight pornography, homosexuality, obscene school textbooks, and other burning issues," and to recruit and train moral political candidates.

REFORMED FAITH AND POLITICS

In this brief set of goals for the decade, the personal and sexual issues for which Moral Majority is chiefly known by the public are mentioned after naming "defeat of left-wing, social welfare bills" and a "strong America." Several articles in *Moral Majority Report* include deregulation of industry and other conservative economics positions that reflect the founders such as Paul Weyrich, Howard Phillips, and Robert Billings, who left Moral Majority to be religious coordinator for the Ronald Reagan campaign. "Walter Williams, conservative black economist, has several articles published in *Moral Majority Report* from Heritage Features Syndicate. Although the magazine has strongly opinioned articles for or against certain political candidates, it editorializes that Moral Majority does not endorse any candidates but only supports principles."

The term moral majority is a highly successful catchword admirably adaptable to media use. The title not only masks its ultra-conservative ideological basis of economics and politics by a concentration on morals and suggests a mass of support which has no factual demonstration, but it has been picked up by journalists to describe the phenomenon of the "religious right" in general. This, too, is confusing, because the religious right has many nuances to which secular journalism is tone deaf.

For example, Christian Voice is a Pasadena-based organization with pre-millenarian and pre-tribulation theological overtones, as is evident by the fact that Hal Lindsey (*The Late Great Planet Earth*) is on its policy committee. It attempts to rally fundamentalist pastors to become politically alert: "We, the chosen shepherds of the flock in these times, share an awesome responsibility, a special privilege, and an even harder calling than those who have gone before" because our nation is a "special target of Satan."[3] Its issues overlap broadly with Moral Majority, although it adds to the long list of sexual and drug abuses and educational shortcomings a concern for governmental betrayal of Christian allies in Taiwan and Rhodesia.

Not only is there huge overlap of issues with Moral Majority and other religious right groups, but there is shared leadership as well. Robert Billings, who was with Moral Majority and the National Christian Action Coalition, is on its policy committee, as are several New Right congressmen who also sit around the Roundtable, where representatives of a number of religious right groups converge. Both Moral Majority and Christian Voice have an elaborate set of sub-organizations to meet the requirements of tax law. For example, Christian Voice operates the Christian Voice Moral Government Fund, which in turn funded a project, Christians for Reagan. The Christian Voice Moral Government Fund is a political action committee that supports specific candidates for office and that is the source of the "morality" ratings often sharply criticized by those who find the definition of "morality" much too narrow and biased. Moral Majority, on the other hand, has its own national "pac" with a network of political action committees in the states, all using the name Moral Majority. It has a Moral Majority Foundation for education, which is tax-deductible. It also has a Moral Majority Legal Defense Foundation, similar to its nemesis, the American Civil Liberties Union. Moral Majority, Inc., the parent body, can claim in bold public ads that it does not support political candidates, because it is the subsidiary political action committees that do this. Political action committees seem in some tension with the advice of the *Moral Majority Report*, "Why Moral Majority Doesn't Endorse Candidates." This article, without a by-line, says:

> It would be a grave error for the national Moral Majority to endorse political candidates on the national or state levels. Endorsement of a presidential candidate would, in essence, mean that Moral Majority was committing itself to a person, rather than to principles. No matter how noble a person or a presidential candidate might be, he is still a human being. He could lose the election. He could go into office and reverse his position on moral issues, and with his moral failure, Moral Majority efforts would be stopped. If we chose to endorse candidates, those candidates could easily lose their election bids. Therefore, our effort would die with them.[4]

A somewhat different organizational tactic is used by Intercessors of America, a tax-exempt prayer chain organized by means of a newsletter that "focuses on subjects requiring national attention through prayer such as pornography and fiscal integrity." Accompanying materials make quite clear the Christian position as the basis of prayer, and urges intercessors to "salt" their communities by writing government leaders and newspaper editors. "Putting feet to prayer" includes public speeches and telephone calls to politicians. A similar group, the Great Miami Prayer Chain, has been organized by Bill Bright of Campus Crusade. Bill Bright's Campus Crusade, and the Christian Freedom Foundation, Third Century Publishers, and Christian Embassy (now defunct) have made their hopes for turning the nation into a Christian Republic, led by evangelical born-again politicians, quite explicit. It was Bill Bright, along with electronic preacher Pat Robertson, who co-sponsored the "Washington for Jesus" rally April 29, 1980.

The introduction of Pat Robertson's name to this chronicle is to bring in another set of nuances, because Pat Robertson is a complex person with an equally complex structure, the Christian Broadcasting Network. With a budget over $50 million annually, the Christian Broadcasting Network has become sophisticated, satellite TV with affiliated stations across America and picked up in many parts of the globe. It attempts to rival the "big three" secular networks with a Christian one. Although Pat Robertson has backed away from a close relationship to some of those who sit around the "Religious Roundtable" and who join in the larger Pro-Family Movement, he maintains touch with them, while asserting publicly, "God isn't a right-winger or a left-winger. The evangelists stand in danger of being used and manipulated." A Yale law graduate and son of a Virginia Senator, Pat Robertson is no political neophyte, nor have his political ambitions been laid to rest. Indeed, his Christian Broadcasting Network provides a remarkable organizing tool, should he feel called upon to run. Religiously, Robertson predicts that the catastophic End Times are near, possibly a nuclear war in the Middle East, in which Russia will be defeated and Israel "will be the wonder of the world." Politically, he thinks the Trilateral Commission wants to take over the world and destroy both democracy and Christianity.

Although the electronic church preachers are assumed by those who do not watch such programs to be caught up in the religious right, it is only a certain few who are really politically active. These include Pat Robertson and James Robison, a fiery and articulate Jeremiah of the religious right, as well as the well-known Falwell. Jim Bakker of another television network, PTL, has pulled back from his initial political forays, and preachers like Jimmy Swaggert, Rex Humbard, Oral Roberts, and Robert Schuller have not been politically oriented. Recent exposure of the Arbitron and Nielson ratings of these various electronic preachers has demonstrated that, using the usual techniques for determining popularity of programs as the standard for advertiser support, the figures quoted by electronic preachers are grossly exaggerated. James Robison may claim as high as 50-60 million viewers in his publicity and fund-raising letters, while the ratings show about 575,000 viewers. It is interesting to note that the non-political electronic preachers have consistently much higher ratings than those who have become quite political. For example, Oral Roberts, Robert Schuller, Rex Humbard, and Jimmy Swaggart top the list, above Jerry Falwell. While Oral Roberts has a Nielson rating of 2.1, Falwell has only a 1.35 and the 700 club (Pat Robertson) a .9 rating. Of ten electronic ministries, only one had increased in viewing households from February to November, 1980, and all the others had dropped. Total audience of all ten was estimated by Nielsen as 13,767,000, with Arbitron slightly lower.

Although electronic ministries have been very much in public view, the political strategy takes place in more quiet settings. The Roundtable (first called "Religious Roundtable") is composed of a mixture of right-wing leaders from Conservative Caucus and the Committee for the Survival of a Free Congress, such as Philip Crane, Jesse Helms, and Ed McAteer; fundamentalist, evangelical leaders like Falwell, James Robison, Dr. Charles Stanley of Atlanta, and Tim LaHaye; and business leaders like R.M. Goddard of Georgia, Dale Collins of Houston, John R. Bruehl of Indiana, and most recently, Cullen Davis and Nelson Bunker Hunt, two of the richest men in Texas. Hunt is also a National Council member of the John Birch Society. The military is represented by General Albion Knight and John Fisher of the American Security Council. According to *Group Reports*, the Roundtable has set a 1982 budget of $1,000,000, almost four times that of 1981.

A meeting of the Roundtable in Memphis, April 11, 1981, had Paul Weyrich, director of the Committee for the Survival of a Free Congress, as the chief speaker. The Roundtable, under the leadership of Edward McAteer, intends to have state organizations in all fifty states, with local chapters in 300 communities by the end of 1982 with the purpose of influencing public policy, reported McAteer at that meeting. Ronald S. Godwin of Moral Majority, attending the Roundtable meeting, described his own organization's goal of fifty self-sustaining, functioning state affiliates active down to the county level.

The Roundtable is part of another coalition, Library Court, named after the street where its original meeting place was located in Committee for Survival of a

Free Congress offices. Paul Weyrich was active in forming this group that gathers around family issues. Its centerpiece legislation is the Family Protection Act. Pro-life, public and private school issue groups, family morality groups, anti-ERA, decency in media leadership, along with supportive politicians like Larry McDonald, Jesse Helms, Gordon Humphrey, and Phillip Crane, sit together to devise mutual legislative and public strategy.[5]

There are numerous other coalitions, such as the Kingston group (fifty organizations dealing with business and single-issues, meeting weekly) and the Stanton group (on national defense and foreign policy). Both of these join with Library Court in a coalition of coalitions headed by Paul Weyrich and called Coalitions for America, which serves as a central forum for a total of 120 conservative organizations. Furthermore, Paul Weyrich, with the financial resources potential of Richard Viguerie's direct mail fund-raising company at his disposal, is taking steps to bring the old right and the new right into closer relationship, as indicated in a John Birch Society monthly magazine.

An umbrella group, or super coordinating group of fifty conservative leaders, was formed in 1981 and entitled the *Council for National Policy.* Familiar names compose its executive committee (Viguerie, Weyrich, Phillips) and its council membership (Morton Blackwell, Reagan liaison; Robert Billings, former leader of Moral Majority and now an official in the Department of Education; Joseph Coors who funds Heritage Foundation; Edward Feulner, head of Heritage Foundation; Nelson Bunker Hunt of Roundtable and John Birch Society; Reed Larsen of the National Right to Work Committee; Ed McAteer of the Roundtable; Bill Saracino of Gun Owners of America; and Phyllis Schlafly, head of STOP-ERA). The Administrative president is Rev. Tim LaHaye, who ran Family Life Seminars and served full-time with Moral Majority on the West Coast. The Executive Director is Louis Jenkins, a defeated Democratic senatorial candidate, who, among other affiliations, is on the board of advisors of Heritage Foundation, Conservative Caucus, and American Legislative Exchange Council. After President Reagan's first year in office, Paul Weyrich presided over a press conference at the end of a meeting of his conservative associates, and announced that the President had only C or C-minus rating with them.

The right has indeed discovered the value of coalition building. These coalitions are listed in some detail to illustrate the way ultra-conservative political leaders and religious leaders are interwoven organizationally. It is these close connections that cause other Christians the most concern. Most Christian groups agree that religious conservatives have just as much right to be politically active as religious liberals, and that bringing one's deep convictions about values, meaning, morality, and the transcendence of God to bear on political life is appropriate. There is much anxiety, however, about the sophisticated encouragement by political leaders for the religiously committed political neophyte. Can a newly-involved Christian be expected to know when manipulation is taking place? When Terry Dolan's National Conservative Political Action Committee targets a list of senators and representatives for defeat, will a fledgling political activist understand all the reasons for supporting one candidate rather than another? Who decides the "moral position" of complex issues involving the economy, or Salt II, or MX missiles, or the advisability of a constitutional amendment as the best strategy on the abortion issue? Groups like the National Council of Churches take several years to come to a policy position on a complex issue. These religious rightists have a whole menu of recipes for action, all ready to serve up, but with no certainty about the originating chef.

Another tactic besides coalition building that the religious right has adopted is the economic boycott, again one that has been used by liberals, too. The boycott is being employed by the Coalition for Better Television, headed by Donald Wildmon, against companies that advertise in television programs that do not meet the morality standards of the Coalition. Tensions in approach and priority of purposes may be illustrated by the public separation of itself by Moral Majority from this Coalition, in the name of sufficient progress having been made with the companies in question and with the intention to conduct its own monitoring. Donald Wildmon, not so incidentally, also serves on the policy board for Christian Voice and the Board of Governors of the Council for National Policy.

Recognizing that this is simply representative and not a comprehensive catalogue of religious right organizations that have fallen in the public mind under the rubric of "moral majority," we move to a deeper examination of who constitutes the followers in these groups.

Who are the Followers?

As the introduction indicated, religious rightists tend to be drawn from the ranks of those who are upset with sudden moral changes in the larger culture. Many of them are fundamentalists who, like unwilling immigrants, find themselves in a new country—but they have not moved; the country has moved away from them. They are desperately trying to reconstruct the society with which they can feel at home, and have set up Christian schools, born-again shopping guides, television "worlds," and gatherings in which their views become majority views. Many are becoming politically active for the first time as they hear the urgency of saving the nation from moral decay and Communist overthrow. Because they are neophytes in politics they are prone to manipulation, as Pat Robertson himself notes, by politicians who are willing to include the fundamentalist's moral agenda, but who have an economic and political agenda of their own. Some of them have, in the purifying fire of divine service, been devious or blundering in their political tactics, and have earned the ire and fury of their opponents. Fundamentalists tend to see the world in extremes of good and evil, with very little middle ground, and their opponents are seen as devils or the handwork of Satan, and are thus to be destroyed.

Some pentecostals and charismatics are included in their ranks, particularly as viewers of the electronic church. But, as Martin Marty notes, "pentecostals tend to be gentle, less than militant people . . . preoccupied with praising God, being healed, and—it must be said—entertained by programs like Jim Bakker's PTL Club talk shows."[6] They may often agree with the morality issues raised by the religious right, but many of them withdraw from the realism of rightist politicing. Evangelicals are also only ambiguously related to politics, and journalists have falsely jumped to the conclusion that 30 million evangelicals in this country means a potential of 30 million for the religious right.

Gallup's poll, on the 30 million evangelicals he defines as comprising one fifth of the adult population, was seen in September, 1980, to be 52% for Carter, 31% for Reagan, and 6% for Anderson, at a time when the general population was split 39%-38%-13%. His survey offered a very mixed picture, with born-again Christians favoring ERA—but by a slimmer majority than other Americans—and at the same time strongly favoring required prayer in public schools. Timothy L. Smith, who is the author of *Revivalism and Social Reform* and director of a research project on "The American Evangelical Mosaic," calls to our mind the evangelicals who are the majority in historic peace churches. They are: Brethren, Mennonites, and Quakers, who do not countenance militarism; the Southern Baptist Convention's thirteen million whose heritage treasures the separation of church and state and whose goal is a kingdom of love; the Churches of Christ in America with over 2.5 million evangelicals who are not caught up in the doomsday biblical prophesy that infuses much television preaching; the black evangelicals who may well constitute a third of all evangelicals in this country, but who are only tokenly represented in "I Love America" rallies; and the Salvation Army, the Nazarenes, and some radical Wesleyan groups that are devoted to people trapped by racism or poverty. Smith says that this broad community of evangelicals deplores Falwell's efforts to build a power bloc in its name and marvels that the news media countenance his claim to speak for them.

If we exclude most denominations like the Southern Baptists and Missouri Synod Lutherans on the basis of their strict separation of church and state, and most evangelicals, pentecostalists, and those fundamentalists who have not been stirred from their aversion to politics, and if we eliminate most blacks (who may share many of the moral sentiments but who strongly resist the ideology of the right), we are left with a much smaller population of religious rightists than is publicly perceived.

Alienated, fearful, angry, outraged, frustrated, anxious—they find hope, community, and a reason for being in groups like Christian Voice, Moral Majority, and the "700 Club." Not all of them are lower-middle-class, though figures show a higher percentage of evangelicals are in that category than the general populace, and that a lower percentage have attended college than the public as a whole. Yet, even though the New Right may draw heavily from small town capitalists, Falwell notes that his biggest audiences are in Los Angeles, Philadelphia, Boston and New York, in that order. Dr. George Gerbner, of the Annenberg School of Communications in Philadelphia sees television preachers as having brought these alienated Americans into the mainstream of our society. Jerry Falwell sits in their living room saying just what they, too, have been saying about moral decay in this country, and he invites them to do something about it. He writes back to them, too. And rugged, smiling Pat Robertson chats with successful beauties who love Jesus, with Congressmen who share his sense of the End Times coming but who also seem unafraid, and invites those who are troubled to call him and pledge their dollars for God's bountiful multiplication. Now, not only have they had a Billy Graham and a Jimmy Carter in Washington, but they have a familiar friend on their living room television who assures them that what they think and what they do will make a difference.

A closer look at the members of Moral Majority has been made by a student, Donna Day-Lower, who has surveyed the available data and concluded:

> Those most attracted to the Moral Majority are almost exclusively white, predominantly working to middle class, conservative Protestant in background without a college education. They tend to have more children than the general population (which brings us back to Yaneklovich's theory that a concern for their children in a complex and pluralistic society provides motivation for many to join the Moral Majority). Moral Majoritarians are both middle-aged (and family-oriented) as well as old (retired persons, often living alone who are regular viewers of the electronic church).
>
> Further, a typical member of the Moral Majority has probably come to the organization with a fundamentalist orientation for primarily religious, rather than political reasons. There was nothing in the data to support an image of patriotism bordering on the neurotic, as the stereotype, created by the media and the visible spokespeople of the organization, would suggest. The adherents are found mostly in the large towns/small cities of the South.[7]

She further notes two class groups, the upwardly mobile who are just "making it" in the American Dream and want what they have accomplished and accumulated to be validated and protected, and the economically stagnant, who are angry with those whose power over their lives has kept them from realizing the American Dream.

How Then are we to Assess Them?

Christians and other religiously attuned citizens have an obligation to listen well to the anger or anguish of every group of people. Furthermore, the citizenship rights we exercise are the rights of all citizens, and religious rightists are working within our political system. So our first words must be words of welcome. We tend to be more prone to mute our religious testimony in public affairs the more we are sensitive to the pluralism in our society. I concur with the President of Union Theological Seminary in New York, Donald W. Shriver, who sees this also as a danger:

> On the one hand, people of faith lose their integrity if they refuse to measure social policy by perspectives rooted in their faith. On the other, a pluralistic society protects its citizens' rights to disagree with each other's faith assumptions, readings of fact and preferred public actions. Freedom of speech includes the freedom to propose a religious argument for a public policy. But no human argument is immune to criticism—from one's neighbor or one's God. . . . Let us speak publicly about all our reasons for thinking about or doing public business. Who knows? It might help us understand each other,

to know where we really disagree and agree, even to teach each other wisdom from our respective inheritances.

Before leaping to criticise the bungling, bumbling new fundamentalist political activist too harshly, we have reason to take stock of our own shortcomings. In one of Jesus' more memorable flashes of humor, he calls on people to "take the log out of their own eye before removing the speck from someone else's eye." Perhaps one favor that has been unwittingly performed for other religious leaders has been this demonstration by the religious right of an exaggeration of our own failings, so that the beam in our own eye is visible at last to ourselves.

The remainder of this discussion is a set of observations that have relevance not only for the religious right, but for all who care about the role of religion in public life. It incorporates many of the perspectives that have been voiced by Christians from a broad spectrum of traditions. It is intended to speak to Christians of various political persuasions.

Observations

The pros and cons of righteous indignation: Their self-righteousness tends to put off even those who share some of the views of the religious right. Any group who gives itself wholeheartedly to a moral cause is tempted by this odious perversion of morality. When one has been stirred to indignation and anger by an infringement of the moral order as one perceives it, the energy to act is released. This happened in the civil rights movement and in opposition to the Vietnam War and to slavery. Being sure that one's position is morally sound is necessary for the hard work and risks of challenging the society, but being too sure that one is right can produce smug self-righteousness and a willingness to justify almost any tactics in pursuit of that good. Some of the critics of the religious right are engaged in a clash of two extremes of self-righteousness and moral certainty, and little progress is made in public mediation of these two extremes. One of the spiritual gifts we bring each other at our best in gatherings of diverse, ecumenical religious groups is the restraint upon our individual passionate certitude about a particular issue. There is a tendency in our pluralistic society to talk chiefly to those whose opinions have been ascertained to be "safe," to agree essentially with one's own. Of course, some common basis for concern is needed to bring any group together. In some settings, however, where we have sufficient common faith and concern for a real dialogue to take place, we often confine ourselves to easy areas of agreement and do not test or demonstrate our commitment to each other and our common goals by searching the areas of painful difference or sharp division. If we care deeply about each other, we then become a bit chastened in the absoluteness of our own position.

To put it another way, it is an essential for the functioning of democracy in a pluralistic society and for the functioning reality of ecumenism that we learn from each other to make even our most fervently held position *less than God.* James Wall, editor of the *Christian Century*, says our task as religious leaders is "to be able to lift up the issues that are important, to be able to push forward to solutions to those issues without baptizing those issues as God's will." There will always be those who see the humility of our position as weakness when we refuse to absolutize our position. Sometimes history forces us to take personal unequivocal stands, and our martyrs, heroes, and heroines illustrate such instances which we greatly honor. But one can even die for a cause with the humility of leaving to God the ultimate judgment of one's sacrifice. There is a significant spiritual difference between self-righteousness, which pridefully judges others, and humble obedience to God's humanly perceived will.

Rescuing the nation with patriotic zeal. During the turbulent sixties many people who criticized their country for its Vietnam policy were considered to be very unpatriotic. "Love it or leave it!" snapped the bumper stickers. Now the harsh critics of America are some of the same ones who carried those bumper stickers, as they now describe our nation's shame in its state of moral decay. But their motto now, in effect, is "Love it and heal it." More effectively than those who protested Vietnam, they cloak their criticism of the country in a kind of patriotism. The nation is in danger. God's special nation may lose its special blessing. We must turn the nation around before its corruption and immorality bring on its destruction. There is a sense of urgency, an appeal to patriotism, and a simple program for survival: Bring the nation back to righteousness and provide it with military superiority against its enemies. There is much psychic energy in that message: the time is short, we are the saviours, the evil is clear, and we must gird ourselves against the enemy.

The inconsistency in much of what is said is often not picked up, and perhaps we are remiss in failing to point to it. The country is immoral and corrupt. On the other hand, only America can be trusted with superior military and nuclear power, because of its moral superiority over other nations of the world. We look to God to heal and bless America once again. But we trust our security to military might. As Robert McAfee Brown puts it, "The only consistent thesis seems to be, 'Yes, we can trust God to save us miraculously, if we turn back to Him, but just to be on the safe side, let's arm ourselves to the teeth!'"[8]

On the other hand, many of us resonate with Falwell's Biblical prodding to turn our nation from its wicked ways. Living by God's principles, we also believe, promotes a nation to greatness, and we want our nation to be great. Our problem is with the definition of "wicked ways" and "living by God's principles." We are concerned about a nation that has too many young people living in urban ghettoes who sense no future in the society and the workplace for themselves. We're concerned about the unresolved problems of racism in our land. We're anxious about a nation relaxing into 9% unemployment. We do not see the role of our country as a global arms merchant as strong evidence of "living by God's principles." We see the problems of families as far more complex than the simple moral solutions proposed by the religious right, and we are not prepared for women to bear the blame and brunt in those solutions. We are anguished by the problems of our poor, especially those who are elderly or sick. We may have, in perplexity and sensitivity to the unknowns and ambiguities involved, left unattended some issues related to sex and pornography, but we cannot limit a definition of "morality" to those issues alone.

Protection of economic gains and a hunger for public recognition. Sociologists tell us that there have been since the fifties some considerable improvements in the economic position of many who are a part of the religious right. Yet the society has been changing so rapidly in values at the same time, that the usually expected shift from sect-type fundamentalism to mainstream religion as one rises in the economic level in society is not occurring for many newly middle-class, even college educated fundamentalists. George Marsden, author of *Fundamentalism and American Culture*, says empathetically that since the Scopes battle over evolution, many conservative evangelicals and fundamentalists seemed to be left in a cultural backwater.

Meanwhile, the nation rapidly has shifted its cultural values so that these people have felt like unwilling "immigrants" in their own country, and they reacted like immigrants, forming their own ghetto-style community. The television "electronic church" makes more visible this encapsulated community within our society. It also provides a sense of public recognition, even a "respectability," despite much popular criticism. The secular new right was shrewd to sense their readiness for a public role and to enlist them to their own political ends through showing concern for the moral issues which motivate them.

None of us is immune to the need for economic security and public recognition of our place in the society. At our best we welcome them into the political fray, because they have a right to be there, and because democracy is healthiest when all of its citizens have free expression and participation. Because of their long sense of alienation, their lack of political understanding, and the insecurities which drive them to overzealousness, we need to be careful not simply to exacerbate their feelings of hostile aggression. How one does this is a case-by-case struggle, and many of us have scars to make our response even more awkward. Some care must be taken not to be overwhelmed, not to be taken over or destroyed by these groups, which may mean some regulatory steps for participation in public meetings that one finds a bit repugnant—or some aggressive counteraction of charges which we do not do with ease or grace. But our long-term goal is to move them toward responsible citizenship.

A nostalgic vision for America. For Christians, something tugs at us when we hear the rhetoric of a Christian America proposed by the religious right. I didn't understand this very well in myself until reading Robert Bellah's books and Robert Handy's careful book, *A Christian America: Protestant Hopes and Historical Realities.* But now I hear in some of Falwell's, Robison's and other religious rightist remarks some echoes from an earlier America for which I may have some nostalgia, but to which I do not think it is possible to return and do not wish to return. Recall, for example, the words of Horace Bushnell in the mid-1800's: "The wilderness shall bud and blossom as the rose before us; and we will not cease, till a christian nation throws up its temples of worship on every hill and plain; till knowledge, virtue, and religion, blending their dignity and their healthful power, have filled our great country with a manly and happy race of people and the bands of a complete christian commonwealth are seen to span the continent." Or recall John Winthrop's stirring words on board ship to Salem in 1630: "We shall be as a city upon a hill. The eyes of all people are upon us, so that if we shall deal falsely with our God in this work, that we have undertaken, and shall cause him to withdraw his present help from us, we shall shame the face of many of God's worthy servants." Winthrop exhorts his people, "that the Lord our God may bless us in the land whither we go to possess."

Hopes for a Christian America have been high among Protestant Christians from the time of the founding of this country. Early rejection of a particular kind of Christianity as an "established" religion came about partly because the earnest desire for religious freedom made it finally politically impossible to place one tradition in the political saddle. It may be noted that the zeal for religious freedom among most groups was freedom for one's own religious expression, not an abstract zeal for freedom of religion for all. What began as a pragmatic desire to avoid the political ramifications of choosing a particular religious position and giving it special state protection and privilege has become a sweeping ideal of freedom for all to be unhampered in religious practice. What began also as a cautious recognition that religion can be divisive as well as uniting, and that the state would do well to stay as clear as possible from religious disagreement, has emerged in some interpretations as a wall separating church and state, which is a rather unfortunate image, because it seems to suggest that perspectives from a religious viewpoint are not germane to political action.

At the time when the first amendment to the Constitution was shaped, the pluralism of America was not very remarkable. In 1800 there were only 12 denominations, all Protestant, although only 10% of the population were active church members. There were 30,000 Roman Catholics as of 1790, although they grew to 600,000 by 1830. Ten years later there were still only 50,000 Jews, however. Today there are almost 50 million Roman Catholics, 72 million Protestants, of which 30 million might be called evangelical and of those 6-7 million are fundamentalist. There are 6 million Jews, 4 million Orthodox, and possibly 3 million Muslims. About 133 million people claim religious affiliation out of a population of 220 million in the nation. A proliferation of new religious bodies adds complexity as well as diversity to our pluralism, because of the difficulty of defining them for government exemptions, and perhaps the test of time is the best judge.

By the time of the Civil War there were appearing some deep divisions about what constitutes a Christian nation and a Christian way of life—as slavery was questioned, and issues of poverty and lifestyle in the cities, the observance of the Sabbath, and other social justice issues became more insistent. But a hundred years later we are asking more basic questions: Given our pluralism today, what dreams for a Christian nation and a Christian world are appropriate, if any? How do we infuse religious perspectives into social discourse and public life while still respecting the views of others? Have we gone too far in secularizing public life as a safeguard of religious liberty—or are we in danger of imposing a particular religious point of view upon society? How does a pluralistic society receive from many religious perspectives without becoming captive to any one of them, or becoming a battleground for them? Have our religious institutions and our homes become ineffective in transmitting religious faith and values in the face of secular forces, such as the media?

Whether or not there were a Moral Majority, we would be confronted with these questions. In an odd way we may be grateful that such issues are forced into our consciousness, because then we must try once again, in new times, to shape our responses. Perhaps we have reached at least the point of calling for a "Golden Rule" of religious liberty. We should seek the freedom of religious expression and practice for others that we would want for ourselves. That leads us to some painful decisions, and some awkward alliances, as well as some limits to our own best dreams for the United States of America.

Endnotes

1. There are times the separation is very blurred, however, e.g. an "Understanding Politics Conference" at Liberty Baptist College, Feb. 8-9, 1982. The key political speakers were Paul Weyrich, Terry Dolan, Howard Phillips, Stanton Evans (*Human Events, National Review*), Connaught Marshner of Phillip Crane's office, Robert J. Billings, and others with similar political orientation.
2. *Christianity Today*, "An interview with the Lone Ranger of American Fundamentalism," Vol. XXV, No. 15 (Sept. 4, 1981), pp. 22-31.
3. Enlistment letter to pastors.
4. Vol. 1, No. 11 (Aug. 5, 1980), p. 5.
5. A more complete list and a summary of the Family Protection Act can be found in my book, *The Bible Vote, Religion and the New Right* (New York: The Pilgrim Press, 1981).
6. *Miami Herald*, Dec. 21, 1980.
7. Unpublished Manuscript.
8. "Listen Jerry Falwell!" *Christianity and Crisis*, Vol. 40, No. 21, (Dec. 22, 1980).

UNDERSTANDING FUNDAMENTALIST VIEWS OF SOCIETY

George Marsden

Introduction: Two Kinds of Understanding

For those of us who are not fundamentalists our first goal in relating to them should be understanding. But how are fundamentalists best to be understood? This question is particularly perplexing regarding their political views. To outsiders their views on politics and society often appear arbitrary and inconsistent. One moment they may be complaining about a "social gospel" and the next they may be proclaiming a program for reforming America from top to bottom. Are such paradoxes best understood as the collective irrationality of angry people who have been left out of the power centers of the society? Or can we make sense out of fundamentalist political opinions on their own terms?

The prevailing approach to understanding fundamentalism has been to explain it as collective irrationality. This approach goes back to the original appearance of fundamentalism early in this century. At that time fundamentalism arose in America as a coalition of evangelical Protestants militantly opposed to "modernism" in theology and the growing secularism in their culture. In the 1920s, much as in the 1980s, fundamentalists made national news, particularly in their political efforts, such as their campaigns to ban the teaching of biological evolution in the public schools. Their liberal opponents indeed applied a model of cultural evolution in explaining fundamentalism itself. Modern culture, they assumed, was progressing steadily through scientific advance. Newer beliefs and older ones were in a sort of struggle for "survival of the fittest." The newer beliefs, armed with the weapons of science, inevitably would win this battle. Fundamentalism, then, was the desperate last struggle of a dying breed of traditionalists. Rural America was frantically trying to preserve a doomed set of values. Once modern scientific education was sufficiently widespread, fundamentalism would disappear. So wrote the *Christian Century* in an editorial titled, "Vanishing Fundamentalism," in 1926: "If we may use a biological term, fundamentalism has been a *sport,* an accidental phenomenon making its sudden appearance in our ecclesiastical order, but wholly lacking the qualities of constructive achievement or survival."[1]

[65]

In the 1950s fundamentalism still was around and so were interpretations that emphasized its culturally determined irrationality. The best of these was offered by historian Richard Hofstadter, who was reflecting particularly on avid attacks by fundamentalists and others on communists and intellectuals during the era of Senator Joe McCarthy. Hofstadter saw the emergence and continuing deep bitterness of fundamentalists as resulting from their experience of crisis in status. White Anglo-Saxon evangelical Protestants had dominated American culture until the late nineteenth century. Their displacement by secularists, supported by the new education of the universities, brought out the paranoid and anti-intellectual traits in their tradition. So their religious style came to be "shaped by a desire to strike back against everything modern—the higher criticism, evolutionism, the social gospel, rational criticism of any kind."[2]

During the cultural turmoil of the 1960s the mood of America changed dramatically. One outcome was that many people realized that the deep diversities of American society would have to be accepted, rather than obliterated or ignored. So, for instance, the "melting pot" ideal regarding immigration gave way to new recognition of the unique heritages of each ethnic group that should be valued and preserved. The "Black is beautiful" theme reflected the same trend—that mere absorption into the white mainstream should not be the goal of a group with its own valuable roots. The same applied to religious heritages. Rather than simply assuming, as advocates of the evolutionary model had, that dissenting groups eventually should be absorbed in the steadily progressing "mainstream" or else die off, dissent was seen as having its own solid roots that might allow it to grow well on its own. In this atmosphere a new interpretation of fundamentalism was suggested, articulated by historian Ernest R. Sandeen. "We exist in a fragmented and divided culture," wrote Sandeen in 1970, "not in one pervaded by consensus."[3] Accordingly, he argued, in his major work appropriately titled, *The Roots of Fundamentalism,* the movement was alive and vigorous just because it had deep ideological roots. Specifically, these roots were in "millenarian" teachings concerning literal Biblical interpretation and the return of Jesus to set up a millennial kingdom. While Sandeen omitted some other important ideological roots, he had made an important point: fundamentalism was an authentic conservative tradition and could be understood best by taking its own ideology seriously.

In the 1980s these two approaches to understanding fundamentalism continue to compete. The one assumes a generally liberal cultural and intellectual consensus and persists in regarding fundamentalism as essentially a cultural aberration. The other sees fundamentalism as a coherent belief system, best understood on its own terms.

The most fruitful way of resolving this debate is to look for the valid insights of each approach. Fundamentalism does indeed grow out of certain cultural experiences. Understanding these will throw light on fundamentalism itself and why it is attractive to many people. These experiences may explain some apparent inconsistencies in the social and political attitudes of the movement. On the other hand, fundamentalism will be misunderstood if it is *reduced* to a cultural phenomenon. Fundamentalism involves commitment to a certain set of views, and until the essential coherence of this worldview is seriously considered, fundamentalism itself can not be understood or appreciated.

Such an approach can bring "understanding" at two levels. First we can "understand" fundamentalism in the sense of gaining an explanation of a strange phenomenon. Beyond that, however, we may go on to "understanding" in the sense of trying to appreciate and empathize with a point of view of a divergent group.

Fundamentalism as a Cultural Phenomenon

The key to understanding fundamentalism as a remarkable cultural phenomenon is to recognize the extent to which evangelicalism dominated the American mentality only a century ago. One hundred years ago *McGuffey's Readers* were standard texts in vast numbers of American public schools. These school books contained explicit evangelical teaching in lessons such as "Respect for the Sabbath Rewarded," "Religion the Only Basis of Society," "The Bible the Best of Classics," "My Mother's Bible," or "The Hour of Prayer." Or think of the novels of Mark Twain. America was in one sense as secular as the wild west, a point that Samuel Clemens enjoyed underscoring. Yet everyone, including a thorough secularist such as Clemens, had an "Aunt Polly" in the background shaping one's conscience. Evangelicalism, which in many respects was very vigorous, controlled much of the American mentality.

Less than half a century later, the picture had changed drastically. By the 1920s secular aspects of the culture had come to the fore in controlling public opinion. Evangelicalism was seriously divided in the fundamentalist controversies and widely discredited by the popular press. "Christendom," said H. L. Mencken, "may be defined briefly as that part of the world in which, if any man stands up in public and solemnly swears that he is a Christian, all his auditors will laugh." "The irreligion of the modern world," said Walter Lippmann in a more serious vein, "is radical to a degree for which there is, I think, no counterpart."[4] Whereas half a century earlier America's leading scientists had been by and large renowned evangelical spokesmen, most educated people now regarded the "warfare between science and religion" as almost a premise of thought.

To understand fundamentalism one must try to imagine what living through such a transition might do to some pious people. Within a generation the values that they had been brought up with—reverence for the Bible and the mores of evangelical Victorian America—had become matters of derision.

Such an experience would be almost like the Anglo-Saxon Protestant equivalent to the immigrant experience. As in the experience of immigrants, the values that were held sacred in one's youth turn out to be widely regarded as quaint and bizarre. America had changed so much, especially in the fundamental values that dominated the public outlook, that it was almost like another country. Evangelical Christians had become strangers in their own land.

As in the immigrant situations, people react differently to such situations. Some adjust to the new cultural setting without great difficulty, blending the old ways and values with the new. Protestant "modernists" of the 1920s would fit this mold. The essence of the Christian tradition, they emphasized, could be found in the best in modern scientific culture. Fundamentalists were those who took just the opposite tact (most Protestants remained somewhere between these two extremes). Like the immigrants who want to preserve everything of the old world tradition, fundamentalists insisted that that which was new in modern culture must be rejected. No compromise could be allowed. Christians were in a warfare between God and Satan, between Christ and Anti-Christ, between Biblical Christianity and modern secular values. It was a fight for life versus death. Heaven versus a culture bent on hell and destruction. Such warfare allowed no neutrality.

While cultural factors in forming such an outlook can be understood best in relation to the dramatic transformation of America in the early twentieth century, the type of experience involved has not been confined to that period. Many persons today have similar experiences. The transformation of the culture in the early twentieth century is recapitulated in the lives of many individuals. They grow up in a relatively protected ethos of evangelical church and social contacts and then are rudely confronted by the cultural values of the larger community that regard such values with contempt. Fundamentalists are those evangelicals who react to such encounters with militancy. Typically experiencing a dramatic conversion that rescues them from some degree of involvement in the secular outlook, they allow no compromise with the old way. Richard Hofstadter describes the typical outlook well as "essentially Manichean; it looks upon the world as an arena for conflict between absolute good and absolute evil, and accordingly it scorns compromises (who would compromise with Satan?) and can tolerate no ambiguities."[5]

Fundamentalism as a Belief System

Valid as such analysis may be, it does not tell the whole story. Fundamentalism is also a coherent belief system representing a combination of a number of longstanding traditions. While social and psychological circumstances may help explain why some people adopt such a worldview, we must not forget that the relationships are reciprocal. Worldviews shape persons' perceptions of reality and help explain strong stances on social questions.

Fundamentalism embodies, first of all, many important themes in the Christian tradition. Central to fundamentalist thinking is a Biblical theme that has been obscured in much of modern Protestantism. The universe is divided, as it surely is in many Biblical conceptions, between the forces of God and righteousness and those of Satan and evil. The warfare is a struggle to the death between God's people and his enemies. This conception is essential, for instance, if one is to see the celebrated acts of Old Testament violence as heroism rather than as atrocities. For today's fundamentalists the practical life and death issues are not found first of all in physical battles, but rather in the battle for the souls of humanity. Holding a classic Reformation and pietist view of the substitutionary atonement, and taking the Biblical cosmic struggle seriously, they see most of humanity as endangered by the punishment of eternity in Hell. Nothing is more important, therefore, regarding one's neighbors, one's nation, or the world, than to convince people to stop serving Satan and to have them accept instead salvation and eternal happiness in Christ. Fundamentalist aggressiveness, which often is viewed by others as self-serving aggrandizement, is seen by fundamentalists themselves as sacrificial service to humanity. Their many arduous missionary efforts evidence the sincerity of such convictions.

This worldview, which as outlined thus far is that of much of evangelicalism, acquires additional characteristics due to its fusion with some other traditions. Very important is a set of beliefs about the ability of Christians to discover the truth with certainty. At a practical level fundamentalist confidence is built simply on the belief that God will lead his people in the truth. Fundamentalists, as well as their close cousins in the pentecostal and holiness movements, often talk of firm knowledge of "the leading of the Lord." But fundamentalists particularly have also expanded this view of truth to include some important theories of how to find truth. The Bible is, of course, the supreme authority for fundamentalists. Moreover, they regard the interpretation of the Bible as an exact science. Thus in establishing the certainty of their views, they rely not on just a general appeal to the witness of the Holy Spirit, but also to a scientific analysis of Biblical teaching.

The combination of such views of knowledge and the Biblical worldview of the clash of cosmic forces has powerful implications. Not only do fundamentalists see the universe as divided between the forces of light and darkness, they also are convinced beyond a doubt that they can identify who or what is on which side. How do they know? Because the Bible tells them so? So what opponents view as arrogance, fundamentalists themselves see as humble reliance on the Bible alone.

The most characteristic product of fundamentalist Biblical interpretation, the system called "dispensationalism," illustrates these points. It also has bearing on some fundamentalist social views. Dispensationalism was devised in the nineteenth century. Reflecting one of the ideals of that age, it was purported to be a thoroughly scientific system of analyzing the Bible. History, as described in the Bible, was divided into seven "dispensations," or ages, in each of which God dealt with his people in a new way. So the requirements that applied to Adam and Eve in the "dispensation of innocence" were different than those that governed Israel in the "dispensation of law," which in turn were different from the New Testament principles governing the current church age. Particularly important for dispensationalists is the interpretation of prophecy. Prophecies are to be interpreted as much as possible as though they were scientific statements of matters of fact concerning the future. "Literal where possible" is accordingly the key principle. This rule means that whenever possible one should interpret a prophecy as referring to an identifiable literal event (for example, the "Beast" in Revelation refers to a future emperor of a restored Roman empire). Particularly vivid in dispensationalists' thinking are a seven year's series of stormy prophetic events, centering around the state of Israel, which will begin any day and will immediately precede the return of Jesus to set up a literal kingdom in Jerusalem for exactly one thousand years.

Dispensationalism has some important political and social implications. Most direct is that fundamentalists tend toward a very favorable attitude toward the Jews and the state of Israel. Dispensationalists correctly predicted the return of the Jews to Israel long before it happened. They do hold that Jews must be converted to Christ, which they predict will happen on a large scale during the seven prophetic years. This fundamentalist zeal for conversions has led many Jews to resent fundamentalists' friendliness. On the other hand, fundamentalists themselves take literally the promise of God to Abraham that "I will bless them that bless thee" and so urge kindness to the Jews.

Dispensationalism also has wider social and political implications. One of its teachings is that the current age is one of steady degeneration. The institutional churches, of which the Roman Catholic is the prototype, are corrupted with worldliness and in unholy alliances with the state or culture. The ideal of "Christendom" or "Christian civilization," say many dispensationalist teachers, was an illusion that the kingdom of Christ could be brought about in this age. Rather, the only true kingdom is that of Christ in the millennial age to come. Meanwhile, Christians should not be deluded by political solutions to the world's problems. Rather, they should separate themselves from worldliness and from worldly churches. One should live, in the words of the Gospel hymn, as though "I am a stranger here. . . ."

Dispensationalists who follow these teachings consistently tend to be apolitical. They insist that Christians should stay away from any social programs. They should rather put all their energies into winning souls to Christ. One should obey the powers that be, but remember that the only really important kingdom is that which is yet to come.

Oddly, however, most American fundamentalists (who are predominantly dispensationalists) do not consistently follow these apolitical implications of dispensationalism. Rather, an entirely different tradition also shapes their social-political outlook. This is the Puritan tradition, which has had a deeper influence in shaping the popular American evangelical mentality than has dispensationalism. By the first half of the nineteenth century, when evangelicalism was a leading force in American culture, this tradition had developed social and political tendencies which are almost the opposite of dispensationalism (which became a widespread view only later in the century). Instead of postponing the kingdom to a future dispensation, the dominant nineteenth-century evangelical view was to regard God's kingdom as growing out of the spiritual progress of the present age. In technical terms this was a "postmillennial" view that said Christ would return only *after* a millennial age which would be the last phase of current history (premillennialists, such as dispensationalists, said Christ would return *before* the millennium.) The nineteenth-century postmillennial views were combined with a more strictly Puritan teaching that America stood in much the same relation to God as had Old Testament Israel. This meant that America was viewed as a chosen nation with a special role to play in history. Many nineteenth-century evangelicals thought that America would have a special leadership role in the approaching millennial age of spiritual blessings. Such views of America's destiny fit the avid nationalism of the era and sometimes fed overestimation of America's virtues in relation to other nations.

Most important for understanding this compelling image of America as a new Israel is that, as with Israel of old, the relationship to God was *covenantal.* The covenant was a national contract with God and the terms of the covenant were that the nation must obey the laws of God. God would continue to bless America only so long as she continued to obey his laws. If she turned from his laws, then surely punishment and destruction would follow.

The relationship of God's law to the nation was thus the key factor in shaping American evangelical social, political, and economic views. The success of the nation depended directly on her virtue. God would bless or curse nations that kept or broke his laws. He would administer these blessings or curses in two basic ways. One way was through special providences. For instance, as happened time and again with Old Testament Israel, he might raise up nations to punish his erring people. The second way of administering justice, however, was built into the nature of things. God had structured the moral law into the universe with many inbuilt rewards and punishments. Perhaps the most popular example was the work ethic. Work was rewarded with prosperity. Laziness and idleness were punished with poverty and misery. Such laws seemed self-evident. Hence it seemed a disservice for the government to reward the poor with welfare payments when they were not working. Charity to the disabled, widows, orphans, and the like was urged; but to give able-bodied people the rewards of work when they were not working was simply to interfere with God's economic laws. Similar principles applied in many other areas. Marital infidelity was punished with misery for oneself and one's family. Intemperance led inevitably to sorrow.

Fundamentalists today accordingly have two traditions to draw on when approaching social and political questions. On the one hand they can draw on the dispensationalist tradition which, when consistently applied, leads away from political action. On the other hand, they can draw from the deeper evangelical tradition of the covenanted nation, where a crucial Christian emphasis is on the importance of national adherence to God's laws, not only in private lives, but in public policy.

From an outsider's point of view, fundamentalists may seem wildly inconsistent in wavering between these two opinions. Sometimes, as we observed at the outset, they attack all political involvement as "social gospel," at other times they are reforming the nation. Sometimes they will speak of America as a doomed nation. At other times it is God's favorite and the greatest nation on earth. Is America Nineveh or Israel? The covenantal theory might resolve this seeming paradox by saying that if the new Israel turns from God she shall be condemned. But then how do the fundamentalist views fit with their dispensationalism where Israel refers only to the literal state of Israel?

Such apparent inconsistency on social and political matters is puzzling and may suggest that interpretations of fundamentalism as essentially irrational are after all the most helpful. Nonetheless, in defense of fundamentalists it should be observed that they are hardly less consistent on such points than are mainline Protestants. One has only to look at the history of the Presbyterian churches in America. During the slavery controversies, for instance, most Presbyterians lined up strictly along regional lines. Those in Alabama or Mississippi saw Christian anti-slavery as a blatant violation of separation of church and state. Border state Presbyterians were usually less certain on the issue. In the North, the closer one's ties were to New England, the clearer it was that a chief duty for Presbyterians was to abolish the slave system. Only rarely did Christians take stances that went against the major social and political opinions held in their region, class, and time. The same is true throughout the history of Christian social and political efforts. Rarely have groups, except some peace churches, long followed a consistent set of principles concerning the relationship of the church to politics. Far more typical has been for such theories to be adjusted to the immediate political interests of the group. So, for example, one of the most common mainline criticisms of American evanglicalism and fundamentalism during the 1950s and 1960s was that it was socially irresponsible, preaching a "private" Christianity. When, however, these same fundamentalists and evangelicals go "public" and turn out to be Republican and politically conservative, the cry is soon heard that they are unduly mixing the Bible and politics. Of course, some such accusations may be legitimate. That is not the present point. The point is only that inconsistency on the church/state issues is not a trait that distinguishes fundamentalists from most other Christians. Probably all of us are guilty of much the same thing.

Understanding the Current Fundamentalist Complaint

If we make this concession, we are in a position to look directly at the current fundamentalist complaint and to attempt to understand the essence of their viewpoint. Since the fundamentalism that we now are looking at is distinctly *political* fundamentalism, it is not surprising that most of the assumptions that shape their outlook (excepting their views on Israel) come from the politically activist covenantal side of their tradition, inherited from Puritanism as transformed in the dominant early nineteenth-century evangelical outlook.

Central to understanding the current fundamentalist alarm, then, is to realize that they take absolutely literally and seriously the idea that America will be blessed or cursed according to how well she keeps God's law. Jerry Falwell makes this point repeatedly. While acknowledging that America is not a theocracy like ancient Israel, "we nevertheless are a nation that was founded upon Christian principles, and we have enjoyed a unique relationship toward God because of that foundation." Specifically, Falwell sees the relationship of God to America as a covenantal relationship. On the one hand, God blesses those who keep his law. "America has been great because she has been good." On the other hand, Falwell quotes the threats of God to Israel for covenant-breaking and argues that "the same warning applies to America today."[6]

The moral issues accordingly are exceedingly practical ones. The success or failure of America depends directly on whether it preserves this moral heritage. Judging by this standard, fundamentalists are understandably alarmed at the moral direction of the nation. To them the open flaunting of God's laws in the open championing of things like abortion, pornography, and homosexuality are sure signs that our nation is on the brink of God's judgment and destruction. As Falwell observes, "If God does not judge America soon, He will have to apologize to Sodom and Gomorrah."[7] So he says in characteristic covenant language, "we're more convinced now that the problem of the nation, the real problem, is a moral one, that the economic problems, the energy crisis, our international embarrassments are all simply symptoms of the fact that God is angry with us as a nation."[8]

To many modern people these might seem like strange causal connections. Will the energy crisis really be relieved if we clean up pornography? Such thinking may seem odd; but Christians should remember that most of the greatest thinkers in their heritage prior to this century held very similar views. If one holds that all of history is controlled by the providence of God and sees the Biblical judgments on nations as real and normative for today, such conclusions are not so outlandish. One might disagree with the premises regarding God's administration of current history, or one might reject some of the specific sins as central requirements of God's laws for modern nations, but nonetheless one must concede that the outlook itself has an impressive heritage.

Fundamentalist thinking accordingly is organized largely around God's eternal laws. "Ours is indeed a clever generation," says Falwell, "but one that is suffering because men are doing what is right in their own eyes and disregarding God's immutable laws." Reflecting directly the thinking of his nineteenth-century evangelical forebears, Falwell sees the laws of reward and punishment built into the order of things as certainly as the laws of physics. "The law of sowing and reaping is as immutable as the law of gravity. . . ."[9] Hence the Moral Majority is to be built on those who share this view of law. So says Falwell. "George Gallup said his findings indicate that a whopping 84 percent today in America believe the Ten Commandments are valid for today, so we began putting together that Moral Majority—a coalition crossing all the lines."[10]

The seriousness with which the Moral Majority take these ideas of immutable law as the basis for God's blessings or punishment is illustrated most clearly by the abortion issue. Whether or not others think fundamentalists are correct in viewing abortion as murder, it is difficult to discredit fundamentalist stances on this issue as motivated out of any obvious self interest. Self interest might suggest that fundamentalists, whose constituency is drawn mostly from the lower middle class and higher, would favor policies that reduced the population of the poor. The fundamentalist stance is just the opposite. The best explanation is that a major motivation is a sincere belief that the whole nation will suffer if such breaking of God's law is condoned.

The family issues, which are central in bringing together the current fundamentalist political coalition, all involve this basic concept of God's immutable laws. The intensity of fundamentalist opposition to the Equal Rights Amendment has been built on this principle. No doubt some less rational factors have been involved as well; but central to fundamentalist understandings is that God has ordained an ideal law-structure for the family. In this structure the husband should be the loving head of the household and the mother should be first of all concerned with childrearing. These structures are built into nature. If they are generally ignored everyone will eventually suffer. As one opponent of ERA put it, "Nature," (unlike the constitution), "cannot be amended."[11]

If we grant, however, that the fundamentalist outlook is built around a coherent concept of a universe governed by God's eternal laws, an important question remains. Have the fundamentalists properly read these laws? Are the positions they are defending all reflections of the immutable laws of God, or are they mixtures of God's laws and culturally conditioned human understandings? Here is a point at which the discussion with fundamentalists can be conducted in their own terms. After all, even if we grant that God's Word is inerrant and that his laws of nature are immutable, almost everyone must admit that one's own understandings of that Word and law can be fallible and mistaken.

Particularly striking if we approach the issue this way is the degree to which the old-time religion reflects the ideals of nineteenth-century America. For instance, the fundamentalist stance on the family, while reflecting some Biblical precedents, also reflects middle-class Victorian patterns and ideals. More clearly drawn from a recent cultural tradition, rather than directly from the Bible, are the economic and political views of the New Right. Unlike their Puritan forebears who thought that government should take an active role in ensuring the economic welfare of the whole community, contemporary fundamentalists favor the free enterprise economics of Adam Smith. Aside from the virtues or defects of this old "liberal" program as an economic system, it certainly reflects a pervasive nineteenth-century American emphasis on the importance of the free individual. While the New Right wants strong government regulation on other moral issues, in economic practice they stress the freedom of the individual to compete for his own success. While they find Biblical justification for an ethic where work is rewarded, the stress on competition for personal success is an American cultural ideal that is in sharp tension with prevailing Biblical themes concerning personal relationships.

Personal success has continued to be a conspicuous motif in twentieth-century American fundamentalism and evangelicalism. One has only briefly to watch some of the giant TV ministries to find that success is one of the main things offered. The entire lifestyle presented evokes this aura.[12] One's prayers for (i.e. gifts to) a ministry are sure to be richly rewarded. Moreover, the new fundamentalism unabashedly identifies with the rich and the powerful, particularly with conservative business interests and their political allies. As Black evangelist Tom Skinner has observed, "There are more than 300 verses in the Bible on the commitment to the poor, to justice and righteousness, but they are silent on that."[13] Despite occasional attention to such themes, the strict Biblicism of the Religious Right clearly has been also a selective Biblicism. There are some signs, however, that because of the Biblicism in the tradition, some elements in the fundamentalist political right may be open to reconsideration of such stances.

In a similar category is the fervent American patriotism and militarism of the movement. A recent mailing from Roundtable Issues and Answers, for instance, provides a list of Old Testament verses dealing with military strength and asks that these be used "to discover His will for the defense of America."[14] Obviously such thinking combines Biblical themes with the cultural assumptions that America stands in the same relation to God as did Old Testament Israel. Fundamentalists also justify such patriotism by stressing that America was founded on Christian principles and hence has a special place in God's plans. Whatever the virtues of such arguments, they involve substantial myopia, the shortsightedness of seeing oneself first and forgetting about one's neighbors. As the fundamentalists' own dispensationalist interpretations would suggest, when viewed from a strict Biblical perspective, the idea of the centrality of America for God's historical plan seems naive and self-serving. Again, some fundamentalists may be open to reconsideration of such points if the questions are framed in their own terms.

All these criticisms are related to a more basic trait of the movement that is not derived from the Bible. That is its tendency to overassurance in identifying God's will with the interests and values of one's own group or nation.[15] Raising such points brings us back to some of the observations made about fundamentalism as a cultural movement. It has appealed particularly to people who divide the universe up into armed forces of good and evil with no middle ground. Moreover, it encourages the presumption that we can identify exactly who is on God's side and who is on the side of Satan. Such overassurance is then combined with the central assumptions of fundamentalist thinking—the understanding of the universe as controlled by God's immutable laws. Nonetheless, it is important for both critics and proponents of such views to notice that the two tendencies do not necessarily have to go together. One might conceive of the universe as controlled by God's immutable laws, revealed in Scripture and confirmed in nature, and yet be ready to acknowledge that one's own understandings of Scripture and nature are severely limited. Such a sense of one's own limitations may help to lead to an attitude of regarding one's neighbor (far and near) as being as worthy as oneself. It may give one a sense that, despite total dependence on God, his Word, and his redemptive grace through the work of Christ, we and our kind may not stand at the center of history nor be the favorites in God's plans.

Such a stance is thoroughly consistent with fundamentalists' avowed premises. It seems fair to suggest, therefore, that cultural circumstance and traditions may be the major factors in leading to the overassurance and seeming self-centeredness of much of the movement. Perhaps, then, the most helpful approach in approaching fundamentalists today is to start by taking their avowed outlook seriously. It is, after all, in principle extremely close to some major traditions still alive in many mainline American churches. Once some sympathetic understanding on this level is achieved, constructive communication may be possible. Under such circumstances, one should expect to find that on some important issues fundamentalists and mainline Christians are basically on the same side in opposition to the destructive forces of much of modern secularism.

Endnotes

1. *The Christian Century* XLIII (June 24, 1926), p. 799.
2. Richard Hofstadter, *Anti-Intellectualism in American Life* (New York: Alfred A. Knopf, 1962), p. 121.
3. Ernest R. Sandeen, "Fundamentalism and American Identity," *The Annals of the American Academy of Political and Social Science* Vol. 387 (January, 1970), p. 64.
4. H. L. Mencken, *Prejudices, Fourth Series* (New York, 1924), pp. 78-79; Walter Lippmann, *A Preface to Morals* (New York: The Macmillan Co. 1929), p. 12.
5. *Anti-Intellectualism*, p. 135.
6. Jerry Falwell, *Listen America*, (New York: Doubleday, 1980), pp. 252, 263, and 49.
7. *Ibid.*, p. 248.
8. Falwell, *Eternity* interview, (July-August 1980), p. 19.
9. Falwell, *Listen America*, pp. 62 and 64.
10. Falwell, *Eternity* interview, p. 19. Of course not all members of the Moral Majority or the New Right are fundamentalists; but fundamentalists are at the core of these movements.
11. Quoted in Donald G. Mathews, "Cultural Fundamentalism: The ERA in North Carolina," paper presented to the American Historical Association, December 30, 1980, p. 7.
12. Virginia Stem Owens, *The Total Image: Selling Jesus in the Modern Age* (Grand Rapids, William B. Eerdmans Publishing Co., 1980) provides a helpful discussion of this theme.
13. Quoted in Peggy Shriver *The Bible Vote, Religion and the New Right,* (New York: The Pilgrim Press, 1981), p. 52.
14. Mailing from Edward E. McAteer, Roundtable Issues and Answers, March 2, 1982.
15. Gabriel Fackre, *The Religious Right and Christian Faith* (Grand Rapids: William B. Eerdmans Publishing Co., 1982) includes helpful discussion of this point.

THE REFORMED TRADITION AND LIBERATION THEOLOGY

by Albert Curry Winn

In a series of essays on the subject of Christian faith and political action, an essay on the liberation theologies is unavoidable. These theologies are patently political, without evasion or apology. They raise the question in its most acute form.

"It is now clear that the major breakthrough in Christian theology in the last decade has been the explosive emergence of political and liberation theologies . . . The theological landscape has been irretrievably changed." Those are the words of David Tracy, a Roman Catholic theologian. He gives the liberation theologies a decidedly mixed review, but is nonetheless aware of their significance.

Up to this point we have spoken of "theologies" in the plural, because there are clear and evident differences between various types of liberation theology. In Latin American liberation theology, the poor are to be liberated from economic oppression. In Black liberation theology, Black people are to be liberated from racial oppression. In feminist liberation theology, women are to be liberated from sexual oppression. Between these theologies there are tensions, even jealousies. They are united by the common theme of oppression, and the common belief that those who have been oppressed can articulate theologies that are more biblical, more valid, more true, than the "traditional" or "dominant" theologies that have been written by the oppressors.

For the limited scope of a brief essay I have chosen to confine myself to Latin American liberation theology, and in particular to the arresting work of Gustavo Gutierrez. I do not mean by this choice to imply that the other liberation theologies are less interesting or important or erudite or significant for our theme of faith and politics. One simply must start somewhere.

I
The Themes of Liberation Theology

What are the principal themes of liberation theology? To attempt a brief answer to that question is a ridiculous effort on its face. Most of us are familiar with the distortion of Calvin's thought that goes under the title "The Five Points of Calvinism." What we have there is a caricature of a theology far richer and more complex than the "five points" would indicate. Just so a listing of "five principal themes" of liberation theology may distort that theology's richness and complexity and produce only a caricature.

Let me record my conviction that we are not dealing here with a mere "regional variant" that we can observe comfortably at a distance, as though it were some brilliant butterfly of the Amazon basin with no particular relevance to daily life in North America. Nor are we dealing with "political ideology" or "an ethical reduction of the gospel." We are dealing with a genuine theology. It has its own theological method, gives an account of its own path to truth. It produces its own understanding of God, of Christ, of salvation, of the church, of eschatology. It intends to be, and is, a part of the ongoing dialogue that includes Augustine, Aquinas, Rahner, Bonhoeffer, Barth, Moltmann, the papal encyclicals, and the documents of Vatican II. Above all, it takes Scripture seriously. Biblical references abound. As it is enlightened by the Word it casts fresh light upon the Word.

So with profound respect, real trepidation, and a saving, humorous awareness that all lists of themes result in caricatures, let us proceed to a thematic outline.

1. *God is on the side of the oppressed.* This is first of all a biblical theme. Gutierrez is keenly aware of the centrality of the Exodus: God is the One who liberated the oppressed slaves in Egypt. Creation and Exodus are indissolubly linked, as Deutero-Isaiah makes clear again and again. Creation is the first act of history, human history; and human history is the story of God's liberating action. The Exodus begins a long march which culminates in the coming of Christ, who brings new creation and new liberation. In the humane legislation of the Old Testament we see God's "tilt" toward the poor. In the incarnation we see God's solidarity with the oppressed.

To be for the oppressed is to be against the oppressors. Here Gutierrez cites a plethora of texts from Job, Isaiah, and all the prophets; from Jesus' words in Luke, and from James. The divine indignation is aroused at the cheating of the powerless, the orphans and widows; at fraudulent commerce and exploitation; at the hoarding of lands; at the violence of the ruling classes; at slavery, dishonest courts, unjust taxes, corrupt officials.

This is clear from scripture. But how can a God who loves all be for some and against others? How can the "universal salvific will" of God, God's purpose to save all, be reconciled with God's own "preferential option for the poor?" Universal love must become concrete, it must embrace some for the sake of all. In the long run, the oppressors can be saved only through the liberation of the oppressed.

2. *In Latin America, oppression is systemic.* It is not enough to describe the crushing poverty of the masses in Latin America. It is not enough to weep in

sympathy for their sufferings. The Latin American reality must be analyzed. Such an analysis is human work, human reflection on facts.

The analysis which makes sense in the Latin American situation is a Marxist analysis. There is a class struggle between those who own and control the means of production and those who own nothing. This is complicated by the dependence of both classes—the poor and the ruling oligarchies—on the great multinational corporations of capitalist North America, the ultimate owners and controllers.

The system is oppressive. It is not enough for religion to transform individuals into persons of good will, whether among the poor, the ruling class, or the corporate directors. Persons of good will are present in all three groups. But they are trapped in an evil system. Nothing will change until the system is changed.

"Development" is a bankrupt term in Latin America. It stands for efforts to help the Latin American nations "catch up" with the capitalist system in North America and Europe. It is "superversion," change imposed from the top, and leaves the power of those on top unchallenged. It does not attack the root causes of the evil. At the end of "the decade of development," the Latin American poor were worse off. The under-development of the under-developed countries is a direct result of the development of the developed countries.

"Liberation" is the proper term for Latin American aspirations—to be liberated from dependence on the developed nations, to be liberated from the smothering power of the elite ruling circles, to be liberated from the grinding, hopeless poverty of the masses. This calls for "subversion," change imposed from the bottom. For Gutierrez this would call for common ownership of the means of production—a socialist state.

Gutierrez would hope that systemic change, "subversion," liberation can come about through the political process, without violence. But he reckons with violence "as a last resort." He does not forget that one of the heroes of liberation theology is Camilo Torres, a Colombian priest who died fighting with the guerrillas. There are three levels of violence in Latin America, he says. There is the violence of the system itself, which kills hundreds of people daily. There is the violence of the police and armies, accounting for the "disappearance" of those who oppose or are suspected of opposing the ruling regimes. And then there is the violence of the guerrillas who can tolerate the situation no longer.

3. *To participate in liberation is salvific work.* To engage in the struggle for justice to the poor is to take part in God's great plan of salvation. Here the question of the relationship between faith and political action comes to a head. How is it possible to relate "liberation," which is so thoroughly political, even to the point of violence, with the great spiritual concept of "salvation?" How can we say that a struggle which is so "horizontal," relating solely to this world, is connected with salvation, which we think of as "vertical," relating to the next world?

Here Gutierrez analyzes the changes that have taken place in the idea of "salvation" within his own Roman Catholic communion. Salvation used to mean "guaranteeing heaven," and the debate was *quantitative*. For how many could the church, which was the sole repository of salvation, guarantee heaven? What about the salvation of the heathen? Gutierrez traces the development of such ideas as "general grace"—grace at work in all people, including those outside the church; and "anonymous Christianity"—Christianity beyond the visible frontiers of the church. At length, through a recovery of the teaching of Thomas Aquinas—that there is present in every human being an innate desire to see God; and above all through a rediscovery of Paul's teaching that all things were created in, through, and for Christ (Colossians 1:16), that all things have been reconciled to God by the blood of the cross (Colossians 1:20), that the grace of God has appeared for the salvation of all human beings (Titus 2:11); the church has begun to teach in the documents of Vatican II "the universal salvific will of God." This is not, as I understand it, the straight-line universalist teaching that all persons are in fact saved. But it declares that God's purpose is to save all, and if any are excluded it is by their own choice, not God's. It is closely analogous to Karl Barth's teaching of the election of all human beings in Christ.

With the quantitative question thus solved, Roman Catholic thought has turned to the *qualitative* question. What is the quality of the salvation that God wills for all and which can be obtained beyond the visible boundaries of the church? Gutierrez repeatedly defines it as communion with God and one's fellow human beings. Sin, then, is not something that cancels the future enjoyment of salvation in heaven. It is what alienates us here and now from our fellow human beings and from God. The overcoming of sin and the restoration of communion becomes a historical, this-worldly project. Heavenly salvation is only the culmination beyond death of what begins here. So there is not "salvation history" and "secular history." There is only one history, human history, in which God is at work to overcome injustice, to break down all that separates people from God and each other. To participate in the Latin American struggle for liberation is, then, to work along with God in the divine effort to save all people.

At several points Gutierrez offers a three-fold analysis of "liberation." First, there is political liberation, the liberation of oppressed classes from their oppressors, about which we have mainly spoken thus far. Second, there is human liberation, in which human beings begin to assume conscious responsibility for their own destiny, seize the reins of their own evolution, become the creators of a new humanity and a new society. Third, there is liberation from sin, which is the root of all alienation and injustice and oppression. Unjust situations do not happen by chance; there is human responsibility for them. But this responsibility is not merely individual, private, interior. It is social, historical fact. Christ dies to liberate us from sin in all its dimensions. Here is a further reason why the term "development" won't do; it dodges the basic issue of sin.

It is clear that if the third level of "liberation" is omitted, we are not dealing with salvation in any full sense of the word. Gutierrez would argue that if the first level is omitted our notion of salvation is equally truncated!

4. *The church must become the church of the poor.* Neutrality is impossible.

Not to side with the poor is to side with those who oppress them. To do nothing and to say nothing is to support the *status quo*. It is pointless to say that the church should not take sides. It has already taken sides with the rich and powerful. What is needed is the "conversion" of the church, a conversion from the side of the powerful to the side of the powerless.

Through the influence of the liberation theologians, the Latin American bishops at Medellin and again at Puebla declared a "preferential option for the poor." Gutierrez attempts to spell out what that means. The *gospel* ought to be addressed primarily to the oppressed, remembering that Jesus declared he was sent to preach good news to the poor (Luke 4:18). The voices of the marginated and dispossessed should be heard in the church; they should take *ownership* and set policy; the owners of this world's goods should no longer be the owners of the gospel. The church should be "the *sacrament* of history," that is, the place where the liberating grace of God, which is the heart of the historical process, can be seen clearly at work. This means, of course, that oppressive structures within the church must be quickly done away. The eucharist should be a *celebration* in the church of the liberation that is taking place outside the church walls.

The church's role is *denunciation* and *annunciation*. The church must denounce all the sinful structures that grind down and oppress human beings. Sometimes the church's voice may be the only one that can speak out. The church must announce the coming of God's kingdom, the possibilities of a more just, humane, and sustainable order.

The church must go beyond being "the church of the poor" to become "the poor church." It must surrender its wealth. Its priests and bishops must live in simplicity. It must express in its life solidarity with the poor.

How can the unity of the church be maintained in the midst of the class struggle? Can rich and poor come to the eucharist together? If the church takes the side of the poor will it not drive the rich out of the church? Gutierrez wrestles with this problem. Is there a real unity to be maintained? Or in a divided world is the unity of the church a myth? Unity is best seen as a gift of God and an achievement of human beings which is still future. Only the commitment to the struggle against all that presently alienates and divides people can make the church an authentic sign of unity.

A strange new ecumenical unity is emerging in Latin America. A common understanding of the misery and injustice that abound is binding different communions together more closely and more quickly than all the slow negotiations about faith and order.

5. *Theology is critical reflection on praxis.* As a result of the four convictions discussed above, the liberation theologians feel that they have discovered a new and better way of doing theology. Theology begins with efforts to change the world, echoing Marx's eleventh thesis against Feuerbach: "The important thing is not to understand the world, but to change it." World-changing does not proceed by a set plan where the end is envisioned from the beginning. It proceeds by "praxis." Praxis is a sort of trial-and-error procedure. You try something.

Then you reflect on what has happened. Then in the light of what you have learned you try the next thing. Praxis is kin to the "action-reflection model" which is discussed so much nowadays by Christian educators. Theology, then, is not an armchair exercise. It can be properly done only by those already engaged in praxis for the poor.

But theology is critical reflection. We do need to understand and criticize our praxis, to examine intelligently what we are doing to change the world. One senses here an indirect parallel to Karl Barth's definition of theology as the church's critical reflection on its preaching. In both cases, theology is not the first thing, but "the second act," as the liberation theologians call it. Theology discerns the positive and negative values in praxis. It makes explicit the faith, hope, and love contained in praxis. It corrects aberrations and one-sidedness. It makes the commitment to liberation more evangelical, more authentic, more concrete, and more efficacious.

It does all this "in the light of the Word." Liberation theology does not wish to abandon scripture. Scripture is not the starting point, because we have read scripture so long through the eyes of the dominant, oppressing group that justification of the way things are is what we will hear if we begin there. We must come to scripture out of our struggle to help the poor. They will teach us to read it from "the underside." We will hear it in fresh ways, and in more authentic ways, because scripture was initially addressed to the oppressed, not to the powerful. This is "the epistemological privilege of the poor."

II
How Reformed Theology Might Be Deepened By Serious Dialogue With Liberation Theology

Up to this point we have been trying to set forth liberation theology as fairly, completely, and succinctly as an outsider can. We have been letting it speak for itself, in the form developed by one of its leading Latin American exponents. We have not engaged in any "critical reflection" of our own.

The time for critical reflection has arrived. In this section we shall reflect positively on what can be learned from this new theology that exploded onto the theological scene in the past decade. In the next section we shall be more negative, emphasizing values in our own tradition that the liberation theologians have neglected to their peril.

First, then, what can we learn from liberation theology? To this question many Presbyterians, if they have read this far, will answer: Nothing! The word "Marxism" triggers in us a completely negative reaction. It stands for atheism, godlessness, tyranny, everything we fear most. It is what many Americans are prepared to combat even at the cost of a nuclear holocaust. How can we "learn" something from a theology that bears so deep a Marxist taint?

The importations from Marxism do indeed need careful theological scrutiny. Regarding some very basic theological flaws we shall have strong warnings to issue in the third section of this paper. But some of what Marx said about the oppression of the have-nots by the haves was said much earlier by Jesus and the

Hebrew prophets. The fact that Marx repeats those things does not make them false. The basic question about the analysis of the Latin American reality made by the liberation theologians is not, is it Marxist? but is it true? In their use of Marxist analysis and in their embrace of the Marxist goal of a classless society, these theologians are clearly neither atheists, godless, nor lovers of tyranny. Reformed Christians should not be so timid and unsure that they fear truth from any quarter.

Other Presbyterians will question whether we have anything to learn because of the taint of violence. This is indeed a vexed and difficult question. But those of us who pay our taxes to support a military system that seeks to uphold our nation's dominance by threatening to annihilate over a hundred million Russians in one thirty-minute salvo can hardly sit in self-righteous judgment over the participation of Camilo Torres in guerrilla warfare as a "last resort." A consistently nonviolent position, applied to ourselves as well as to others, is a Christian option, perhaps *the* Christian option. But so long as we are tainted by violence, let us not refuse to learn from others who are similarly, and perhaps less seriously, tainted.

If we can get beyond these obstacles, we can hear some interesting things from our neighbors to the south.

1. *We can be reminded of our own long history of political involvement.* Those who think it is un-Presbyterian to write their Representatives or Senators should simply take up a copy of Calvin's *Institutes.* The fundamental document of Reformed theology begins with a political letter, addressed to King Francis I of France. In it Calvin, who had fled France as a subversive, warns his former sovereign that France is so filled with the fury of wicked persons that there is no place in it for sound doctrine. He speaks of the violence of the established government and the courts, which have condemned, imprisoned, exiled, burned, exterminated innocent people. He speaks of the lies, frauds, and slanders that have been spread. He expresses the belief that the king has been ill advised and urges him to make his own independent investigation of the facts. He dares to say that a king who in ruling over his realm does not serve God's glory exercises not kingly rule but brigandage. He puts his hope in the strong hand of the Lord which will surely appear in due season, coming forth armed to deliver the poor from their affliction and also to punish their despisers, who now exult with such great assurance.

Those who think it is un-Presbyterian to attend the open meetings of City Council should study the constant, unending, exhausting dealings that John Calvin had with the local authorities in Geneva.

Though he never held public office, John Knox was as deeply involved in the politics of Scotland as anyone living; he was the chief political counter-force to Mary, Queen of Scots.

The Westminster Assembly of Divines was appointed and paid by Parliament, in the midst of a civil war between Parliament and King Charles. Its task, to prescribe uniformity of belief, church government, and worship for England,

Scotland, and Ireland, was an essential building block in a grand scheme of political unification.

When George III remarked that Cousin America had eloped with a Presbyterian parson, he was not praising the Presbyterian Church for its apolitical stance.

When Presbyterianism divided North and South in these United States, the ostensible issue was highly political: whether loyalty to the federal government should be a requirement for church membership. The underlying issue was even more political: slavery.

There has been an almost schizophrenic split between the rhetoric of Reformed theology and the action of Reformed churches and people. Calvin's rhetoric in his chapter on "Civil Government" is ostensibly anti-revolutionary. Leaning on Romans 13, he defends the necessity of civil government and the divine sanction for it. Regardless of the form it takes, Christians should be compliant and obedient to it. He argues at length that obedience is due even to unjust rulers. Christians should not rebel, but suffer patiently and trust God to vindicate the right. But, says Calvin, God uses human agents to punish unjust kings, some by an express command, others unwittingly. "The Lord accomplished his work through them alike when he broke the bloody scepters of arrogant kings and when he overturned intolerable governments. Let the princes hear and be afraid."

The last quotation could have been written by a liberation theologian. And the action of American Presbyterians in the American Revolution was based there rather than on the main thrust of Calvin's chapter.

The rhetoric of the Westminster Confession of Faith is decidedly apolitical. The saying most frequently quoted is that synods and councils "are not to intermeddle with civil affairs which concern the commonwealth unless by way of humble petition in cases extraordinary." Yet the Westminster Assembly was sitting at the aegis of a Parliament which finally beheaded a lawfully crowned king, an event which sent shock-waves through Europe that extended to the French Revolution and the Russian Revolution.

That Reformed political actions have been at times unwise and at times inexcusably violent is beyond question. But a stance of political apathy, of political non-involvement, while it may seem to be sanctioned by Reformed rhetoric, is not in accord with Reformed history from the beginning to the present time. When the United Presbyterian Church in the U.S.A. adopted its Book of Confessions, including the *Barmen Declaration* and the *Confession of 1967*, it took a bold step to bring Reformed rhetoric into line with Reformed history and tradition.

Liberation theology, with its overtly political stance, can shake us out of our political apathy and remind us what our tradition has been all along.

2. *We can be reminded that Reformed theology was originally a theology of the oppressed.* In the letter to King Francis I, referred to above, Calvin says: "What mean and lowly little men we are . . . in men's eyes most despised—if you will the offscouring and refuse of the world, or anything viler that can be

named . . . Some of us are shackled with irons, some beaten with rods, some led about as laughingstocks, some proscribed, some most savagely tortured, some forced to flee. All of us are oppressed by poverty, cursed with dire execrations, wounded by slanders, and treated in most shameful ways.''

Geneva was a city crammed with refugees from almost every European land. Money, supplies, and food were short. Survival was a constant problem. When the refugees returned to their homes, they often met with fresh oppression. Such was the case of John Knox and the Scottish refugees. In the preface to the Scots Confession they write: "But such has been the rage of Satan against us . . . that to this day no time has been granted us to clear our consciences, as most gladly we would have done. For how we have been tossed until now the most part of Europe, we suppose, understands.''

The burning bush of Exodus 3 figures prominently on most of the seals of the Reformed churches. The church is aflame with persecution, but it is not consumed; it survives. The oppression experienced by the Reformed churches was not primarily economic or racial or sexual; it was plain, straight-line religious oppression.

The Reformed theologians were just as sure as the liberation theologians that God is on the side of the oppressed. That conviction is one root of the strong doctrine of *election* that is so characteristic of Reformed theology. The oppressed are the elect, and the oppressors are the reprobate. It is one of the ironies of history that in the course of the centuries this became reversed. In many Calvinistic cultures the rich became the elect and the poor became the reprobate; the Scotch-Irish frontiersmen were the elect and the Native Americans whose lands they seized were the reprobate; the Calvinist Boers were the elect and the South African Blacks were the reprobate; the Southern slave-owners were the elect and the slaves were the reprobate; the comfortable, educated church members who fill the church on Sunday are the elect and the street people who come for soup on Monday are the reprobate. This is a perversion of primitive Reformed theology. Initially the Reformed church was the church of the poor. It was, as Calvin called it, "the poor little church.''

There are Reformed churches which are oppressed today: in places like Czechoslovakia, Taiwan, Korea, LeSotho. In many cases it is because they have exercised a "preferential option for the poor," because they have had a ministry of denunciation and annunciation. I have a notion Calvin would be more at home in those churches than in the middle-class comfort of our North American Calvinist churches. More important, I suspect Jesus would be, too.

3. *We can be helped to take seriously neglected portions of the Bible.* Robert McAfee Brown, perhaps the best North American interpreter of Latin American liberation theology, has remarked more than once on the sort of canon within the canon utilized by Gutierrez and his colleagues. There is the Exodus, of course—the original record and all the reassessments of its meaning that mark the rest of the Old Testament. There are the prophets, with special weight on such passages as Jeremiah 22:13-16: to do justice is to know God; and Isaiah 58:6-7:

the true fast is to let the oppressed go free. Then there is Jesus' sermon at Nazareth in Luke 4:16-30 and the picture of the last judgment in Matthew 25:31-46. And don't forget the passage in James 5:1-6 about the wages of the laborers kept back by fraud.

Everyone knows those passages, but they are not really foundational to traditional Reformed theology. When Calvin the commentator dealt with them he spoke as movingly for the poor and the oppressed as anything Gutierrez ever wrote. For Calvin the widow, the orphan, the plundered poor were "us," not "them" as they are for modern, middle-class Reformed exegetes. But Calvin the theologian founded his system on the Pauline Epistles. And that has dictated the shape of Reformed theology ever since.

This can be understood in terms of what Brown calls "the interlocutor." Every theology takes its shape around its questioners and the questions they ask. Calvin's interlocutors were the Roman Catholics on one side and the left-wing Reformers on the other, with second-generation Lutherans nearer the middle. This becomes clear if you look at the Index of Names in a good edition of the *Institutes*. It then begins to account for the Table of Contents. And finally it explains the Index of Scripture References. Calvin was driven to those parts of scripture that helped him answer his interlocutors.

After the Enlightenment, the interlocutors became the nonbelievers. And this dictated subtle changes in the structure of Reformed theology and in its canon within the canon.

The interlocutors of liberation theology are the non-persons, the poor and oppressed ones whose humanity and personhood has been denied by the system. It is their questions which dictate the form of liberation theology and drive it to certain scriptures as foundational.

Should Reformed theology recognize non-persons as interlocutors? The prophets did. Jesus did. It would broaden and deepen our grasp of scripture to do so.

4. *We can be driven to reconsider the connection between Calvinism and capitalism.* What disturbs many North Americans most about liberation theology is its indictment of capitalism as the root cause of oppression and suffering in Latin America. We react as though someone had uttered blasphemy. That reaction reveals the religious value we tend to give to capitalism. Blasphemy is an irreverent insult to a god. If a charge against capitalism, however reckless or unfounded, strikes me as blasphemous, have I made capitalism a god, an idol?

The material benefits that the capitalist system has brought to most North American Presbyterians are obvious. We live in unprecendented and unparalleled affluence. The source of the affluence may well be primarily the exploitation of the nonrenewable resources of an incredibly rich continent. But those riches could not have been unlocked and delivered to our doors without the aggressive competition which is characteristic of capitalism. Until recently we have been able to believe that the same escalator that carries some to untold riches and power lift the mass of people at least a few steps higher in income, prosperity, and comfort.

With the vanishing of the frontier and the cultivation of consumer demand that outstrips our resources, things have changed. In a "zero-sum" economy the rich can grow richer only if the poor grow poorer. Fortunately there are laws which seek to limit and cushion the brutality involved in this competition. But in the international order there are far fewer limiting and cushioning laws and mechanisms. As the rich nations grow richer the poor nations grow poorer in a ruthless, brutal fashion. This is why, as we saw earlier, the under-development of the under-developed countries is a direct result of the development of the developed countries.

The capitalist system, which is now so strongly attacked by the liberation theologians, has been closely linked with Calvinism. Max Weber explored this linkage in his famous essay, written early in this century, entitled *The Protestant Ethic and the Spirit of Capitalism*. It has been much criticized as over-simplistic, but a re-reading even today reveals its power and insight.

Weber makes a case for Benjamin Franklin as a quintessential capitalist. He quotes the familiar maxims: "Time is money"—any time you are not working is costing you the money you could have made. "Credit is money"—for six pounds a year you may have the use of hundred pounds. "Money can beget money"—he that murders a crown destroys all it might have produced, even scores of crowns.

Here is a working, secular religion. The first and greatest commandment is to work as hard as you can as many hours as you can to make as much money as you can. The cardinal sin is waste of either time or money. The monastic, ascetic discipline is that the money thus made is not to be spent on amusement or comfort but straightway invested to beget more money. The cardinal virtues are thrift, industry, prompt payment, keeping contracts—all of which increase your credit and enable you to have the use of the money of others. This religion seems almost designed to achieve the accumulation of capital. We have all known and observed its devotees.

Franklin's father was a Calvinistic Puritan. And it was Calvinistic Puritanism, says Weber, that fathered the secular religion we have described. The great question for Calvinists was: how can I know that I am one of the elect? Pastoral advice to those tortured by that question was two-fold. First, you must consider yourself chosen and beat down all doubts, since doubts betray a lack of faith. Second, you must engage in intense worldly activity to give evidence of your election. Since the making of money is an objective measure of the extent and effectiveness of worldly activity, wealth becomes the most tangible sign of election. Here is the theological root of capitalism. But the theology can be abandoned and you will still have the driving zeal to make money for the sake of making money, without regard to luxury, comfort or the other things money can buy. It is a contest, a game, and money is the way you keep score. "Enough" is always "more."

It is interesting to compare "the spirit of capitalism," as described by Weber and recognized by us in ourselves and others, with Calvin's own views about money and business. He did regard business as a legitimate way of serving God and working for the greater glory of God. This was because the circulation of money and goods and services is a concrete form of the communion of the saints. Those engaged in business should aim to help the poor and to reduce the gap between the poor and the rich. Calvin thought it would be good to restore the Year of Jubilee, a periodic redistribution of wealth so the gap would never become permanent. This is a far cry from the response of a multinational corporation to a church-sponsored stockholder resolution: "The use to which our products are put is not our concern; the maximization of profit is."

It is not impossible that Calvin would agree with the liberation theologians that capitalism of that stripe is indeed a source of oppression. If Calvinism is the unwitting father of capitalism, is it now called upon to be the corrector of the abuses that have arisen within capitalism?

5. *We can be reminded that praxis, doing the truth, is an old Calvinist custom.* Long before Marx wrote that the important thing is not to understand the world, but to change it, Calvin was trying to change Geneva from a brawling, licentious town to a just, humane, sustainable city, a city ordered according to the Word of God. Truth, he believed, is in order to goodness. The successive editions of the *Institutes* that issued from his pen were colored by those efforts, that praxis. He would probably want to turn Gutierrez's definition around and say: "Theology is mediation on the Word in the light of praxis." But he would agree that uninvolved, armchair theology is worthless.

III
How Liberation Theology Might Be Deepened By Serious Dialogue With Reformed Theology

It is a false humility to assume that because Reformed theology is old and encrusted with tradition it has nothing to contribute to contemporary theological discussion. God bestows gifts on all, even on us. It is part of our obedience to the Fifth Commandment to honor and value the particular gifts given to our fathers and mothers in faith. So we move on to discuss certain aspects of our heritage which the liberation theologians have neglected and which we feel they should not have neglected. One form of love between different parts of the church universal is the duty of serious theological dialogue.

1. *We would remind the liberation theologians that good theology always struggles to be universal.* Calvin's goal in writing the *Institutes* was not to compile a handbook of the peculiarities and special insights of the Reformed churches but to set forth the Christian religion, the faith of the one holy catholic church, what has been believed everywhere, at all times, by all. Every Reformed Confession does the same. Karl Barth wrote his massive *Church Dogmatics*, not Swiss Dogmatics, or Reformed Dogmatics.

The liberation theologians remind us that we cannot really do this. The theology we write is inevitably colored by our time, our situation, our geography, our economics. If we are the oppressors our theology will unconsciously seek to justify the oppressive *status quo*. If we are the oppressed our theology will cry for change and liberation.

This problem was recognized years before the liberation theologians by Richard Niebuhr, who wrote eloquently about the relativism that affects physics, philosophy, economics, politics, and theology. In each case all knowledge is conditioned by the situation of the knower. We need to face this, take it seriously, admit it freely.

But should we rejoice in it and glory in it? Or should we struggle against relativism and try to attain such inclusiveness and universality as we can? The liberation theologians have abandoned the attempt for even a measure of universality. They write Latin American theology or Black theology or feminist theology. The latter two have even excluded from the conversation those who do not have their particular experience. That is understandable, but it is a cop-out. How can the church be reformed and always reforming if the ongoing dialogue is not open to everybody, and if the central attempt is not to include as many segments of the community of faith as we possibly can?

2. *We would remind the liberation theologians of the reality and pervasiveness of sin.* The Achilles heel of Marxism is its inadequate doctrine of sin, its unfounded optimism regarding human nature. If only the social order can be changed, if only the proletariat can seize control of the means of production, if only the classless society can come into existence, then greed, lust, selfishness, violence, oppression—all the undesirable aspects of humanity will wither away. Utopia will arrive. That no Marxist state has been able to demonstrate even the first faint beginning of this "withering" process does not seem to diminish the naive optimism of the devoted Marxist.

Gutierrez seeks to protect himself from this error by his three-fold analysis of liberation, in which the third point is liberation from sin. Should that not be the first point?

The main problem, however, is in the second point: liberation for the self-development of a new humanity. Let us quote directly Gutierrez's still sexist language, because that contributes to the *hubris* that is expressed: "Man, the master of his own destiny"; "liberation from all that limits or keeps man from self-fulfillment"; "liberation from all impediments to the exercise of his freedom"; "man constructs himself"; "man takes hold of the reins of his own destiny"; "man makes himself throughout his own life and throughout history"; "the goal is the creation of a new man."

There is seemingly no sense here of partial depravity, let alone total depravity; no sense of humanity's inability to save itself; no real sense of sin. The New Testament knows of a soaring hope for a new humanity (II Corinthians 5:17). But this is not a self-creation; it is a new creation of God.

The sense of the universality of sin and the vanity of all efforts to re-create ourselves ought not to be used as a defense of the *status quo*. We do not want to argue here: if the masses seize power they will be just as selfish and greedy as the present ruling elite; therefore let things stay as they are. We know they would be sinful. We do not know they would be *as* sinful. In the few test cases we can observe, such as the recapture of political power by Blacks in certain counties and cities in the South, the new rulers have not been on the whole as venal or ruthless as their predecessors. Life would be measurably better if power positions were exchanged many places in the world. Mary's dream is a good one: "God has put down the mighty from their thrones and exalted those of low degree" (Luke 1:52). But the Magnificat does not speak of "man making himself, seizing the reins of his own evolution." We would like to challenge the legitimacy of such language in Christian theology. If Gutierrez finds it hard to listen to Calvin, let us quote to him the repeated refrain of Anselm in his own tradition: "Have you considered how weighty sin is?"

3. *We would remind the liberation theologians of the proper place of the Word of God.* The Word has a place in their definition of theology: critical reflection on praxis in the light of the Word. But is this the proper place? In the beginning is the first act: praxis, the trial-and-error process of work for the liberation of the poor. Then comes the second act: critical reflection on what has been happening—in Hegel's phrase, this reflection rises when the sun goes down. Finally comes a third act: "in the light of the Word." At length we employ scripture in order to examine the reflection we have made on the action we have taken. This rises as the moon sets.

Reformed theology is a theology of the Word of God. It issues in a church reformed according to the Word of God. The Word of God has a priority position in the theological process. Liberation theology correctly warns us that if we come quickly and carelessly to the Word we are apt to read it as members of Pharaoh's court, not as enslaved Israel. Thus we should have a "hermeneutical suspicion" about our own hermeneutics. We should acknowledge the "hermeneutical privilege of the poor." We should listen intently and patiently to what the poor find there. But we should also trust the inherent ability of the Word to break down prejudices and false readings. It is, after all, "the hammer that breaks rocks in pieces" and "the sword that pierces to the division of soul and spirit." This is true when it is given priority in the theological process, even by those in Pharaoh's court.

The Word needs to guide praxis, not just to examine our critical reflections on praxis. The Word needs to guide critical reflection, not just to examine it after moonset. The Word needs to be living and active throughout the whole process.

Gutierrez's practice is better than his theory. His work is studded with references to Scripture. He obviously knows his Bible very well. Our question is why can he not give it a larger place programmatically?

When the dust settles on this confrontation between liberation theology and Reformed theology, what can we say in conclusion? At least this. Political neutrality is impossible. While political involvement can be risky and sinful, political noninvolvement is even more risky and sinful. It supports forces that oppress the poor, and God is on the side of the poor.

For centuries the political involvement of the Roman Catholic church was primarily to defend its privileges as an institution and to obtain the power of the state to enforce codes of personal morality which the church could not enforce through its own influence. This is not the kind of political involvement that is in line with liberation theology or the best Reformed theology. For Protestant groups to engage in this type of political involvement does not improve it or make it more praiseworthy.

Political involvement in behalf of the oppressed, in solidarity with the poor, will also be tainted with sin, but it bears the sign of grace. It lines up with the long purpose of God. North Americans who choose such involvement may become the opponents of their own class, their own race, their own sex, their own lifestyle, their own government, their own economic system, or at least of the obvious abuses to which it has led. Our cross is not laid down in Latin America, but here. Will we deny ourselves, take up that cross, and follow Christ?

CHURCH AND STATE: A BRIEF INTRODUCTION FOR CONTEMPORARY PRESBYTERIANS

Jane Dempsey Douglass

Church people today are asking very difficult and important questions about the relation of church and state: To what extent does religion need government support? Is it government's proper role to protect religion and morals? Must government officials be Christian to be moral? Do tax-exempt churches have the right to criticize government policy? Should government decide which religions are legitimate religions?

Because many such questions are not really new questions but perennial ones rooted in our particular theological and social history, it may be helpful to acquire some historical perspective on the way in which church and state have been related through the centuries. For the sake of brevity, we will focus on the western Christian tradition out of which American Presbyterianism has come.

Christianity has spent most of its history in a world of state religions. The rulers to whom Christians are so emphatically urged to be obedient in Romans 13 and I Peter 2, probably the most quoted New Testament texts on the subject down through history, were in the first century neither Christian nor "secular" rulers but rather the Roman emperors who were worshipped as divine in the Roman state religion.

Already in the New Testament we see the tension between Paul's reassurances that, "There is no authority except from God, and those that exist have been instituted by God," (Rom. 13:1) on the one hand, and on the other, Paul's regular use of the confession, "Jesus is Lord." Some scholars believe this confession of Christ's lordship carries with it implicitly a denial that Caesar is lord. Kelly cites a very ancient document, the *Martyrdom of Polycarp*, which describes a state official trying to negotiate with the bishop Polycarp just before his execution, saying. "Why, what harm is there in saying 'Caesar is Lord', and burning the incense, and so on, and saving yourself?" But Polycarp refused the advice and went to his martyrdom.[1] This episode reflects the New Testament sense that civil authority is part of God's plan and ruling, but it is not in itself divine. Only God is lord, never Caesar!

Christians' refusal to worship the Roman gods aroused hostility and charges of "atheism." Such irreverence was feared because it might bring down the wrath of the gods upon the whole empire. Christians were also believed to be guilty of a variety of forms of immorality. This hostility to the Christians soon led to persecution by the state, at first local and sporadic, but by the third century becoming general and systematic.

In response Christian apologists attempted to interpret to the society at large the nature of their faith. One apologist around 200 A.D. tried to explain Christian life in this way:

> For Christians are not distinguished from the rest of mankind in country or speech or customs . . . Though they live in Greek and barbarian cities . . . and follow the local customs in dress and food and the rest of their living, their own way of life which they display is wonderful and admittedly strange. They live in their native lands, but like foreigners. They take part in everything like citizens, and endure everything like aliens . . . Like everyone else they marry, they have children, but they do not expose their infants. They set a common table, but not a common bed . . . They obey the established laws, and in their own lives they surpass the laws. They love all men, and are persecuted by all men . . . they are put to death, and they are made alive. They are poor, and they make many rich . . . They are reviled, and they bless . . . To put it briefly, what the soul is to the body, Christians are to the world.[2]

At the beginning of the fourth century, the Emperor Constantine was converted to Christianity and made Christianity a legal religion. But not till nearly the end of the century did it become the sole state religion. As you can imagine, many leaders of the church were ecstatic at the new possibilities for evangelism open to them and saw the Constantinian era as a turning point in history, a glorious moment in the plan of salvation. Yet tension persisted: other Christians were very concerned that entanglement with a corrupt state would destroy Christianity. The number of desert fathers and mothers in the wilderness of Egypt grew rapidly in the early years of the Christian empire; they were seeking to fulfill their baptismal vows to renounce the devil and all his pomps.

Influential Christians in the newly Christian empire tried to transform moral and social life and humanize the law codes. For the first time Sunday became a civil holiday. In time there developed the glories of the medieval "age of faith": a unity of faith, culture and society, Latin as a universal language of western Christendom, theology as the queen of the sciences in the new universities, magnificent art, music, drama, and architecture dedicated to the worship of God, kings anointed by bishops or popes in a quasi-sacramental induction into their offices, laws designed to protect Christian morality, and nearly everyone in the Empire a baptized Christian.

But there is another face to medieval society: religious intolerance and anti-semitism. Blasphemy against God became a civil offense as well as an ecclesiastical offense. The church turned heretics over to the secular officials for their punishment, often death.

Some persons who were called heretics had indeed strayed far from the church's tradition; others by modern standards had not. Take, for example, the Waldensian sect, a twelfth-century community which espoused apostolic poverty and preached to the poor, studied the Bible assiduously and repudiated contemporary ecclesiastical authority; it was severely persecuted as heretical, surviving only by fleeing to the mountains of northern Italy. Yet in the sixteenth century its affinity to Protestantism was recognized. Since the Reformation the Waldensians have identified themselves with the Reformed tradition.

Those of the Jewish faith who refused to convert to Christianity were increasingly isolated and victimized. The IV Lateran Council in 1215, an ecclesiastical council meeting in Rome, decreed, for example, that Jews and Muslims in every Christian province must at all times wear distinctive clothing so that Christians could not by accident mingle with them and perhaps be deceived. They were not to appear at all in public on certain days, particularly Passion Sunday. The council goes on, "Since it is absurd that a blasphemer of Christ exercise authority over Christians, we on account of the boldness of transgressors renew . . . what the Synod of Toledo (589) enacted . . . prohibiting Jews from being given preference in the matter of public offices, since in such capacity they are most troublesome to the Christians."[3]

One of the ongoing debates of the middle ages is how the civil authority should relate to the ecclesiastical authority. Papal advocates argued that the power to rule the state is given by God to kings through the church. Therefore a pope can withdraw the imperial authority from a disobedient ruler. On the other hand some theologians argued that God grants the power to rule directly to kings. These tensions, along with the existence of special clerical privileges, contributed greatly to the anticlericalism of the later middle ages.

As a matter of perspective we should remember that even during the middle ages Christianity lived in quite different relationships to the state in different regions. For example, outside the Roman empire Christianity had been firmly planted in India in a Hindu culture before the beginning of the Constantinian era, and it continued to grow there. The church around the Mediterranean Sea survived under Islamic rule; and by the high Middle Ages, missionaries had carried the Gospel east all the way to China.

It was precisely the stresses and strains of the western medieval age of faith that produced the Protestant Reformation of the sixteenth century. For more than a century before Luther, calls for reform of the church and society had dominated the church's life; but by the sixteenth century when Luther began to write, there was considerable disillusion with previous methods of reform. Luther himself saw his reform rooted in years of Biblical study which led him to believe that Christians are justified before God by grace alone through faith. This teaching, though at odds with the most popular school of theology in the period, need not in itself have created the upheaval which in fact resulted. After all, there had been theologians teaching very similar doctrines in the tradition of Augustine throughout the middle ages. But the consequences of the doctrine of justification by faith and of related Biblical insights which Luther and his followers saw as necessary for the life of the church and society were far-reaching: a new stress on the importance of individual conscience, the priesthood of all believers, removal of clerical privilege, popular education so that all could read the Bible, a commitment to the practical service of one's neighbor in society not as a means of earning merit before God but as an expression of thanksgiving for God's gifts.

Luther sided with the theologians who believed that civil authority comes directly from God, not through the church. Therefore any ruler, whether Christian or not, could be a "mask of God" both hiding and revealing God's ruling of the world. Luther thought he had a higher view of the ministerial role of civil authority than just about any theologian ever had. When he was explaining the Lord's Prayer, commenting on the petition, "Give us this day our daily bread," he said:

> When you pray this petition turn your eyes to everything that can prevent our bread from coming and the crops from prospering . . . You pray, therefore, against the devil and the world, who can hinder the grain by tempest and war . . . because in time of war we cannot have bread. Likewise you pray for government . . . Grant, Lord, that the grain may prosper, that the princes may keep the peace, that war may not break out, that we may give thanks to thee in peace. Therefore it would be proper to stamp the emperor's or the princes' coat-of-arms upon bread as well as upon money or coins. Few know that this is included in the Lord's Prayer.[4]

So highly did Luther regard the office of civil authority that he advocated the transfer of laws regarding marriage from the church to the state. Most of the later reformers followed his views on this matter.

Luther's doctrine of Christian vocation for all the baptized at work in the secular realm as well as in the church strengthened Protestant awareness of the goodness of all creation. In fact his model of sainthood is the Biblical picture of a faithful Hebrew patriarch, ruler over lands and flocks, concerned with social and economic matters, laughing in his tent with his wife and children, rather than a medieval monk in the desert with a rock for a pillow.

In the early years of the Reformation, Luther was quite clear that religion is a matter of the conscience and should never be coerced by the state. In later years he yielded to more conservative colleagues in recognizing the state's responsibility to protect true religion. He seems never to have seriously questioned the medieval understanding of the Christian society where citizenship and baptism are so closely related. Only the Anabaptist movement of the sixteenth century and a few free spirits rejected that concept at the time, and the mainstream Reformers disagreed with the theological foundations of their position.

Part of the power of the Protestant movement sociologically was that it spoke directly to the profound spiritual anxiety of the period but also to the concerns of the rising middle class, to new nationalisms of the period which had been challenging papal overlordship on political grounds, and also to the Renaissance spirit then moving over the Alps into northern Europe.

Calvin came to Protestantism out of a remarkable French Catholic reform

movement stemming from the Renaissance. He finally identified with Protestantism not many years before the publication of his first edition of the *Institutes* in
1536. While passing through Geneva soon after the City Council had declared
itself for the Reform in 1536, with some difficulty Calvin was persuaded to stay
and assist with the reforming of the city. Calvin had a theology very close to
Luther's in its main outlines, but Geneva was sociologically very different from
Wittenberg. Whereas Luther still lived in an essentially feudal society, Geneva
already had overthrown episcopal temporal authority over the city before Calvin
arrived and had become an independent republic with a tradition of representative government. Yet the medieval vision of a Christian society where church and
state cooperate to defend the faith and public morals remained fundamental to
Geneva's view of itself. So Reformed Geneva inherited a complex interweaving
of church and state, along with the tensions created by it. Separation of church
and state was no more intrinsic to early Calvinism than it had been to Lutheran-
ism.

The popular image of Calvin as tyrannical despot of Geneva contains a large
measure of unfortunate myth, however. The governing councils of Geneva were
well established, certainly a match for the persuasive powers of Calvin and the
company of pastors. The government even once exiled Calvin along with two of
his colleagues, largely because of their troublesome attempts to provide more
freedom for the church. Calvin was persuaded to return three years later. But he
succeeded only after almost twenty years of effort in persuading the City Council
to relinquish to the church the right to excommunicate, and he never did succeed
in reintroducing weekly communion as he had hoped. As a matter of fact, the
first elders of the church in Geneva were chosen by city councils from their own
membership. Civil government was very deeply involved in church matters in
Geneva.

On the other hand Calvin, his fellow pastors, the elders, and the deacons as
officers of the church felt ethically responsible not only for the spiritual but also
for the social and economic life of Geneva. Calvin's Biblical commentaries and
sermons abound with discussions of contemporary social problems. The deacons
supervised the city hospital which also served as an orphanage, senior-citizen
home, and refugee-reception center. The City Council appointed Calvin one of
the members of a commission to develop a cloth-making business at the hospital
to provide a means of support for some of the residents. The proper functions of
church and state were clear theoretically but difficult in practice to distinguish.

The final chapter of Calvin's *Institutes* is a discussion of civil government.
In the tradition of Luther, it is a strong statement of the dignity of civil government as instituted by God, but it goes on to include a new Reformed element, a
preference for shared governing over rule by one person as safer and less likely
to permit tyranny. But the climax of the chapter—and the book—is the powerful
reminder that obedience to earthly rulers must never lead to disobedience to the
King of Kings, to whom all human authorities must bow. Calvin cites Peter from
the Book of Acts, "We must obey God rather than human persons." (Acts 5:29;
Inst. IV, xx, 32)

We must remember that the *Institutes* had been dedicated to the king of France, under whose rule Protestants were suffering severe persecution. Geneva in Calvin's day was receiving thousands of refugees for religious reasons, an influx which taxed the ability of the city to house and feed them. Calvin himself was one of these refugees. He and the readers of the *Institutes* knew full well that the penalty for obeying God rather than human rulers could be imprisonment, exile, or death. For toleration of religious dissent on *major* issues was hardly considered a virtue by Catholics or by most Protestants in the sixteenth century. One of the very rare rulers who practiced religious toleration in this period was a Reformed woman, Jeanne d'Albret, Queen of Navarre, who wrote: "I have forced no one with death, imprisonment or condemnation . . . I do not condone outrages committed in the name of religion and I would punish the offenders."[5]

Late sixteenth-and early seventeenth-century Calvinist political theory was much concerned with the problem of the wicked ruler and became increasingly revolutionary, earning Presbyterians a reputation for feisty defense of the people's rights. Calvinists, lay and clergy alike, felt called to pour energy into reconstruction of a social order so that it could more closely resemble the promised kingdom.

In a sermon to the House of Commons in 1641, the Puritan minister Thomas Case urged:

> Reformation must be universal . . . reform all places, all persons and callings; reform the benches of judgment, the inferior magistrates . . . Reform the universities, . . . the cities . . . the countries . . . reform the Sabbath, reform the ordinances, the Worship of God . . . you have more work to do than I can speak.[6]

Here we see the peculiarly Calvinistic activism moving toward a more hopeful future. Not just the church or the civil government, the pastor or the magistrate, but the whole Christian people bears responsibility for creating a new society.

It was with the Age of Enlightenment, the eighteenth century, that toleration of religious dissent, with fuller respect for freedom of conscience, really came into focus. And this was the period when both American government and the American Presbyterian church were developing their definitive forms. Although established Lutheran, Anglican, and Reformed churches in the older European tradition had come to America with some of the original colonies, other colonies on principle had permitted no established religion. As the colonies moved to nationhood, a decision had to be made about the role of religion at the federal level. The decision to establish *no* religion for the new nation was a remarkable shift away from tradition, probably for a variety of reasons: the memory by many of religious oppression, the practical inability of government to suppress dissenters under circumstances of the frontier, a new intellectual climate of rationalism favoring individual freedom, some genuine religious commitment to religious freedom, and some pragmatic willingness to give up privilege for one's own church to avoid having to grant privilege to other churches. The result of this decision in time was the disestablishment of religion also at the state level and the emergence of the phenomenon of American denominationalism.

American Presbyterians in a series of official actions in the course of the eighteenth century made it clear that they no longer wished the privileges of establishment for themselves and would not approve them for others. They approved the principles written into the First Amendment. The Synod of New York and Philadelphia in 1788 published Preliminary Principles for church government which are still part of chapter I of our *Book of Order*, including the following paragraph:

> They are unanimously of opinion: That "God alone is lord of the conscience, and hath left it free from the doctrines and commandments of men which are in any thing contrary to his Word, or beside it, in matters of faith or worship." Therefore they consider the rights of private judgment, in all matters that respect religion, as universal and unalienable; they do not even wish to see any religious constitution aided by the civil power, further than may be necessary for protection and security, and, at the same time, be equal and common to all others.

The American religious diversity of the eighteenth century was mostly, though not exclusively, Protestant. New waves of immigration in the late nineteenth century from eastern Europe and the Mediterranean area brought increased numbers of Catholic and Orthodox Christians and of Jews. Twentieth-century immigration has considerably increased the number of Muslims, Hindus, and Buddhists. In face of this increasing religious pluralism, American Presbyterians have continued to affirm the separation of church and state created in response to the American experience. They have also affirmed religious liberty as a basic human right for people of every nation.

Most American Presbyterians have not understood the separation of church and state to remove from the church an ethical responsibility for supporting social justice. This concern grew to new prominence in America at the end of the nineteenth century when the social problems resulting from industrialization and slavery became so apparent to the church, and it continues strongly today. Our concepts of social justice have been slowly and painfully refined since then. Some believe that precisely because in our own time the role of government has become so much greater than in the eighteenth century and because all institutions of society are so interdependent, the church's roles as monitor of social justice and as prophetic social witness are more important than ever. But increasingly this is an ecumenical witness, drawing on the strength of many religious traditions.

Despite the variety of historical experiences of church-state relations, Presbyterian people have rather consistently relied on the following principles:

1. The church is both holy and sinful, always in need of reformation. Though endowed with the gift of the Holy Spirit, the church cannot claim to be infallible in lifestyle or in its decisions. Matters of order in the church *should* be adapted to changing cultures and circumstances so that the church's ministry can be carried out most effectively.

2. Every human person bears the image of God and thereby lays a claim upon us. The structures of both church and society must lend themselves to the creation of human community while safeguarding human dignity and liberty of conscience.

3. Civil government, whether or not it is in the hands of Christians, is to be respected as a gift of God, bringing order in society. It can be held account-able for justice. But in a sinful world it cannot create a perfect society, and it cannot demand ultimate loyalty. Where requirements of the state are seen to be in conflict with the will of God, Christians must choose to obey the will of God.

4. *All* Christians through their vocations *in the world* are called to serve the neighbor by their skills and by their love and to transform the structures of soci-ety so that God's justice will be shown to the world.

Presbyterians have been hard at work in this reformation of the world for centuries. But the task before us seems as great as ever. Our ancestors did not always perceive as sinful, for example, the racial, sexual, and economic inequal-ities which we now believe to be sinful. They more readily accepted the neces-sity for violence and coercion than we do. As our awareness of the nature of freedom, of justice and injustice, becomes more sensitive, we see that there is still much work to do!

Endnotes

1. J.N.D. Kelly, Early Christian Creeds (London: Longmans, Green, 1950), p. 15. Quo-tation from "The Martyrdom of Polycarp," *The Apostolic Fathers*, trans, E.J. Good-speed (New York: Harper and Brothers, 1950), p. 250.
2. "The Address to Diognetus," in *The Apostolic Fathers*, op. cit., p. 278.
3. "Canons of the Fourth Lateran Council, 1215," in *Readings in Church History*, vol I, C.J. Barry, ed., (Westminster, Md.: Newman Press, 1968).
4. Luther, "Sermons on the Catechism," in *Martin Luther: Selections from his Writings*, J. Dillenberger, ed. (New York: Doubleday, 1961), pp. 222-223.
5. Roland Bainton, *Women of the Reformation in France and England* (Minneapolis: Augsburg Publishing House, 1973), p. 60.
6. Michael Walzer, *The Revolution of the Saints* (Cambridge, Mass.: Harvard University Press, 1965), pp. 10-11.

This address was given as an introduction to the address by Mr. William P. Thompson at the Purdue meeting of United Presbyterian Women, July 1982.

FAITH AND POLITICAL ACTION IN AMERICAN PRESBYTERIANISM, 1776-1918

Louis Weeks

Many Presbyterians today simply assume that the churches have a responsibility to address political issues. Human rights, peacemaking, self-development of peoples, and at least a score of the other primary programs and issues in which the major Presbyterian denominations are involved, have political ramifications, if indeed are not outright political matters. Presbyterians in their General Assembly of the UPCUSA in 1976, for example, voted to "Urge the U.S. Government promptly to recognize the effective sovereignty of the Republic of Panama over all Panamanian territory including the present Canal Zone. . . ."[1] That same year the General Assembly of the PCUS adopted a "Public Policy Statement on Indian Affairs," which declared that "we in the Church should exercise our power and influence in society and before the Federal and State Governments so that legislation designed to terminate reservation states without consent of the Indian tribes may be repealed, or defeated. . . ."[2] These two actions and many others on matters such as world hunger, the Central Intelligence Agency, the war in Lebanon, and Vietnamese refugee assistance asked Presbyterians individually and collectively to lobby, petition, pray or otherwise try to influence the governments of the USA and other nations of the world.

On the other hand, many Presbyterians question the propriety of such political involvement. "The Church ought not get mixed up in politics!" is their exclamation. They cite, particularly in the PCUS, "the spirituality of the Church" as a theological doctrine.

Have the major Presbyterian denominations entered into a new era of political involvement, denying their tradition and embracing the ways of the world as though Christian gospel? This paper seeks to report a brief survey of some general streams in the history of Presbyterian faith and political action in United States history.

Beginning

In the words of John T. McNeill, a careful historian of Reformed communions throughout the world, Calvinists "have participated energetically in political and social action."[3] Presbyterians in North America proved no exception to the rule. Throughout their history the mainline denominations of connectional Calvinism have been deeply involved in political life, sometimes distinguishing citizenship in a colony or nation from that in the Christian community but more frequently seeking to transform temporal structures in light of Christian values and commitment.

McNeill claims that Presbyterians have "adopted a variety of political attitudes." Characteristically, though, they have supported representative government and "rejected various forms of absolutism."[4] Thus it seemed natural in American colonies for most Presbyterians to thirst for a representative form of government. When a strident Continental Congress declared a day of fasting in May, 1776, the Synod of New York and Philadelphia postponed its regular meeting so ministers could that day lead their congregations in worship.[5] Most Presbyterians sided with the revolution, and many served as leaders in it—John Witherspoon among them.[6] At the successful conclusion of the War for Independence, a joyous, newly-formed Presbyterian General Assembly sent a formal communique expressing "unfeigned pleasure" at the election of George Washington as President of the new, United States of America. "We are happy that God has inclined your heart to give yourself once more to the public," they declared. "We pray Almighty God, to have you always in his holy keeping."[7]

Early National Life

Presbyterians began responsible participation in the new nation's life rather confidently. Though numerically a rather small minority, Presbyterians occupied positions of power in most areas of the country. Only about twenty thousand members were counted as the denomination formed in 1789, in a nation with a population of about four million.[8] But when the legislature of Virginia had, for example, appropriated Western lands for a new school in Kentucky, Presbyterians led the agitation, saw the legislation through to enactment, and helped staff the board of directors of the new Transylvania Seminary.[9] The Rev. John Todd of Hanover Presbytery, his nephew Col. John Todd of the legislature, and Caleb Wallace, a Presbyterian minister-turned-lawyer, oversaw the founding of the "public school."[10]

Separation of church and state, which most Presbyterians affirmed and the remainder conceded as a political necessity, did not mean a retreat by Reformed Christians from any arena of politics.[11] It merely meant that religious liberty would be guaranteed by the state, that secular government would not interfere with the church. According to John Witherspoon, who embodied initial Presbyterian involvement in matters of state, responsibility of the civil magistrate was to protect the rights of conscience while punishing impiety and profanity.[12]

At the turn of the nineteenth century, Presbyterians numbered among both Federalist and Republican parties. Alan Heimert, in *Religion and the American Mind*, states that "Religion and politics were never again so closely intertwined" as during the early 1800's.[13] Some scholars go so far as to argue that the Presbyterians enjoyed the preferential treatment of an "established" church, the way congregationalists still did in Massachusetts and Connecticut.[14] Whether of preferred status or not, Presbyterian clergy and lay leaders exercised "moral trusteeship" fearlessly. Lyman Beecher, while Connecticut's "big gun of Calvinism" and before he became a Presbyterian, said that governments must be a "terror to evil doers, and a praise to them that do well." "Civil government is a divine ordinance," he proclaimed.[15]

Moral stewardship involved Presbyterians in all the major issues of the day—foreign policy, war and peace, social issues of slavery and temperance, etc. Generally the pattern of voluntarism prevailed with societies formed for every benevolent enterprise. Some involved more social, some more ecclesiastical goals. But almost all were seen to be working together for political amelioration as well as for evangelization of the American (and other) people. Among the first wave of benevolent societies were the American Bible Society (1816), the American Education Society (1816), the American Tract Society (1814), and the Association for the Relief of Respectable, Aged, Indigent Females (1814). The American Colonization Society sought to elicit individual acts of emancipation by slaveowners, but also the enactment of laws supporting the freeing of slaves for settlement in Liberia.[16] The Association for Relief of . . . Females, working mainly in New York, lobbied muncipal and state authorities. Even the American Bible Society enlisted Presbyterian political figures to spotlight their cause.[17]

Among the second wave of voluntary societies were the American Home Missionary Society (1826), the American Temperance Society (1826), the General Union for Promoting the Observance of the Christian Sabbath (1828), and the American Anti-Slavery Society (1833). The chief end of the General Union . . . in its early years remained to force the cessation of mail delivery and the closing of post offices on Sunday. Gradually, the members of the Temperance Society and their colleagues in agitation moved to demand state and federal laws regulating or banning the manufacture and sale of liquor.[18]

Presbyterians in all these efforts tried to bring denominational power to bear upon government in order to accomplish their desired ends. Annual remonstrances against Sunday mail delivery, petitioning Congress to close post offices, became a regular feature of Presbyterian General Assemblies, for instance.[19] Temperance advocates also kept a steady stream of political pressure upon elected officials, particularly as the issue changed from one seeking moderation to one demanding abstinence from "demon rum." By 1828, those reformers backed for office "their men," and discouraged voting for incumbents who failed to respond to pressure.

Although few Presbyterians agitated in behalf of what might be termed "pacifism" in those early years of U. S. history, a number spoke out strongly against the War of 1812 and the repression of freedoms of citizens that accompanied it. Most notably, De Witt Clinton, mayor of New York City and a staunch Presbyterian, embodied political resistance to the re-election of James Madison that year. His running mate, Jared Ingersoll, also shared allegiance to the Presbyterian Church.[20] And when Madison defeated Clinton in a close race, proceeding to prosecute the war, he faced resistance from Presbyterian ministers whenever he proclaimed national fast days in behalf of that war. James Blythe of Kentucky, for one, took the occasion in January, 1815, to chide politicians and to urge members of his congregation to give such allegiance to God alone.[21]

Not all Presbyterians pressured the national, state, or local government in behalf of issues they perceived to be moral ones. Indeed, one of the few generalizations appropriate to Presbyterian history uniformly is that "all Presbyterians did not agree on the matters." The Covenanters had anticipated participation in an avowedly Christian country. When the U. S. Constitution failed to express Christian loyalty, and when the government made a treaty with an Islamic nation expressly denying America's Christianity, they failed for many years to acknowledge the U.S. as a national entity and presumably stayed out of the PCUSA because it did.[22] Other Presbyterians, members of the PCUSA, considered much of the political action inappropriate for a church body. The vast majority of Presbyterians, however, seem to have approved of some corporate political action and opposed other such activity. It should also be noted that a great many Presbyterians shared a general Protestant bias against churches actively supporting certain political candidates.[23]

The Cumberland schism of 1804-1810 apparently had little effect upon the political "meddlesomeness" of Presbyterians. After the division between Old and New Schools in 1836-38, however, the New School Assembly addressed political matters more frequently and in greater detail than did the Old School. But Old School Presbyterians, such as Robert J. Breckinridge, did not hesitate to involve the church in issues considered moral ones. Both denominations continued to make corporate statements and to give denominational weight to certain political stances. Breckinridge, who served simultaneously (1847-53) as Pastor of the Lexington (Kentucky) Second Presbyterian Church and State Superintendent for Public Instruction, argued that leaving the political arena in the name of Christianity denied the very incarnation of Jesus Christ.[24]

To call these Presbyterians "theocrats," as some scholars have done, really overstates the case for religious involvement in politics.[25] A few of the clergy may have been so presumptuous as to assume their interpretation of the Bible and ethical sensibilities coincided with God's purpose for the world. Most, however, had simply realized the importance of giving moral direction to society. Presbyterians, especially strong in the middle colonies and subsequently in the most pluralistic of the states, in large measure shared a vision of the United States as a nation God both blessed and judged.[26] They sought to lead American life in "paths of righteousness," recognizing that Jesus spoke of both sheep and goats. They sought the Lord as a shepherd.

The Issues of Slavery: One Example

The question about relationships between faith and political action can be approached from several different angles. The study of individuals, for example, will show that many underwent immense change in the course of their lives. The tracing of biographies also shows the immense variety among Presbyterians in points of view and demonstrations of those perspectives. A study of corporate actions also yields insights about denominational attitudes and actions. But a consideration of the various issues, with Presbyterian response to each, seems thus far to yield excellent results. The "peculiar institution" of Black chattel slavery in the United States offers just one, albeit most important, example of the ways in which Reformed faith informed political activity.

Note for example the variety of perspectives held by Presbyterians in the early 1800's on slavery—some sought to have the institution overturned; some upheld it; many considered the welfare of individual slaves and sought to have them freed, but left the institution alone; many others sought to evangelize slaves and free Black people, but supported slavery and owned slaves. Many thousands of slaves were Presbyterians; and probably thousands more free Black people belonged to Presbyterian congregations.[27] Some sessions did not record the names of Black members; and almost none recorded more than Christian names, so it is impossible to tell numbers accurately.

Every Presbyterian, Black or white, had a stake in slavery. Most, in the early years of the century, opposed the institution. David Rice, pioneer minister in Kentucky, agitated fiercely to exclude it when a constitutional convention met in 1792.[28] He stood election as a member of the convention, and he published an anti-slavery broadside on the subject. "Human legislatures should remember that they act in subordination to the great Ruler of the universe, have no right to take the government out of his hand, nor to enact laws contrary to his. . . ."[29] Rice lost, with many Presbyterians on his side; but many also opposed the outlawing of slavery. Subsequently, a comparatively strong anti-slavery movement existed within Kentucky Presbyterian circles. When another constitution was proposed in the 1840s, another Presbyterian minister led the anti-slavery forces unsuccessfully in an attempt to bar the practice of slavery.[30] Yet a third Presbyterian pastor led what little movement for immediate abolitionism still existed in the hostile years immediately before the Civil War.[31]

It is also helpful to see the changes that occurred over time among Presbyterians. John Holt Rice, the Virginian who founded the seminary that became Union, for example, spoke out strongly against slavery in 1817, calling it an evil and assuming people only disagree on how to end the institution. As time went by, however, Rice grew to defend slavery and to publish his opinions for all to see. Although he knew many Black people well—indeed when he pastored at Cub Creek one-fourth of his congregation were slaves—Rice moved to defend the institution in the U.S. and urge free Blacks to move to Liberia. As he grew more pro-slavery in his attitudes, Rice wrote that "religion" needed to keep to its "own peculiar sphere." "It was never the intention of Jesus Christ and his inspired apostles that there should be any collusions . . . between the church and the state," he insisted in 1826. "For this reason they entirely abstained from intermeddling with the affairs of worldly policy."[32]

On the other hand, James G. Birney of Kentucky and Alabama moved from accepting ownership of slaves in 1816 to a time of questioning the institution, to an ethical stance in 1834 in which he manumitted his own slaves and advocated colonization. By 1837, he had become an out-and-out abolitionist, indicted for harboring a fugitive slave in Cincinnati. As a Presbyterian, Birney became leader of the "Western" branch of abolitionism, the political wing that sought to force the South to end the practice. He became a candidate for the U.S. presidency in 1840 and 1844, nominated by the Liberty Party.[33]

The changes in political involvement and the changes in attitudes on slavery that individuals experienced came also to Presbyterian judicatories. General Assemblies and lower courts during the 1810s made several political pronouncements on the evils of slavery. The most famous of these statements, quoted and cited by subsequent courts, was that made by the Assembly of 1818. Recognizing slavery as an evil, it celebrated early Presbyterian attempts to end slavery. It called for a total abolition of slavery while recognizing that the manner of emancipation should not destroy the society. Pleas of necessity were not to be made an excuse for hindering efforts that were lawful and practicable in ending the evil. Consideration of the happiness of the injured parties took precedence over considerations of expense or inconvenience.

The statement bore also some recommendations and admonitions to members of church sessions and presbyteries—to support the American Colonization Society, to educate slaves, and to discountenance all cruelty in treatment of slaves.[34]

As theological issues and questions of evangelical ecumenism divided Presbyterians in the 1830s, so too did denominational attitudes and actions on slavery. Not incidentally, slavery had become more profitable by that time; and slave states had begun to coordinate political strategies for its maintenance. The Old School-New School division had certainly as a secondary cause the anti-slavery sentiments of the New School leaders. Subsequently, most New School Presbyterians came to protest the continuance of legal slavery, a stance that provoked the withdrawal of New School Southerners from the communion in the 1850s. Old School Presbyterians generally avoided references to slavery, especially as the Southern wing of the denomination prospered. Presbyterians actively engaged in the "underground railroad," seeking political redress from prosecution for their efforts, organized in 1847 the Free Presbyterian Church which centered in southern Ohio and extended to Iowa.

Perhaps best remembered of the Presbyterians politically engaged in opposition to slavery, Elijah P. Lovejoy, was martyred for the cause.[35] Converted in 1832 and licensed to preach after attending Princeton Seminary, Lovejoy chose rather to edit a newspaper in St. Louis. When Lovejoy championed anti-slavery, particularly when he decried mob violence against a Black man, he was forced to move his paper to Alton, Illinois, in a free state. In Alton, Lovejoy claimed the rights "of an American citizen" to free speech; but a mob destroyed his printing presses and threatened his life should replacement presses again print abolitionist views. The friends of Lovejoy tried to defend him, but he was shot and killed in the midst of mob violence in November, 1837, as he protected the new presses.

Granted Lovejoy's abolitionism, of particular note is the involvement of the Presbyterian Church in the affair. Lovejoy was supported in his abolitionism chiefly by Presbyterians in Illinois, especially by Edward Beecher, President of

Illinois College. Beecher led the meetings at the Alton First Presbyterian Church and Upper Alton Presbyterian at which anti-slavery sentiment received hearings. Later, when Lovejoy had received threats, Benjamin Godfrey, a Presbyterian elder, and probably the wealthiest person in town, wrote that the Presbyterian Church building had become an abolitionist stronghold.

> There is So Much Excitement in our Place on The Subject of Abalishionism That really I am Confused I am told that our Presbiterian Church in Alton has been turned in to a depasitory of armorey from this it Would Seam as if our Presbiterian Brotheren have lost Sight of the Swords of Life and restorted to humain weepons to do the will of there Master This May be the praper way - but for My Self I Can not Subscribe to it. and I really feeall unhapy and am anxiaus to Unite My Self with Some Denomination of the lords people that appear in the Sight of the World to be Less Clameraus.[36]

Thus while many in that local church supported Lovejoy, others considered the involvement of the church in politics inappropriate. In this regard, Alton Presbyterian Churches offered a microcosm of the U.S. situation historically. Opposition to church involvement in social and political issues coalesced particularly for Southern Presbyterians with the forming of a doctrine of "the Spirituality of the Church." That doctrine stands a full examination, more attention than it has received thus far.

Spirituality of the Church

As previously indicated, ministers such as John Holt Rice held that separate spheres of church and state meant separate sacred and secular activities of believers. Characteristic of his expressions was the admonition that the church "should confine itself to making good Christians."[37] In the 1859 words of James H. Thornwell, the Presbyterian Church

> "is exclusively a spiritual organization and possesses only a spiritual power. Her business was the salvation of men; and she had no mission to care for the things, or to become entangled with the kingdoms and policy, of this world."[38]

Only the written warrants of scripture should authorize church action. It should be noted that Thornwell spoke within the Old School Assembly, and the "spirituality of the church" became a formed doctrine only after the Civil War. But it became an explicit norm for the Presbyterian Church, U.S.

It may well be, as historian Jack Maddex recently argued, that a full blown articulation of the doctrine came from Stuart Robinson, a Louisville pastor and the leader of a border movement from the PCUSA into the PCUS during the late 1860s.[39] Robinson, a fascinating preacher, social critic, and astute business leader, doubtless modeled for all Presbyterians the fact that one could advocate political and social neutrality in church courts while at the same time seeking social reform as a political citizen (and, by the way, growing wealthy in the process).[40] Whatever its origins, the doctrine did capture much of the theological imagination of the Southern Presbyterian Church and rendered corporate activity very circumscribed, at least from 1867 until the late 1930s. Even into the 1950s PCUS statements and activities usually began with an interpretation of the primary spiritual function of the church that permitted the intrusion of worldly concerns. The Southern Presbyterian "liberal," E. T. Thompson could argue in 1961 that for twenty-five years, the PCUS "has officially accepted the idea of social responsibility."[41] But he was forced to choose his words carefully, because most Assembly positions on race, industrialization, urbanization, labor, human rights, and other such issues had avoided dealing with many actual impingements while speaking of some ethereal ideals.[42]

The PCUSA after reunion between what had been Old and New Schools apparently depended on no such slogan or doctrine to characterize relationships to social and political issues in the latter decades of the nineteenth century. Indeed, as Robert Ellis Thompson sought to speak of the denomination in his own day, he said that in 1895 "the Presbyterian Church still holds a central position in the religious life of the nation."[43] Thompson complained a bit that many in his day proposed "that the church shall take the whole social burden on her shoulders, and hold herself responsible for the right conduct of affairs which properly belong to the state."[44]

But he took as a "sign of good" the interests of institutional churches in social problems and their development of programs and advocates in behalf of meeting those problems. He lauded the work of people like Sheldon Jackson, who mixed politics, education, social services and Christian ministry.[45] Jackson, ordained by Albany Presbytery in New York in 1858, at first served as a missionary among the Choctaws and other tribes in the U.S. In 1884, he became superintendent of Presbyterian missions in Alaska; and a year later, he was appointed concurrently superintendent of public instruction for that region. He brought reindeer into Alaska and stocked herds. He wrote extensively on political, social, educational, and mission matters. In brief, he embodied the religious and social values of the Presbyterians in the territory, supported by the federal government—"the civilizing and Christianizing" that many turn-of-the-century Americans considered synonyms.[46] In approving of Jackson and other such leaders, Thompson doubtless reflected the general attitudes of leaders in the PCUSA, who elected Jackson Moderator of their General Assembly in 1897.

Another historian, Jacob H. Patton, in 1900 made observations similar to those of Thompson, although Patton did not focus on Sheldon Jackson. Patton claimed he had been drawn to the study of Presbyterians in the U.S. because of its influence "during the current growth of our national life."[47] He highlighted the need for Presbyterians to continue their involvement in social, political, and economic affairs, pointing to consequences for the church:

> The financial and industrial policies of the general government extend their influence throughout the land, and are, therefore, a great power for evil or for good in respect to the support of the institutions of the church, thus indirectly promoting or retarding its legitimate operations. Unfortunately, in our time, too many intelligent Christians of the different denominations are

quite often derelict as citizens in not fully realizing that it is their duty to inform themselves in relation to the financial and kindred measures of the government, in order that they may vote intelligently should there be mismanagement in consequence of incompetent men being in control of public affairs.[48]

However different the theological expressions may have been, the PCUSA and the PCUS bore great similarities in the issues they confronted and the stances they took regarding those issues. The actions and attitudes of the United Presbyterian Church of North America probably conformed also to essentially the same perspective.

Major social issues of the day for Presbyterians included temperance and Sabbath observance, both more forcefully advocated than ever and both consuming most of the reforming energies of the denominations. Of course, some advocacy of public education continued; and many individuals worked in behalf of other reforms. Both were perceived by all three Presbyterian denominations as issues falling within the purview of the church. Southern Presbyterians argued that both temperance and Sabbath observance were commanded in scripture, therefore appropriate concerns for corporate Christian action. Other Presbyterians, not inhibited by the doctrine, nonetheless gravitated toward these issues as central ones for pressing civilization and Christian ethics in national life. Thus in a sense the doctrine of "spirituality of the church," though it became a focal point of expressing distinctive differences between denominations, had a limited effect in the addressing of faith and political action in American Presbyterianism. Those without the doctrines chose corporate involvement in the same two major issues.

Temperance and Sabbath Observance

Presbyterians were deeply involved in both temperance and Lord's Day movements during the last decades of the nineteenth century and the early years of the twentieth. Space limitations permit only a glimpse at the scope of that activity. A more thorough presentation of the history will be offered in the study now underway.

The PCUSA had already offered a number of resolutions and admonitions to its members by the time it moved to establish a full Permanent Committee on Temperance in 1881. The committee was charged to produce resources, to gather and report statistics, but also to "seek to quicken and to unite our Synods and churches in suitable measures for promoting the Temperance Reform." The committee quickly perceived the political implications of such a commission, and among the "suitable measures" it advocated the following year was that Presbyterians support members of the House of Representatives who sought to investigate the "traffic in intoxicating drinks."[49] Since the issue had been addressed by previous Assemblies as early as 1812, annual reports beginning in 1882 emphasized the tradition of involvement and the history of collaboration with voluntary societies.

Gradually, however, reports moved to more specific political endorsements and advice. The Committee in 1891 said that it had concentrated on sending literature to Nebraska, where a "Prohibition struggle was in progress." It also advocated sending "petitions, remonstrances, and other evidences of disfavor" until state legislatures acted to prohibit the traffic.[50] The report of 1898 claimed that chairs of Presbytery Temperance Committees across the country had been informed of the Ellis Bill, pending in Congress—a measure suppressing liquor sales on government property. The secretary in behalf of the Permanent Committee wrote to key Senators and Representatives urging them to support that bill.[51] By 1907 annual reports included progress reports on "the Status of the States," whether "dry," "local option," or "wet." It declared some limits on the involvement of the denomination as a body, but it affirmed the collective right to petition on behalf of particular bills.[52]

It is interesting to observe the way in which the PCUSA distinguished appropriate from inappropriate activity. In 1891, the committee said simply

> With politics pure and simple, the Church of Jesus Christ, as such, may have nothing to do, but with the right, as God gives her to see the right, she has everything to do and she has no right to lay the responsibility on the shoulders of independent organizations which she herself is bound to assume.[53]

By 1907, the "Sphere of the Church" was said to exclude organized interference in political primaries, or advocacy of particular candidates.[54] But in the 1928 election some years later, Presbyterians, including the Moderator of the Assembly endorsed publicly the candidacy of Herbert Hoover over Al Smith, because Smith represented the "Wets." Robert M. Miller has contended that Presbyterians with other Protestants gave quasi-official backing to Hoover, especially in denominational and independent publications, because of the temperance issue more than anti-Catholic sentiment.[55]

The involvement of Presbyterians in the politics of temperance led also to their lobbying efforts on matters of foreign policy. In 1893 the General Assembly instructed the Permanent Committee on Temperance to petition Congress to cooperate with other Western powers to stop the sale of liquor (and weapons) in Africa, the New Hebrides, and Alaska. In 1901 the General Assembly protested against the opium traffic in China. And in 1906 they made another political statement about the availability of liquor for the Nez Perce Tribe and the need to change structures for dealing with them.[56]

Southern Presbyterians differed somewhat in their involvement in the politics of temperance. Rather than follow that history, however, it might prove more helpful to trace the Sabbath observance issue among them. The two issues remained inextricably bound, and examples of the one frequently were used to inspire work in the other. But if anything, the Sabbath observance movement spurred more thoroughly political involvement than did temperance.

The Sabbath observance issue, as temperance, had a long history of Presbyterian action. In earlier decades of the nineteenth century, however, church attendance had been respected and fashionable in America. Railroads had even complied, and the nation in effect stopped its regular business on Sundays. So while temperance advocates felt, at least until well into the 1920s, that they were winning their battle, those seeking mandatory Sabbath observance considered the reform consistently in jeopardy and the forces of godless secularism winning the contest. Worthy of note is the ambiguity of the Bible on both accounts; but as mentioned already, Sabbath observance received explicit warrant from scripture. Isaiah 58, and other such conditional statements of God's covenant, served to warn advocates of the political consequences should they fail.[57]

In 1878, the PCUS established a Permanent Committee on the Sabbath, which reported the following year and thereafter annually. Typically, their reports called upon the people in the PCUS to work with political leaders to insure Sabbath laws, necessary for both national survival and Christian freedom. In 1893, the General Assembly itself protested to the government that the Columbian Exposition in Chicago remained open seven days a week.[58] The issue became pointedly political again in the presidency of a son of the Southern Presbyterian manse—Woodrow Wilson. The Assembly Committee congratulated him on his stemming the tide of Sabbath desecration in the armed forces.[59] Several times the committee reports addressed particular bills, congratulated particular politicians, and even suggested particular avenues of redress against those insensitive to the issue.

In both cases, the Southerners on Sabbath and the PCUSA on temperance, a rather full range of political activity was advocated and reported as having taken place. As the twentieth century progressed the complexity of political and social life increased. So too did the Presbyterian involvement in American politics become more complicated. One can also detect a bit more modesty in most of the denominational stances and arenas of action.

Twentieth Century Faith and Politics

The American religious experience, anomalous in many respects, has been characterized by two opposite and almost equal movements in recent decades. On the one hand, gradual secularization has occurred in a seemingly relentless process. Religious belief has been perceived as a matter of individual, private concern. On the other hand, mainline denominations (and most recently even sectarian churches) have participated thoroughly in political life, addressing a growing range of issues and even persons in the courts and legislative halls of the country.[60] New issues have cropped up thanks to education, technology, and communication—every issue seemingly a moral one.

Presbyterians North and South had addressed other issues at the turn of the century besides Sabbath observance and temperance. Southern Presbyterians were drawn into the arena of international politics when two of their missionaries, William Henry Sheppard and William McCutchen Morrison, were prosecuted for libel in 1909.[61] Sheppard and Morrison, pioneer missionaries in the Belgian Congo, reported atrocities related to colonial oppression of the tribes with which they labored. Their libel trial became a *cause celébrè* for Southern Presbyterians and for Protestants in general. National protest meetings were held, letters and petitions inundated both elected representatives and State Department officials. They were acquitted in Leopoldville, returned upriver to their work as heros among the tribespeople; and some reforms actually did take place in colonial administration. At least the oppression became more subtle. In this and several other complicated issues, the Southern Presbyterians despite their "spirituality of the church" became increasingly public in their connectional life.

Presbyterian U.S.A. leaders moved toward more institutional embodiment of political concerns about the same time. One issue that came directly from America's increasing pluralism was put in the form of a question to the 1909 Assembly. "Is this a Christian nation?" the narrative asked. From the question, the narrative moved to describe early settlers: "Our continent was not settled by bands of atheists or infidels having no religion, nor by Jews or Mohammedans refusing the name of Christ, but by colonies of Christian people acknowledging Jesus Christ as Lord."[62] It then proceeded to advocate political adherence to this tradition, affirming the constitutional language of the new states. And it landed the opinion of the U.S. Supreme Court in The Church of the Holy Trinity v. the United States (1892). Religious language "speaks the voice of the people."[63]

The 1907 Assembly also heard a positive report from the Department of Church and Labor, established two years previously as the first formal denominational organ to relate churches with the labor movement. By naming and publicizing "Labor Sundays," the department considered they were both doing evangelistic work among working people and interpreting for all including Presbyterians the needs of workers.[65] Then, of course, the Assembly received regular reports on both Temperance and Sabbath observance as previously.

But the student can note in the denomination increased attention to the political and economic implications of church actions. A statement on Home Missions noted that property values in Eastern Kentucky doubled for land immediately surrounding new academics and churches. Reports from many of the various foreign missions gave political information and implications for the work of the missionaries.

The Department of Church and Labor of the PCUSA may have arisen from the insights and perceptions of those connected with the Social Gospel movement, with its triumphalism and its emphasis on progress. The greater part of early twentieth century involvement apparently came with some reluctance, however, as the implications of an evangelical faith meant Presbyterian support of political ideas and effects. An impressive pastor such as Francis J. Grimké, Black PCUSA leader in the 1910s and 1920s, seemed more at home preaching about Jesus Christ and human salvation. But he did enter into the political fray necessarily—to argue for increased social welfare, legislation and a legal end to America's color line.

As events and issues became more complex, Presbyterians (as others in mainline churches generally) struggled to come to terms with them. George Marsden and others studying fundamentalism have discovered that even among that wing of the Presbyterian communions, many varied stances characterized the actions of those previously thought to have attempted escape from complication in pat phrases and reductionist politics.

World War I: An Example

Most American Presbyterians supported Woodrow Wilson, renowned Reformed politician, as he moved toward engagement on the side of the Allies. Fellow Presbyterian William Jennings Bryan campaigned in behalf of Wilson throughout the midsection of the country, and he accepted the position of Secretary of State in the new cabinet in 1917. But as Wilson severed diplomatic relations between the U.S. and Germany in February, 1917, Bryan spoke to a mass meeting in New York of peace advocates and pacifists. There he said that the United States would not "get down and wallow in the mire of human blood." Bryan, evidently from ethical and religious sensibilities more than from political sagacity, separated himself from the Wilson administration's position though he remained within it.

On the other hand, Presbyterian Billy Sunday, (yes, he was one!) endorsed the War effort and enjoyed whipping up patriotic hysteria. His 1918 prayer before the U.S. House of Representatives symbolized his union of the cause of Christ and the nation's interests. He referred to the German nation as "vile, greedy, avaricious, blood thirsty, sensual, and vicious." He prayed that every citizen would "stand up to the last ditch and be willing to suffer . . ." in the great battle against the "wolfish Huns."[67]

The stance of the PCUSA General Assembly of 1917 represented something in between the positions of Bryan and Sunday. They endorsed the report of a Special Committee on the State of the Nation which urged "unreserved support of all our people" for the effort.[68]

By the same token, the Assembly addressed a letter to Wilson that called war "irrational inhuman and unchristian."[69] The text of the report particularly showed the extent of ecclesiastical support for the nation:

In the development and progression of the ideals and institutions of the American Republic, Presbyterianism has been a vital and significant force. That force is challenged anew by the crisis that now confronts this generation. The conflict into which we have been irresistibly drawn is one that is so manifestly for the maintenance of righteousness and in behalf of humanity that it should command the courageous and unreserved support of all our people. By every thrill of loyalty to our sacred heritage, by every memory of the sacrifice and suffering of our fathers, by every compelling motive that inspires unselfish action, the Presbyterian Church is summoned to do its part in redeeming the world from its bondage to autocratic rule, and from its prison house of armaments, into a life free to express its own natural good will and fellowship with all men.

The One Hundred and Twenty-ninth General Assembly of the Presbyterian Church in the United States of America records its loyal allegiance to the Government of the United States of America and its unfaltering support of the President in the prosecution of this war for freedom and peace.[70]

In perhaps its most important action of the Assembly, a National Service Commission was appointed "to make to the Government of the United States formal offers of the services of the Presbyterian Church, and upon any request that may be made by the Government, the Commission be authorized to call upon any or all of the agencies and resources of the Church, as in its judgment may be wise or needful.''

The prosecution of the war affected both home missions and foreign missions. In 1917, reports from these boards expressed less distance from politics than did that of the special committee. Home Missions, for example, reported that, "A Christian democracy here, so pure and so virile as to set up standards and ideals for all aspiring peoples, is our incomparable missionary opportunity."[71]

The work of the National Service Commission during 1917-1918 proved extensive indeed. Evangelist J. Wilbur Chapman, Moderator of the denomination, gave practically the whole year to its prosecution. He traveled throughout the country urging ministers and elders to cooperate in the various efforts. Among other things, the Commission nominated chaplains for service, sequestered offices and staff to solicit money, built chapels and "tabernacles" at various army camps, urged food conservation by Presbyterians for the supplying of soldiers," safeguarded the morals of our soldiers and sailors" with a White Zone around camps forbidding saloons and other "dens of sin," called on the government for "seasons of prayer," aided in selling bonds, and assisted in recruitment of young men.[72] To the 1918 Assembly, the commission made several recommendations which were adopted. Among these was a call to "all the churches" in the PCUSA to "offer the fullest measure of cooperation with the Government of the United States and its agencies in furthering the objects and strengthening the agencies engaged in this war." The U. S. labored, according to the commission, "against a conspiracy that is the negative of all things sacred. . . ." They urged the Presbyterians "to secure the acceptance of the law of Christ in social, national, and international life."[73]

Assembly reports of committees on home missions, foreign missions, education, publications, church erection, and all the rest, mentioned the impact of the war; but some did not dwell upon it. Evidently all PCUSA committees purchased some quantity of Liberty Bonds. Home Missions personnel centered on the good morale Presbyterians could provide, and the Board of Foreign Missions lauded the involvement of China, Persia, and Siam on the side of the Allies, claiming partial responsibility for those governments' decisions.[74]

The PCUS, much more reserved in its Assembly statements of 1917, telegraphed Woodrow Wilson that it

> united in earnest prayer that he and those associated with him in authority might be given Divine guidance and strength; and that the Assembly, in sympathy and faith, commends him, our army and navy, and all our distressed homes to God and the Word of His grace, that they may be enriched with faith and patience, comforted and guided in this day of trial and need.[75]

By 1918, the Assembly's telegram expressed only support for the president and the prosecution of the war:

In this crucial hour of Christian civilization, the General Assembly of the Presbyterian Church in the United States commends you to the God of all grace; we are confidently relying upon you, as the spokesman for the moral forces of the world, to carry on your gigantic task to righteous consummation.

We express our earnest sympathy and assure you of our Christian fellowship and all possible and proper support in these days of trial, and pray God's wisdom may guide you.

We believe that, with your superb courage and sublime faith, you will be used as the means of saving to us and to humanity the Christian principles which are our priceless heritage from our fathers.[76]

Southern Presbyterians also established a Select Committee to prepare a letter to the churches about "our soldiers." That letter advocated cooperation with the government and with other denominations to support the War Work Council and other enterprises. The Board of Foreign Missions also mentioned the impact of the war, but in general the PCUS leadership did not evidence as thorough involvement as did the PCUSA.

Support for the government did not prove universal among Presbyterians however. One historian counted seven clergy of note in the PCUSA who remained pacifists, advocating U.S. non-alignment in the War. Norman Thomas, the most famous, became a leader in the newly-formed Fellowship of Reconciliation and tried to convince fellow clergy in the Presbyterian Church that it should "transcend nationalism." Its actions moved Thomas during that time to resign from the Board of Home Missions, of which he had been a member.[78]

But other Presbyterians who did not embrace the doctrines of pacifism, Francis Grimké among them, protested that ministers and churches should neither enlist men for military service nor buy Liberty Bonds.

Generally the Presbyterians fully endorsed the actions of the U. S. government and their Assemblies, Boards and Agencies established little or no critical distance between values and actions of Church and State. Note, however, that both so-called "liberals" and so-called "conservatives" backed unequivocal political involvement; and representatives from both streams criticized the actions.[79]

Summary

U. S. Presbyterians North and South, East and West, have been deeply involved in political action throughout the history of the nation. Many have at various times given univocal support to the government, and they have sought to change its direction through the use of petitions, boycotts, public demonstrations, lobbying for specific bills, and backing particular political candidates. They have worked corporately as well as individually in the various enterprises.

At the same time, many Presbyterians rather assiduously distinguished social and political from religious issues. Their ethical discernment frequently was not based upon escapism or mere self-interest. Although, as in the case of slavery and human rights, it sometimes has proved convenient to argue differing citizenships when Presbyterians have supported morally questionable (sometimes downright indefensible) positions.

The careful student of Presbyterian history in the U.S., as shown in the sketches of various issues, can make few generalizations beyond those of McNeill. Indeed, commitment to Calvinism and its theological offspring means that Presbyterians have participated with energy in many social and political actions. Other papers which accompany this one explain something of the theology and world perspective underlying this commitment. And McNeill's wisdom in pointing to the variety of attitudes politically cannot be doubted. From the time of the Revolution until the present, no significant social or political issue has been perceived uniformly by Presbyterians in the U.S.

Perhaps the reader can argue, further, that as issues in the twentieth century have become more complex, as human knowledge has increased of the whole world's situation, and technology has presented myriad novel images of life and political activity, Presbyterians true to their tradition of "meddlesomeness" have confronted the complexity and sought to cope with it. The chief issues of the final portion of the nineteenth century—temperance and Sabbath observance—have remained important during the twentieth. But Presbyterians have discovered that the Sabbath observance issue has many sides to it, and they have learned that legal prohibition did not resolve the temperance issues either. At the same time new, worldwide issues confronted U. S. Presbyterians, and by the time of the first decade of the twentieth century almost all realized the relationships between political and evangelical matters in various mission fields.

In the twentieth century also, religious pluralism in the U.S. has become much more diverse. The presence of various styles of Judaism, Eastern Orthodoxy, and Christian sects—not to mention the faithful in Buddhism, Islam, Hinduism, and so-called "new religions"—has forced a readjustment in Presbyterian self-understandings. Overall, however, Presbyterians have remained comparatively confident and comparatively powerful in the U.S. political activity despite their situation as a small minority, which is how they began.

Endnotes

1. *Minutes of the General Assembly of the United Presbyterian Church in the United States of America*, 1976, I, P. 132. Seven commissioners recorded their dissent to this action. (p. 133).
2. *Minutes of the General Assembly of the Presbyterian Church in the United States*, 1976, p. 208.
3. John T. McNeill, *History and Character of Calvinism* (New York: Oxford University Press, 1960) p. 411.
4. *Ibid*, pp. 411, 412, 418-420.
5. *Minutes*, May 22, 1776, located in Guy S. Klett, editor, *Minutes of the Presbyterian Church in America*, 1706-1788. (Philadelphia: Presbyterian Historical Society, 1976) p. 549.
6. For an excellent description of Presbyterians and the Revolution, see the *Journal of Presbyterian History* (52) 1874, Number 4.
7. *Minutes of the General Assembly*, 1789, *Assemblies 1789-1820* (Philadelphia: Board of Publication, 1821) p. 12. Washington replied that he desired Presbyterians to

accept his "acknowledgments" for their "laudable endeavors to render men sober, honest, and good citizens, and the obedient subjects of a lawful government." *Minutes . . .* , 1790, p. 24.

8. It should be noted that before the Great Revival (1799-1804), only about ten percent of the population belonged to any church. In addition, there were many who worshiped with but did not belong to Reformed communions; and with the Plan of Union of 1801, Presbyterians and Congregationalists together represented a sizeable portion of American Christian communicants. See Edwin S. Gaustad, *Historical Atlas of Religion in America* (New York: Harper and Row, 1962, 1976) pp. 21, 89; U.S. Bureau of the Census, *Historical Statistics of the United States, Colonial Times to 1957* (Washington: Department of Commerce, 1960) pp. 227-229. Scot Covenanters and German Reformed also populated various areas of the country.

9. Robert Davidson, *History of the Presbyterian Church in the State of Kentucky* (New York: Robert Carter, 1847) pp. 288-293.

10. On their contributions, see W. H. Whitsett, *The Life and Times of Caleb Wallace.* (Louisville: Filson Club Publications, Series 1, 4, 1888).

11. One succinct study of the larger issue is offered by Clyde Manschreck, "Church-State Relations—A Question of Sovereignty," in Manschreck and Barbara Brown Zikmund, *The American Religious Experiment: Piety and Practicality* (Chicago: Exploration Press, 1976) pp. 1-13.

12. James H. Nichols, "John Witherspoon on Church and State," in George L. Hunt, editor, *Calvinism and the Political Order* (Philadelphia: Westminster Press, 1965) pp. 130-139.

13. Alan Heimert, *Religion and the American Mind* (Cambridge, Mass.: Harvard University Press, 1966) p. 541.

14. Peter Williams, *Popular Religion in America* (Englewood Cliffs, New Jersey: Prentice-Hall, 1980) p. 109, 110.

15. Beecher, . . . Sermon on Dueling (1809) quoted in Clifford S. Griffin, *Their Brothers' Keepers: Moral Stewardship in the United States,* (New Brunswick) N.J.; Rutgers University Press, 1960) p. 10.

16. P. J. Standenraus, *The African Colonization Movement, 1816-1865* (New York: Columbia University Press, 1961).

17. Charles I. Foster, *An Errand of Mercy* (Chapel Hill, N.C.: University of North Carolina Press, 1960).

18. Griffin, *op. cit.,* pp. 119-131.

19. *Minutes,* General Assembly, 1815, p. 59, 67.

20. William Gribbin, *The Churches Militant: The War of 1812 and American Religion.* (New Haven: Yale University Press, 1971) pp. 31-39. It should be noted in fairness that elections took on a very local character then, and some of Clinton's supporters argued he would defeat the British handily. Clinton, though, became the prototype of the avowedly pious politician—a new breed in the U.S. at the time.

21. See Neils Sonne, *Liberal Kentucky, 1780-1828* (New York: Columbia University Press, 1939) pp. 108-134. Sonne names other Presbyterians "highly critical of public policy," including James McChord, a prominent Lexington pastor, and James Fishback, editor of the *Western Monitor.*

22. Robert E. Thompson, *A History of the Presbyterian Church in the United States* (New York: Christian Literature Co., 1895) pp. 56-58.

23. Lois W. Banner, "Religious Benevolence as Social Control: A Critique of an Interpretation," *Journal of American History* LX (1973) pp. 23-41.

24. Robert W. Hartness, "The Educational Work of Robert Jefferson Breckinridge," (Unpublished dissertation, Yale University, 1936). In Virginia, John Atkinson, President of Hampden-Sydney, led the movement for public education. Henry Ruffner, a Presbyterian minister, planned implementation. In North Carolina, Calvin H. Wylie, a Presbyterian elder, was most influential.

REFORMED FAITH AND POLITICS

25. John R. Bodo, *The Protestant Clergy and Public Issues, 1812-1848* (Princeton, N.J.: Princeton University Press, 1954).

26. See my "Gods Judgment, Christ's Command: Biblical Themes in Nineteenth Century American Political Life," to appear in James Johnson, ed., *The Bible and American Politics* (Philadelphia: Fortress Press, for the Society of Biblical Literature, 1983).

27. Andrew Murray, *Presbyterians and the Negro* (Philadelphia: Presbyterian Historical Society, 1966).

28. Robert Bishop, *Outline of the History of the Church in the State of Kentucky* (Lexington: Thomas T. Skillman, 1824).

29. Rice, "Slavery Inconsistent with Justice and Good Policy," (1892) in Bishop, *op. cit.*, p. 402.

30. Robert J. Breckinridge. See Robert W. Hartness, "The Educational Work of Robert Jefferson Breckinridge," (unpublished Ph.D. dissertation, New Haven, Yale, 1936).

31. John G. Fee, who moved finally from the New School denomination to become a Baptist.

32. John H. Rice, "Inquiry into the meaning of the word *doulos* in the New Testament," *Evangelical and Literary Magazine*, Vol. ix (1926) pp. 411-20. See my "John Holt Rice and the American Colonization Society," *Journal of Presbyterian History*, 46 (1968) pp. 26-41, for a full discussion of the changes.

33. See Dwight L. Dumond, *Letters of James G. Birney, 1831-1857* (Washington: American Historical Association, 1938) 2 Vols. "Introduction," pp. v-xxiii.

34. *Minutes of the General Assembly, 1818*, pp. 692-694. That Assembly also called on all Presbyterians, individually and corporately, to "suppress this abominable vice," Sabbath-breaking. (p. 678).

35. Merton L. Dillon, *Elijah P. Lovejoy: Abolitionist Editor* (Urbana: University of Illinois Press, 1961).

36. Capt. Godfrey to Theron Baldwin, President of the Female Seminary in Godfrey, Ill., Nov. 4, 1837; available in John Gill, *Tide Without Turning: Elijah P. Lovejoy and Freedom of the Press*, (Boston: Starr King Press, 1959) p. 188.

37. William Maxwell, *A Memoir of the Rev. John H. Rice* (Philadelphia: J. Whitham, 1835) p. 313.

38. Benjamin M. Palmer, *The Life and Letters of James Henley Thornwell* (Richmond: Whittet and Shepperson, 1875).

39. Jack P. Maddex, "From Theocracy to Spirituality: The Southern Presbyterian Reversal on Church and State," *Journal of Presbyterian History* 54 (1976) pp. 438-457.

40. See my "Stuart Robinson: Kentucky Presbyterian Leader," *Filson Club History Quarterly* 54 (1981) pp. 360-377, for one account of his life.

41. E. T. Thompson, *The Spirituality of the Church* (Richmond: John Knox Press, 1961) pp. 45, 46, and *passim*. Writers from both the PCUS and the PCUSA cite the doctrine as one reason why reunion did not take place between these denominations.

42. Thompson himself admits that some years the committee was just "fighting for its very existence." p. 43.

43. R. E. Thompson, *op. cit.*, pp. 303ff.

44. *Ibid*, p. 240. Thompson's work has been cited frequently as a classic, dependable study from the period.

45. *Ibid*, p. 196. He granted words similar in approbation to Amanda McFarland, "for years the only representative of our Christian civilization in the neglected territory of Alaska, and even presided over a constitutional convention called by the natives to set up a government. . . ." p. 191.

46. See Alvin K. Bailey, "The Strategy of Sheldon Jackson in Opening the West for National Missions, 1860-1880," unpublished Ph.D. dissertation, Yale University, 1948); Theodore C. Hinkley, "The Alaska Labors of Sheldon Jackson, 1877-1890" (unpublished Ph.D. dissertation, Indiana University, 1961).

47. Jacob H. Patton, *A Popular History of the Presbyterian Church in the United States of America* (New York: R. S. Mighill, 1900) preface.
48. *Ibid*, pp. 554-556. The great bulk of Patton's text on the church after 1870 concentrated on the heresy trial of Charles A. Briggs.
49. *Minutes, PCUSA Assembly*, 1882. pp. 67-73.
50. *Reports to the General Assembly*, 1891, pp. 1-11. In that year, some reservations were expressed about the methods of the Women's Christian Temperance Union and especially the Anti-Saloon League.
51. *Reports to the General Assembly*, 1898, pp. 1-15.
52. *Reports to the General Assembly*, 1709, pp. 1-29.
53. *Report*, 1891, p. 7.
54. *Report*, 1907, p. 15. Also of note is the involvement of women in the temperance movement especially. See Ruth Bordin, *Women and Temperance, the Quest for Power and Liberty 1863-1900* (Philadelphia: Temple University Press, 1981). She points out that even the United Presbyterian Church "traditionally cool to women activists, formally expressed approval of the [WCTS] in 1885," p. 129.
55. Robert M. Miller, "A Footnote to the Role of the Protestant Churches in the Election of 1928," *Church History* 25 (1956) pp. 145-159.
56. *Reports*, 1907, p. 14.
57. See my article, "The Scriptures and Sabbath Observance in the South," *Journal of Presbyterian History* 59 (1981) pp. 267-283, for a more complete review of the subject.
58. *Minutes, General Assembly, P.C.U.S.*, *1893*, p. 8.
59. *Minutes, General Assembly, P.C.U.S.* 1919, p. 123.
60. Martin E. Marty, *Righteous Empire: The Protestant Experience in America* (New York: Dial Press, 1970), makes another distinction between "private" Protestantism and "public" Protestantism (p. 179.) But, the stress on parties among Presbyterians seems less helpful than a stress on "forces" or "processes."
61. Stanley Shaloff, *Reform in Leopold's Congo* (Richmond, Va.: John Knox Press, 1970) pp. 84-106.
62. *Minutes, General Assembly, PCUSA, 1909*, p. 258.
63. *Ibid*, p. 259.
64. *Minutes, General Assembly, PCUSA, 1907*, p. 292.
65. Sabbath Observance became an ecumenical committee called "Lord's Day Alliance."
66. Bryan, *New York Times*, Feb. 4, 1917, quoted in Ray Abrams, *Preachers Present Arms*, 3rd Edition (Scottsdale, Pa.: Herald Press, 1969) p. 44.
67. William G. McLaughlin, Jr., *Billy Sunday Was His Real Name* (Chicago: University Press, 1955) p. 260.
68. *Minutes, General Assembly, P.C.U.S.A.*, *1917*, p. 236.
69. *Ibid*, pp. 155-158.
70. *Idem*.
71. *Ibid*, Part II, p. 6.
72. *Minutes, General Assembly PCUSA, 1918*, pp. 60-80.
73. *Ibid*, p. 81.
74. *Ibid*, Part II, *passim*.
75. *Minutes, General Assembly, PCUS, 1917*, pp. 23, 24.
76. *Minutes, General Assembly, PCUS, 1918*. pp. 13, 14.
77. *Ibid, passim*.
78. Murray B. Seidler, *Norman Thomas: Respectable Rebel* (Syracuse, N.Y.: University Press, 1961) pp. 18-30.
79. I am indebted to the work of George M. Marsden, *Fundamentalism and American Culture* (Oxford: University Press, 1979), for many of his insights explored in this section.

CHURCH AND STATE IN THE UNITED STATES

by John C. Bennett

It is hard for us in the United States to realize what a break with our European past the American doctrine, structures, and policies in this connection were when the First Amendment to our constitution was adopted. It was even a break with the law and practice within several of our states which continued for several decades. It was not until this century that the First Amendment was applied to practices within the state; it applied originally only to the national state. Today in countries that have long had religious establishments there are strong movements in the direction our country chose.

There are fascinating survivals of the old religious establishments, but the movement away from them has come as an inevitable result of both religious pluralism and secularizing trends. One of the chief marks of the establishment in England has been the fact that the government has formally chosen bishops, deans, canons and even some professors of theology. Most often this has been a formality but there have been a few cases in this century in which choices were made that were objectionable to the Church of England. Now the church is seeking changes in the way such leaders are chosen. In 1927 the Parliament which regarded itself as a lay assembly of the church vetoed a revision of the Book of Common Prayer agreed on as a result of processes within the church. Ever since it has been assumed that if the Parliament were to take such an action again that would be the end of the establishment.

One example of the fascinating survivals was the recent royal wedding when for a few hours we saw the re-enactment of Christendom with all the symbols of a Christian nation. Obviously it would be impossible to have such an event in the United States and American Christians do not desire it. Another survival is the fact that in West Germany the state collects a tax for the churches. People can avoid the tax by formally leaving the churches but they are not inclined to do that in large numbers.

There are three essential grounds for believing in the separation of Church and State. The first is the need of religious institutions to be free from control by the state. The second is the need to protect citizens from interference with their religious liberty through the use of the power of the state by a church or group of religious institutions that seek to bring about discrimination in their favor. The third is that we have learned from experience that separation from the state is favorable to the health and vitality of churches.

1. Churches, if they are to be true to themselves, should demand freedom from control by the state. This means freedom for religious faith and worship and witness, including public worship and public witness. It means freedom of assembly and freedom for the ordering of the corporate life of the churches themselves. It means that they should have freedom to propagate their faith and the people should have freedom to change their religious commitments. It means freedom to act in accordance with religious beliefs and commitments.

In many countries when religious people take some of these forms of freedom they are persecuted, though often the acts for which believers are persecuted are called "political." This is true of nations on both the extreme right and the extreme left politically. Even in a nation as tolerant of diversity and dissent as ours, religious freedom can lead to conflicts with the state, and these conflicts require care and sensitivity on both sides. The acceptance by the state of the right of citizens to be conscientious objectors to military service is a good illustration of an *ad hoc* concordat between the state and many churches. This is still true because of the importance of the initiative of churches even though such conscientious objection is no longer limited to those cases for which there is either a churchly or a theological basis. An absolute moral commitment which can be translated into a religious commitment in terms of Tillich's understanding of religion as "ultimate concern" can be accepted legally as the basis for conscientious objection. Conflicts come over the right to object to particular wars and this may become more important since the Roman Catholic hierarchy has recognized the right of conscientious objection to "unjust wars" and this in principle would be selective objection.

There is no problem in this country now concerning freedom of religious teaching and witness, and the burden of proof is on any interference by the state with any action in accordance with religious belief in society. It is a very heavy burden of proof backed by the First Amendment.

That such religious freedom from any limitation by the state is not absolute is well illustrated by the terrible events in Jonestown. After those events it is easy to see there should have been protection of people against such exploitation and even lethal abuse by a religious leader, but it is not easy to say exactly at what point and by what method the state should have entered the picture. Today there is a great deal of debate as to how far the state should investigate the financial operations of a religious institution or community, and this issue is raised in the case of such organizations as the World Wide Church of God.

The state's enforcement of law within the life of the Church is accepted in some situations. When there is a split in a denomination the state has often acted to determine which group should own the property that is involved. Should dissenters who have controlled local church buildings be allowed to retain them when they vote by a large majority in particular units to separate themselves from the denominational body? In the past the courts have followed the law of the denomination concerning the ownership of local church property in line with the Supreme Court of *Watson and Jones* (1871). Recently there has been some confusion about this when general assumptions about ownership of property have been found to be unsupported by clear written legal provisions. The United Presbyterian Church has acted to clear up this matter.

Churches are not creatures of the state though they do live under the law of the state in external matters. The great word for Christians has been the declaration of the Apostles: "We must obey God rather than men" (Acts 5:29). The fact that this may mean disobedience to the state involving legal penalties does not alter what should be the general expectation that a just and healthy state should lean over backwards to respect the freedom of religious people and religious institutions to be true to themselves. One of the most important of the services of the Church to the state is to keep the state under independent criticism. The healthier the state, the more this will be welcomed as a contribution.

2. The second reason for welcoming and preserving the separation of Church and State is that it protects the state from ecclesiastical control and its citizens from the use of the power of the state by a Church or a group of churches to abridge their religious liberty.

Before the Second Vatican Council, when Church-State issues were discussed with most emotion, the concern that many Americans had was that the Catholic Church might use the state to discriminate against non-Catholics. One of the great Catholic social liberals who was active in the first half of this century was Father John A. Ryan. He had much to do with the development of religious support for the New Deal in the 1930s. He wrote a book that appeared under more than one title (one title was *Catholic Principles of Politics*) which contained a paragraph that indicated that if Catholics were to become a significant majority they might use their power to limit to some extent the religious freedom of non-Catholics. Father Ryan did not like this possibility at all for it was against his liberal spirit. He assured the reader that it would never happen, that it was only a theoretical possibility. Non-Catholics did think that it might happen in a state with a large Catholic majority. I can remember that this paragraph was often cited as an illustration of the threat of Catholic power hanging over this country. Paul Blanshard in the 1940s and 1950s wrote books warning the country of the dangers of Catholic power.[1]

As recently as 1960 when John Kennedy was running for the presidency the relations between Catholics and many Protestants were ugly because of this fear. Many Protestants resisted this fear. In my home there is a picture on the wall of Reinhold Niebuhr and myself holding a press conference in our apartment in Union Seminary opposing the Protestants who were stirring up religious opposition to Kennedy. This fear has vanished as a serious concern of American non-Catholics. The experience of a Catholic president who proved to be independent of the hierarchy (he ran less risk of being called bigoted for opposing the hierarchy than a Baptist!) and the Declaration of the Vatican Council on Religious Freedom created a new situation. There was never any worry about the Catholicism of Eugene McCarthy, Robert Kennedy or Edmund Muskie.

The Vatican Declaration said the following: "This freedom means that all men are to be immune from coercion on the part of individuals or of social groups and of any human power, in such wise that in matters religious no one is to be forced to act in a manner contrary to his own beliefs. Nor is anyone to be restrained from acting in accordance with his own beliefs, whether privately or publicly, whether alone or in association with others, within due limits." That last phrase was merely a recognition of the fact that there are limits to forms of anti-social behavior which may be given religious justification and it has not been used by the Catholic Church as an escape clause. Quite the contrary, this Vatican Declaration has had a profound effect on the Catholic Church and on the attitudes of non-Catholics to it. It is well known that the Catholic Church is the greatest defender of human rights including religious freedom for Christians and non-Christians in many countries, especially in Latin America. No longer is it emphasized that error has no rights. Rather it is said that persons or consciences in error have rights. I wonder if the declaration of a Church Council of any kind has ever so soon changed the spirit and policies of a great Church or has had such beneficent effects on society.

The most debated question during the 1950s was whether or not public funds should be used to provide various kinds of services to parochial schools. The issue at stake in the minds of many was the religious freedom of non-Catholics who did not want to be taxed to support a Catholic religious program. Some marginal benefits such as transportation and some textbooks and health services were allowed, but the Supreme Court has been rigid in making impossible substantial contributions to the teaching of non-religious subjects in parochial schools.

3. The third reason why we should welcome the separation of Church and State is that it is favorable to the health and vitality of churches. It puts them in a situation that requires self-support. This in our country has given the laity a very important role and generally the churches have developed strength based upon lay initiative that is not found in the state churches. In this country the statistics concerning church attendance and concerning the amount of money raised for churches are remarkable. Many more people are present in our churches in proportion to the size of the population than is the case in nations with religious establishments.

In American history there was a very interesting episode in 1818 when in Connecticut the Congregational churches were disestablished. One of the great religious leaders of that time, Lyman Beecher, fought hard against disestablishment, but after he had been defeated he changed his mind. Professor Winthrop Hudson describes this change in these words: "He (Beecher) found himself forced to acknowledge that what he feared as the worst thing that could happen had turned out to be 'the best thing that ever happened in the State of Connecticut'. For, as he said, 'it cut the churches loose from dependence on state support' and 'threw them wholly on their own resources and God', there was created a moral coercion which makes men work.''[2]

The Catholic Church in the United States has been very dynamic and in many ways has flourished more than has been the case in official Catholic states. I wonder if this experience did not help to prepare the way for the Declaration concerning religious freedom.

Twentieth-Century Issues

A number of issues indicate that our constitutional provision for the separation of Church and State is far from being a finished product. In every generation, new questions about its meaning arise which call for answers. There has been a succession of answers by the Supreme Court and in some cases it has changed its mind. It is surprising that it was not until the 1920s that the First Amendment was applied to the states, and that this was done by way of the Fourteenth Amendment. It was not applied to Church-State relations until 1947, when there was a series of Supreme Court decisions concerning religious schools. (It had been applied to Utah in cases involving polygamy in the last century, but Utah was then a territory under the direct control of the federal government.)

1. There is a fundamental problem arising from the relationship of the two clauses of the First Amendment: "Congress shall make no law respecting an establishment of religion, or prohibiting the free exercise thereof." Sometimes what is said about separation seems to raise difficulties in regard to positive forms of the free exercise of religion. Religious freedom is not primarily freedom from religion!

The relation between the establishment clause and the free exercise clause in the First Amendment is well illustrated by a decision of the Supreme Court, in December 1981 (Widmar et al v. Vincent et al). The University of Missouri in Kansas City had forbidden the recognized student groups interested in religion to use rooms for meetings even in hours when they would not be otherwise used because the university authorities thought that for them to do so would be in violation of the establishment clause of the First Amendment. This case finally reached the Supreme Court and the Court with eight justices agreeing decided that this action of the university violated the free exercise clause, that so long as many other student groups with a variety of interests were allowed to use the rooms such discrimination against religious groups was unconstitutional. Justice Stevens said that "if school facilities may be used to discuss anti-clerical doctrine, comparable use by a group desiring to express a belief in God must also be permitted." The court noted that religious groups sometimes engaged in worship but did not allow that fact to justify their exclusion from use of the facilities. The court laid down some guidelines to indicate when such activities might be inconsistent with the establishment clause but there was a clear tendency to give the benefit of the doubt to the right of religious groups to use public facilities. This is a very important decision that should free public institutions of higher learning from inhibitions that have led in practice to unfair obstacles put in the way of religious groups on public campuses.[3]

In 1947, the court gave a new interpretation of the establishment clause in the Everson case which dealt with the use of school buses by parochial school children. It gave permission for them to use school buses under some conditions but in the development of its argument the court said: "The establishment of religion clause of the First Amendment means at least this: Neither a state nor the federal government can set up a church. Neither can pass laws which aid one religion, aid all religions, or prefer one religion to another." When the words, "aid all religions," were first published many of us were shocked. I had myself assumed that the establishment clause meant that no church should have a preferred position. The words about not aiding all religions seems to suggest that the state did not take a positive attitude toward religion, but was indifferent to the welfare of religious institutions and communities, that it made a special point of not doing things that might create conditions favorable to the free exercise of religion by most people in the nation. This attitude seemed to be a false reading of our history and of our nature as a people. It seems to me now to reflect a different spirit from that suggested by the case in the previous paragraph.

I came to see that there is one thing to be said for this statement about not aiding all religions: it was an attempt to be fair to that minority in the population that is not committed to any religious faith or to any religious community. There has been some fear that the First Amendment might be regarded as consistent with the idea of a *multiple religious establishment*.

However, five years after the Everson decision the court in an opinion written by Justice Douglas in regard to the New York released time case (actually it was "dismissed time") said the following and in doing so provided a better balance than the words of the Everson opinion:

"When the State encourages religious instruction or cooperates with religious authorities by adjusting the schedule of public events to sectarian needs it follows the best in our traditions. For it then respects the religious nature of our people and accommodates the public service to their spiritual needs. To hold that it may not would be to find in the constitution a requirement that the government show a callous indifference to religious groups. That would be preferring those who believe in no religion over those who do so believe. Government may not finance religious groups nor undertake religious instruction nor blend secular and religious education nor use secular institutions to force one or some religion on any person."

It is interesting that while as late as 1931 the Supreme Court declared that we are a "Christian people,"[4] Justice Douglas in the case from which I have quoted said that we are a "religious people." He added, "and our institutions presuppose a Supreme Being." It is doubtful that the Court will ever go back to the claim that we are a Christian people. Awareness of the presence of such a significant Jewish community would almost certainly make that impossible. Whether the claim will continue to be made that our institutions presuppose a Supreme Being is bound up with the current discussion of our "civil religion."

The issue at stake here is that on the one hand there should be the avoidance of a multiple establishment of religion and on the other hand the state, most of whose citizens have some religious commitment or relationship, should not hinder their religious expression or set itself up as alien to their religious interests. It should do what can be done, without being unfair to the convinced secularists in the population, to facilitate the free exercise of their religion by our people. There are sure to be many sensitive borderline situations and there are times when mutual tolerance is better than legalistic rigidity that decides too readily what cannot be done.

A good example of what the state does in this regard is its provision for chaplains in the armed services on the ground that only so can it enable those who are separated from their civilian communities to exercise their religious freedom. Many religious groups would prefer a different status for chaplains, that they not have military rank, but even if such a change were made the state would have to cooperate with the churches in making religious ministry available.

While there should be the avoidance of a multiple churchly establishment, there should still be the opportunities now often provided for the expression of what may be called "civil religion" in the context of government. There is objection to the phrase "civil religion" but I think that what I mean will be evident from the illustrations that follow. There should not be an artificial inhibition of all religious expression by the president and others who represent the state. The provision for chaplains of Congress and many other legislative bodies shows how deeply rooted a recognition of civil religion is in our institutions. We never have such inhibitions against religious expression on such occasions as the inaugurations of presidents. Robert Bellah calls attention to the significant references to God in John F. Kennedy's inaugural address.[5] Lincoln's Second Inaugural was one of the greatest American religious utterances, and our tradition would be much poorer without it.

Thanksgiving proclamations of the president are taken for granted as being appropriate but one may hope that they may become less expressions of national self-righteousness and self congratulation.

Do we prefer a complete inhibition in this area, the preservation of a religious vacuum through silence about religion on all public occasions or do we prefer some openness so that sometimes the nation points beyond itself to the God who transcends it and in whom most of its citizens believe? If there is to be a public expression of civil religion, it should be under the criticism of churches and synagogues to keep it from becoming a form of national idolatry. Perhaps it is too ironic to use our money as the medium through which the nation says: "In God we trust!"

The American civil religion at its best is a source of judgment rather than a source of national idolatry. However the interaction between the civil religion and the specific religious faiths, Christianity and Judaism especially, is very important. In January 1972, there was one of the prayer breakfasts in Washington that must be unique in the world. Three thousand of the most powerful people in the nation were present. At the head table were President Nixon and Billy Graham and such respectable atheists as the Soviet Ambassador and the Mayor of Moscow graced the occasion. Also at the head table was Senator Mark Hatfield who brought to the occasion what could only come from a specific religious tradition.

In Hatfield's speech which must have seemed out of tune with the occasion he said the following:

> "If we leaders appeal to the God of civil religion, our faith is in a small and exclusive deity, a loyal spiritual advisor to power and prestige, a defender of only the American nation, the object of a national folk-religion devoid of moral content. But if we pray to the Biblical God of justice and righteousness, we fall under God's judgment for calling upon his name but failing to obey his commands. We sit here today as the wealthy and the powerful. Today our prayers must begin with repentance. Individually we must seek forgiveness for the exile of love from our hearts. And corporately, as a people, we must turn in repentance from the sin that has scarred our national soul."

We can be sure that Hatfield was thinking among other things of the war in Indo-China which he had strongly opposed. The civil religion is not self-sufficient. It needs to be renewed and corrected by the specific faiths among the American people. The free exercise of religion guaranteed by the First Amendment includes this kind of religious witness in the context of the state.

2. Turn to a second area of discussion: The relation between religion and politics. In our history the separation of Church and State has never meant the separation of religion and politics. Not only citizens as individuals but churches and synagogues have found ways to express their convictions about great political issues. Very often religious institutions have supported the dominant powers in society, but it is seldom suggested that they are being political when they do this. Whenever they go against the stream and engage in criticism of the state or of economic powers, they are accused of being political.

In a democracy decisions of great moral and religious significance are made by means of the political process, and the churches should not separate themselves from that process. There can be debate about what is appropriate action especially in connection with partisan politics and the choice of candidates. Hard problems arise when candidates so completely embody issues from opposite points of view that we cannot separate decisions on issues from decisions on candidates in a particular election.

In spite of what I have said, there is a common assumption that any voicing of political opinions by any unit of the Church is a violation of the principle of separation of Church and State. Recently I heard an interview by a very intelligent reporter of Bishop James Armstrong, the president of the National Council of Churches. Bishop Armstrong was there to explain the opposition in the churches to our government's support of the Duarte government in El Salvador. He was asked by the interviewer: "Don't you believe in the separation of Church and State?" At present this issue is raised very often in the context of the activities of the so-called "Moral Majority" and its allies in the "Religious Right" because of their very much publicized activities in politics.

There is a phase of this subject that is too often neglected: some discrimination concerning the various units of the Church that take action. No one doubts that Christians as citizens should act politically and this would apply to members of the clergy and other conspicuous leaders of the Church as citizens, though they are often criticized because they have difficulty in separating themselves from their representative role. One other form of Christian activity that has been very common in the life of American churches is the work of unofficial movements or organizations that may take the name of Christian or even the name of a denomination but which do not speak or act in behalf of any ecclesiastical body. There are or have been many such movements, movements for peace, for racial justice, for various economic goals, for laws in regard to the control of the liquor traffic,[6] some of the pro-life movements, etc. In the 19th century the movements for the abolition of slavery were unofficial and denominations as such usually avoided such decisive political action. One movement today that functions in this way is CALC (Clergy and Laity Concerned) which began as a movement that was opposed to the war in Indo-China. Then there is the official action often taken by the judicatories of the denominations and in the Presbyterian system these bodies have an important representative role.

There is another level of action which is taken by ecumenical bodies such as the National Council of Churches and the World Council of Churches or even state-wide or local councils of churches. These have a dual role. To some extent they are representative because most of those who participate in them are appointed by denominations and this gives importance to what they say and do. However, in practice what they say and the message that may be embodied in what they do are directed to the churches more than they are taken to represent the churches. There is some ambiguity here, but their decision-making bodies are far enough removed from the members of any one church that it is best to emphasize this "speaking to" rather than "speaking for." There is even another variation when a conference is called officially by ecumenical institutions and it is charged to speak and act unofficially, to speak only for those present to the churches. Sometimes there are *ad hoc* groups of leaders of the church that speak to the church and expect that the public will overhear. This overhearing by the public is always involved. Churches that have bishops have more visible leadership in practice than other churches and that makes the actions of the Roman Catholic bishops even when they speak as individuals or *ad hoc* groups very influential. But even when the Pope speaks one cannot count on the members of local churches hearing him!

When we are thinking about the activity of Christians in politics it is desirable to take account of these distinctions. Bodies that officially speak for large constituencies are not as free as movements and organizations that are unofficial and speak for themselves. The degree of representativeness depends on the polities of denominations. Yet, even the most official and representative bodies should not act on the basis of a kind of Gallup Poll of the membership. Representativeness does involve exposure to ideas that may not be expressed in a great many local situations, to the implications of Biblical and theological teaching, to the experiences of people who live in quite different situations from those that influence the minds of the members of one part of the Church, and to processes of discussion. The churches in any one country through these processes are able to begin to see the world as it is experienced by Christians in other countries. The more official the body that speaks or acts the greater the need to emphasize the difference between action about political issues and action in support of particular parties or candidates. Greater hesitancy to speak or act when partisan differences are involved in contrast to what is said or done about issues that do not separate parties is not necessarily related to matters of church and state but rather to the fact that partisan issues reflect more hardened differences in the churches themselves. It is appropriate for a denomination or any other unit of the Church to call attention to the facts about agreements or disagreements between the positions that candidates have taken or that are expressed in party platforms with positions that have been emphasized in the teaching of churches.

Various levels of political action by churches are as old as the Republic. One interesting example was the furious opposition to Jefferson and his party by the clergy of New England. Denominations were split by the issues that led to the Civil War. In the depression of the 1930s there was an enormous amount of speaking and acting on economic issues by units of the church. In recent times two kinds of issues were emphasized both by unofficial movements and later by the judicatories of the churches: those related to civil rights and interracial justice and those related to the Vietnam war. In both cases, though controversies in the churches remained, denominations and also ecumenical bodies took sides in favor of civil rights legislation and in opposition to the Vietnam war. This was emphatically true of the United Presbyterian Church.

Today a great deal of attention is given to the political activities of the "Moral Majority." What they have done most of the time has been formally no different from what we can expect of the mainline churches, including the Roman Catholic Church. Those who disagree with them should argue about the substance of the positions which they take rather than about their right to be political. They can be criticized for the extent to which they have pushed partisan political action in "single issue" politics. They concentrated on defeating several senators in the 1980 election and were successful. Sometimes the single issue was the Senator's support of the Panama Canal treaties; more often it was the position of senators on laws outlawing almost all abortion. Jerry Falwell, the leader of the Moral Majority, says that in the next period abortion will be the issue of highest priority. It is not unconstitutional to engage in "single issue" politics, but it does distort the political process and is unfair to candidates who have records on many issues.

Among the positions which the Moral Majority takes, at least two raise very serious questions in relation to the establishment clause of the First Amendment. One of these is the attempt to persuade legislatures to pass laws calling for the teaching of Biblical creationism as science together with what is taught about evolution. So far they have been successful in two states. It is intolerable for legislatures to dictate the content of teaching in schools and in this case they are asked to endorse a religious doctrine as having scientific claims. Teachers who are compelled to use textbooks that include such teaching will in many cases feel bound to correct the text and that will expose themselves to legal prosecution. I doubt if such legal action will be taken often because the memories of the Scopes trial in 1925 probably suggest limits to the public's tolerance of such repressive policies. The other position that the Moral Majority takes that raises church-state issues is their demand for the right of schools to sponsor prayers. I shall return to this later. There are ambiguities about what is often called "voluntary prayer" and those who support prayer in the schools may claim that the "free exercise" clause of the First Amendment is on their side.

3. A third area of discussion is about the use of public funds to give some support to parochial schools. Most parochial schools, of course, are Catholic, but there are well established Lutheran schools and Jewish schools to mention those that are most numerous. Recently, partly because of the work of the Moral Majority and allied movements, there has been an explosion of Protestant parochial schools primarily for religious reasons. There have been many such schools established to preserve racial segregation, but I do not suggest that is the primary motive in the case of most of these new Protestant schools.

The heat of the argument about giving any public support to parochial schools a generation ago (and it was very hot!) was a result of fear of Catholic power among many sophisticated people combined with a crude anti-Catholicism which has had a long history in our country. One of the high points in the influence of both was the campaign for the election of John F. Kennedy in 1960. That election proved that a Catholic president might not be subservient to the bishops or the Pope in the performance of his duties as president, and at the same time Pope John XXIII and the Second Vatican Council reassured non-Catholics that Catholicism would not be a threat to their religious liberty. There is today much less emotion expressed in the discussion of this subject. There is a new factor which raises many new problems: the proposal for public support for private schools including parochial schools by means of the voucher system or tax credit for tuition in private schools. Both of these proposals have caused less furious debate than the earlier proposals for support for parochial schools, but they raise more serious problems in relation to the well-being of the whole system of public education.

The parochial schools provide not only religious education but general education which is acceptable to the state. They bear the financial burden for the education of millions of children and the public authorities would find it very difficult to get along without their help. It is difficult to see any reason why the state should not provide help to the parochial schools for the teaching of non-religious subjects, especially for the sciences which require laboratories and other expensive equipment. There might be a kind of released time in reverse with parochial school children going to the public schools for part of their education. The Catholics would have to make a concession in distinguishing part of their educational program as secular. The non-Catholics need no longer fear that parochial schools indoctrinate children with anti-Protestant or anti-Jewish teaching. This fear used to be a large factor in the attitudes of non-Catholics on this subject.

A good case can be made that the Supreme Court has been too rigid in its interpretation of the First Amendment in relation to experiments in cooperation between public schools and parochial schools. If all that we had to consider was the Church-State context of the problem of public and private education, it should not be impossible to come up with new procedures that would be much fairer to all concerned. We have a new situation today with all kinds of private schools mushrooming because of the disillusionment concerning the public schools, because of opposition to busing, and because of the attacks on public education by such groups as the Moral Majority which have led to a great increase in the number of Protestant Christian schools.

We need to ask two questions at least in this new situation. The first is a question concerning how we are to distinguish between well-established systems of private education under religious sponsorship and all sorts of new private schools that have no history and that are not likely to meet desirable educational standards and which would spring up to collect publicly supported tuition payments. The second question has to do with the effect of tuition tax credits or vouchers on the total structure of elementary and secondary education. Would not either of these provisions encourage the mushrooming of schools and an enormous scattering of the energy and resources of the community available for education? Would these measures not make impossible in many places any stable structure of public education? There would be no confidence in the continuity either of the use of expensive buildings or in the use of the personnel of public education, especially teachers. The problems of public education, especially in the inner city, are very great, but would not these new measures rob the city schools of resources and thus make their problems worse? My chief suggestion is that we ought not to deal with these proposed measures—tuition tax credit or the voucher system—primarily as a Church-State issue but rather in terms of their effects on the quality of education in all kinds of schools.

It is unfortunate that because of this new situation it may be difficult to move toward a more just policy in relation to the well established parochial schools, Catholic and Protestant and Jewish, without bringing about the results of the broad use of the tax credits and vouchers that I have mentioned.

4. The issue of the use of law to prohibit almost all abortions is often regarded as involving Church-State relations. I used to think that it was chiefly a Protestant-Catholic issue and that the Catholic authorities were using their political clout to impose a Catholic position on the nation as a whole by law. I gained

this impression, in the late sixties, when I was a member of Governor Rockefeller's commission on abortion legislation. The commission was itself split as between Catholics and others, and there is no doubt that the bishops in New York State did throw their whole weight against a law that permitted abortion in several situations. Catholic pressure on the legislature was very strong.

Today we can discern some realities that were not present in the sixties. The Moral Majority is more Protestant than Catholic and a very restrictive constitutional amendment concerning abortion is their highest priority. The Republican Party is still more Protestant than Catholic and its platform also came out for such an amendment with the support of Ronald Reagan. The top Catholic authorities are more adamant on this subject than the leaders of most Protestant denominations but polls show that the Catholic constituency is very much divided. There are differences among Catholic moral theologians; for example, between Bernard Häring and Charles Curran who are of the same spirit on many other issues.[7] The differences among Catholics about the use of law in regard to abortion are very clear with Father Robert Drinan, the former Congressman, giving leadership to the opponents of a restrictive law.

When there is debate concerning the use of public funds to enable poor women to have abortions, one sees an absolute conflict of conscientious convictions. Those on one side are outraged by almost all abortions and they believe that their tax money should not be used for this purpose. On the other side many are outraged and this is also a moral outrage because the society in refusing to use funds in this way is creating a situation for poor women which is in effect discriminatory. Middle or upper class women are able to pay for abortions and, if necessary, to travel to a state or to a country where they are permitted. Poor women, including adolescents who are too immature for the responsibilities of motherhood, will be forced to bear children under circumstances unfavorable to the well-being of the children themselves or to have abortions under unsafe conditions. Those on both sides of this issue can hardly communicate; they are like ships that pass in the night.

The debate concerning when human life begins related to legislation before Congress seems, to me, to have to do with a metaphysical description of what is human more than with a theological position, though that point is debatable. The issue is poorly phrased as being about when human life begins. There is life from the beginning and there is no other than human life involved. The real problem is when does this life become a human being that has the same claims as persons who are born.

Instead of making this issue a Church-State issue because of its relationship to Catholics and Protestants, I think that it would be better to ask both sides to be restrained in the use of law because of the profoundly different conscientious positions separating them. It is a fact that the judicatories of many Protestant denominations have come out in favor of a law that permits abortion under several conditions. This is true of the Presbyterian denominations, both the United Presbyterian Church in the North and U. S. Presbyterian Church in the South, of the United Methodist Church, the Episcopal Church, the United Church of

Christ, the Lutheran Church in America, the Reformed Church in America, and there may be others. This is true of most of the Jewish community. An absolutistic law against abortion would force many people in these religious traditions to act against their consciences, but the absence of such a law does not force anyone to go against his or her conscience.

There, however, is this difficult situation: those who regard abortion as murder may as a matter of conscience feel that they must call upon the law to stop a murder from being committed down the street. Those who think in these terms generally hold the view that the human being with full claims begins at conception.

5. My fifth controversial issue is raised by the very widespread desire of the public for permission to have what are called voluntary prayers in the public schools. Public verbal prayer in schools has been declared unconstitutional by the Supreme Court. The polls show that the idea of school prayers is very popular with the public, but many of our churches and the National Council of Churches are opposed to it.

Private voluntary prayer is constitutional now! A serious issue is raised when prayer becomes a public event, especially an event involving the use of words. Who is it that is expected to make the voluntary choice? A teacher, a faculty, a superintendent, a class, a school board? Whoever makes the choice, such an event would go against the convictions of a minority in many situations. The fact of prayer itself would do so in some cases and the content of the prayer might do so in others. Those who might absent themselves would probably feel under pressure to conform and in some cases they might feel the scorn of the majority. This would in a sense be an interference with the religious liberty of the minority.

There is also a serious practical problem about the content of the prayer. Is it not clear that no representative of the state should dictate the content of the prayer? If the wording of the prayer is chosen by *ad hoc* groups in each community, who would say whether or not the wording was appropriate? A Christian prayer or a Biblical prayer would be too sectarian. A vague prayer with little meaning would discredit prayer. I can see numberless debates in local situations about the words chosen for a prayer, and these debates would be anything but prayerful. In New York State there was a prayer authorized by the regents and the prayer was so general that people really committed to religious faith lost interest. What right had the regents to determine the content of prayer? Fortunately, the Supreme Court, in connection with the New York case, decided that prayer in the schools was unconstitutional.

There was a fascinating case in New Jersey in which the local school board in Netcong very ingenuously instituted a program in which the prayer of the chaplain in either the House of Representatives or the Senate for the day was read from the Congressional Record and the pupils were given the opportunity to meditate on it. This was making use of a prayer under the auspices of the State that was accepted as legal in another situation but the State Board of Education ordered the local board to terminate the practice and when the local board appealed to the United States Supreme Court, the appeal was denied. That shows how ingenuous a local group can be and how determined the Supreme Court is on this subject.

If there were some way of having a moment of silence before the mystery of our existence that transcends particular faiths and that transcends the confident affirmations of secular knowledge, it might be appropriate. Whether the schools could generally provide an atmosphere that would not spoil the occasion is a question. Churches and synagogues should emphasize the danger that words of prayer under the auspices of the schools may come to express a minimal civil religion that might come to have a life of its own. There is a special danger that since patriotic symbols do not raise Church-State issues they might be used to fill a religious vacuum and that out of the effort to have an occasion for religious awareness would develop national idolatry. These problems connected with prayer in the schools should remind us of how essential it is that the content of religion be given by religious communities that are independent of the State.

Church and State Conflicts

Conflicts between Church and State are continuous and pervasive. In countries with an established non-Christian religion there is often a perpetual struggle to create or preserve any space for the church at all. There are innumerable variations in the degree to which this is possible and especially in the degree to which the Church can function at all outside the sanctuary. There are such conflicts and struggles in nations that are politically and culturally totalitarian but again the variations are numerous. In communist countries there is a spectrum ranging from as closed a society as North Korea or Albania to nations where the churches have such strength that they can be limited but not suppressed. Poland would be at the latter extreme and close to it would be Hungary and Yugoslavia. In the Soviet Union there is considerable freedom for worship in the sanctuary but there are great limitations on religious education for young people in the Church, and there are no regular opportunities for public teaching or witness. The Churches keep what freedom they have within their own life by supporting the policies of the regime and its structures. There are many authoritarian countries on the right in which units of the Church are led by their faith to resist the state at particular points and whenever religiously motivated dissent threatens the government it is repressed. Again there are all degrees of this. We need to keep remembering that Christian witness on matters of justice, on the protection of basic human rights is often very costly. This is true in nations which our government supports because they are anti-communist such as South Korea, Taiwan, South Africa, Chile, Argentina, Guatemala, El Salvador, to name only a few. It was very often true in Brazil where the Church is strong and where there is now some moderation in the repressiveness of government. The number of nations in which Churches have assured religious liberty that includes liberty of public witness on issues of justice and freedom is unfortunately very small.

In this chapter, we are concerned about the churches in the United States.

We are fortunate that religious liberty is protected by the First Amendment and by the ethos of our society and that this liberty most of the time includes liberty of witness and action on social issues. In some periods in recent history there have been episodes of repression and of costly struggles to use freedom. During the period in which Joseph McCarthy was intimidating agencies in the government, there was fear of dissenting from positions favored by McCarthy and others who were recklessly accusing people of being subversive. Though churches suffered, this did not involve central conflicts between Church and State but rather tendencies to be fearful of unofficial pressures from public opinion, often local public opinion. Units of the Church strongly attacked these repressive tendencies defending freedom for themselves and for society as a whole.[8] The nation finally overcame this repressive menace. There were always portions of the press and of the electronic media that took freedom to illumine what was taking place and appeals to legal protections of freedom were always available. We did not have a central conflict between Church and State.

There were many conflicts in our society over the issues of civil rights and racial justice, and Churches were very much involved. These did not involve a central conflict between the Church and the national State. They did involve many conflicts of units of the Church and many movements inspired by Christian faith with local ordinances or police and state governments. One of the events which most vividly called attention to the issues in this many-sided struggle was the arrest of Martin Luther King, Jr. and his remarkable letter written in the Birmingham jail.[9] This letter was actually addressed not to the government but to a group of ministers who had sought to persuade King not to engage in such a confrontation with the authorities. Dr. King made clear that he believed in civil disobedience to unjust laws, that in willingly accepting punishment under such laws one "is in reality expressing the highest respect for law." Dr. King also made clear that he was appealing from an unjust local ordinance to the federal law which he honored. So again there was no conflict between Dr. King and the national State. Also, the Church was ambiguously involved for the ministers whom he addressed were on the opposite side from King although a very large part of the constituency of the Churches gave full moral support to King's action. In relation to civil rights we may say of the Churches that, while they were engaged in innumerable cases of local resistance to authorities, their main strategy was to work for the enactment of the major laws protecting the rights of minorities in the 1960s. In the case of the Civil Rights laws of 1964, a very influential senator in the South who opposed the law blamed its enactment on the "preachers."

I think that the chief central conflicts between Church and State in the next period are likely to be in relation to foreign policy and especially in relation to the use of nuclear weapons. It is reassuring concerning the health of our society that during the Vietnam war there was remarkable freedom for dissent. Within the churches this dissent grew steadily from 1964 until about 1971. There were unofficial movements which organized most of the public expressions of opposition to the war, but by 1970, the judicatories of many denominations had opposed the war including the General Assembly of the United Presbyterian Church. In November 1971 the hierarchy of the Roman Catholic Church said that the war was an unjust war which was a change from its earlier attitudes toward the American government. The press remained free during this period and opposition to the war was expressed on very high levels of the establishment, for example in Congressional committees. Some *acts* of protest which were formally illegal, such as those of the Berrigans, were punished; these were not the acts of churches though there was widespread sympathy with them in the churches.

I have referred to the provisions by the state for conscientious objectors to military service under the draft. The courts have come to provide a broad basis for this so long as the objectors are opposed to all wars. Today the problem that will be raised more than ever before will come from objectors to particular wars. This was the case with most of the objectors to the Vietnam war who were sent to prison or who chose exile. In the future there will be two new factors that will increase the number of resisters to particular wars. One is that Roman Catholic authorities, both the Vatican Council and a statement of the American hierarchy, have given support to the principle of conscientious objection to military service. In their case this must generally involve conscientious objection to particular wars because the Church has never given official support to pacifism in principle but has taught that some wars that meet particular criteria may be "just wars." The other new factor is that the prospect of nuclear wars will produce large numbers of Christian nuclear pacifists among both Catholics and Protestants.

These two factors are closely related because of the dramatic opposition to the use of nuclear weapons by Roman Catholic bishops. If a nuclear war should come about and lead to an exchange (bloodless word) of massive attacks between two countries the war might end in days or weeks and the whole issue of conscientious objection would hardly arise. The point at which conscientious objection to the use of the nuclear weapons may arise is when people are drafted to fight in what is initially a conventional war with a threat of becoming a nuclear war at a later stage. Objection to becoming part of a military system that is committed to the use of nuclear weapons under some conditions, even to initiate their use, may be the form that conscientious objection to nuclear war takes. Also, at many points in the military establishment individuals, when they see that they may be required to give signals for the use of nuclear weapons, may become conscientious objectors. There is taking place at this time an astonishing amount of rethinking of the moral issues involved in the use of nuclear weapons. We can be sure that there would be strong support by units of the Church for those who become objectors in the situations that I have mentioned.

Prior to the decisions of many individuals to become conscientious objectors to nuclear war, we can expect that many units of the Church will oppose policies of the government that are likely to lead to the use of nuclear weapons. I expect that unless there is a profound change in the attitudes and policies of our government we shall see deeper conflicts between units of the Church and the State than has been known in our country. Of course, these conflicts will also be conflicts within the churches themselves, for members of the churches are part of the public opinion that supports the policies and some of them are responsible for the policies. It is always difficult to sort all of this out. Both theological and ecclesiastical leaders are already beginning to be involved in this conflict with the government or, more accurately, with the administration, for Congress is also divided.

Defense of those who become conscientious objectors will be an important part of the agenda of the churches. This was so in the case of many churches during the second world war and in the Vietnam war and it is a significant mark of development of thought in the churches that this was a radically different attitude than their attitude in the first world war. So far as the basic conflict is concerned judicatories will probably not be the first to move, but public witness within the churches on this subject is already building to a surprising extent, surprising because we had had such a long period of a fatalistic silence about the use of nuclear weapons.

Churches that are giving high priority to peace will find themselves dealing moie realistically with the prevention of nuclear war. Often they have dealt in too general terms about peace without emphasizing current political choices. They will not be able to avoid the moral question concerning the use of nuclear weapons or the political questions concerning the social influences and political forces within both superpowers which unless counteracted may push them into the dreaded catastrophe.

The emphasis upon the negative task of preventing nuclear war does not mean that the churches should not stress the positive goals of peace, the goals of reconciliation between peoples, but these goals will elude us if we do not move away from the nuclear arms race, if nations, beginning with our own, do not abandon their readiness under some circumstances to use nuclear weapons, thus initiating the nuclear stage of a war. Must we not say that working for these ends is the first immediate social responsibility of our churches? In the early stages of this commitment we may find that it does involve conflict with agencies of our government, but we may hope that, since it is our whole society that has such a stake in the prevention of nuclear war, the churches and the government will come to be on the same side.

My final comment is that there is one inherent difference between Church and State. The government of a state has as its immediate responsibility the security and true well-being of the nation for which it is a trustee. It can come to broader and more universally humane interpretations of the sources of that security and also of the content of national well-being. The churches within the nation can do much to bring about these changes. It is significant that the Presbyterian Confession of 1967 after considerable debate said of national security the following:

"God's reconciliation in Jesus Christ is the ground of the peace, justice, and freedom among nations which all powers of government are called to serve and defend. The church, in its own life, is called to practice the forgiveness of enemies and to commend to the nations as practical policies the search for cooperation and peace. This requires the pursuit of fresh and responsible relations across every line of conflict, *even at risk to national security,* to reduce areas of strife and to broaden international understanding.''

The Confession goes on to say about nuclear war:

"Reconciliation among nations becomes peculiarly urgent as countries develop nuclear, chemical and biological weapons, diverting their manpower and resources from constructive uses and risking the annihilation of mankind.'' (9.45)

People for whom national security is the absolute concern usually give disproportionate emphasis to its military defense and in doing so choose policies that are self-defeating and in their own way risk national security. These words of the Confession written fifteen years before the rise of the current anxiety about nuclear weapons are a good example of what the witness of the Church should be to the State.

The Church by its very nature is a universal community. Its faith is in God who has no favorites among the nations. This means that the Church begins with a concern for the people of all nations. Yet its members are citizens of one nation and have special responsibilities for its well-being and for the well-being of their nearer neighbors. A nation may extend its vision so that it includes in its conception of its own interest the chance to live in a peaceful and just world, the point at which the Church begins. When members of the Church become aware of the claims both of their loyalty as citizens and their loyalty as members of the universal community they know that they face problems, even conflicts within themselves. This is as it should be.

Endnotes

1. Especially Paul Blanshard, *American Freedom and Catholic Power,* (Boston: Beacon Press, 1949).
2. Winthrop S. Hudson, *The Great Tradition of the American Churches,* (New York: Harper and Brothers, 1953).
3. For an account of this action see Roy E. Young, "Religious Liberty on Campus," (April 9, 1982).
4. In the case of the application of Prof. Douglas Clyde MacIntosh for citizenship as a selective conscientious objector to war (United States vs. MacIntosh, 1931).
5. Robert N. Bellah, *Beyond Belief,* (New York: Harper and Row, 1970), Chapter 9.
6. The Anti-Saloon league was founded in 1895 and was enormously effective in organizing people in a number of Protestant denominations in support of Prohibition. It brought great political pressure on candidates and on Congress and state legislatures to secure the ratification of the 18th Amendment.
7. Bernard Häring, *The Law of Christ,* vol. III (The Mercer Press, 1967), p. 205ff. Charles Curran, New Perspectives in Moral Theology (Fides Publishers, Inc., 1974) Chapter 5.
8. A notable example of the witness by a church on McCarthyism was a letter from the Presbyterian General Council (USA) to all Presbyterian churches in 1954 about the consequences of the hysteria created by McCarthyism. Since it was published in full in

the *New York Times*, it is a good example of the public's overhearing what is said to the churches.

9. Published in Martin Luther King Jr. *Why We Can't Wait* (New York: Harper and Row, 1963). Also in James M. Gustafson and James L. Taney (editors) *On Being Responsible* (New York: Harper and Row, 1968).

The most comprehensive and authoritative book about Church and State in the United States is Anson Phelps Stokes, *Church and State in the United States* (three volumes), (New York: Harper and Brothers, 1950). This book was issued in 1964 by the same publisher in a revised one volume edition by Stokes and Le Pfeiffer.

THE POLITICS OF THE EIGHTIES

Dorothy Dodge

The 1980s present the American voter with a number of new political patterns. The presidential selection process has been revised significantly, a number of new political actors such as the political action committees and the mass media have come upon the scene. The traditional two-party system has weakened and new political coalitions appear to be forming. Finally, new political alignments over issues from both the left and the right suggest substantial revision of the structure of American society. Faced with such an array of major political revisions, the American voter may view the 1980s as a period of potential turbulence and upheaval equaling that of the 1960s.

The Changing Environment

The Primary and Convention System

Over the fourteen years since the 1968 Democratic Convention nominated Hubert Humphrey, a number of major revisions in presidential selection styles have occurred. In contrast to the traditional so-called "smoke-filled room" system prior to the 1968 convention, in which candidate selection was made by party leadership and nomination at the party national convention, the 1980 style has been revised to a selection process in which the individual candidates themselves became the major actors. Party conventions after 1968 were reduced to virtual rituals. Although the traditional political trappings appeared to be assiduously followed, the previous 150 years of nominating style is gone. Replacing the traditional style is a new system in which individual candidates, playing to opinion polls, the media, and the primary voters seek to become the recognized "front runners." Virtually ignoring both party leadership and party structure, the candidates for the White House now take their cases directly to the voters. In the new expanded primary system candidates pursued committed delegates to assure their nomination. Eliminated was the older practice of courting the party leadership and the party regulars in order to gain their support for party nomination.

What were the rule changes encompassed in the new primary system that so significantly altered the role of parties and party leadership in presidential selection? A major change was the expansion of the number of primaries held throughout the United States, replacing the party caucus and state convention as the selection process for candidates. A second change was in the rules regulating delegate selection for the national nominating conventions. The Democratic Party, in particular, required division of delegates committed to candidates in proportion to the support such candidates had received in the state primaries or local caucuses. Proportional division also was required at the local level and within every congressional district. Proportional division of delegates was intended to assure that participation by all segments of the society would be promoted. The Republican Party did not adopt rules for proportional division of delegates as strict as those found in the Democratic rules. Ninety per cent of Democratic delegates at the presidential convention were under a strict proportional representation requirement. However, new party rules being discussed by the Democratic National Committee suggest a return to a less strict proportional requirement and a practice closer to that followed by the Republican party.

The new expanded and proportional primary selection process tends to work to the advantage of the nationally-known candidate who has built already significant popular support among the voters throughout the country rather than in favor of local or regional favorite son candidates. Favorite son nominations at the conventions were discouraged since there was little likelihood that the convention would shift to a dark horse or compromise candidate. Only those candidates with time for lengthy nomination campaigns, well-developed and effective campaign organizations and staff, and adequate resources to finance extended campaigns were likely to make any kind of showing in the primaries or to gain the desired number of committed delegates at the national conventions to succeed as the party's eventual nominee.

The new primary system of selection forces early announcement of candidacy by those desiring the presidency. In assessing their chances of success in the nomination, candidates may delay too long and be eliminated from consideration. Gerald Ford suffered this fate in the last election. Some decide not to make the race in the face of unknown opponents and the need for early response to issues and events with no chance of changing your mind in the face of altered circumstances. The most able may be eliminated from candidacy out of the fear of being defeated by second-raters or a turn of events out of their control.

Early support also counts heavily in the eventual success of a presidential hopeful. The tide tends to run with the front-runner. Voters don't wish to waste their votes on the loser. The early front-runners often limit the alternatives for voters in later primaries as they eliminate candidates from the field. Celebrities have the edge in becoming the front-runners since their names are recognizable to the voter before the campaign begins. Facing a field of opponents, a celebrity may carry a primary with less than a majority of the vote, but be declared "the winner" in the voter's mind.

Elected office-holders often are discouraged from becoming active candidates since their political roles place time constraints upon their ability to campaign actively over a long period of time. Although they may have a known name and possible celebrity status, they also become criticized for neglect of their elected duties in pursuit of higher office. Thus the experienced and informed may be eliminated before the race for nomination begins.

The new primary system not only forces early announcement, it requires that candidates organize their own campaign structures and staffs at least two years before the nomination race begins. A new breed of candidate is produced under this system. They have been referred to as "middle-aged athletes." Personally the candidate must have physical stamina, a tolerance for travel, an ease in meeting crowds all over the country and in eventual settings, a media presence which is compelling, and an issue to be repeated thousands of times at meetings all over the country. The primary means the end of the dark horse and the last minute draft. The informed, thoughtful, and experienced candidate does not always combine these qualities. Media presence and crowd appeal does not automatically assure knowledge of the issues. Some critics of the new primary system of nomination complain that the United States has not had an able presidential candidate since the smoke-filled room was abandoned.

Availability of campaign resources is critical for the hopeful candidate. A long nation-wide campaign is expensive. Provision for federal funding of campaign expense reduced the necessity for candidate reliance upon party fundraising. But total federal allowance for campaign spending was set at $17.6 million. This sum is not adequate for the necessary campaign expenditures, especially if a candidate is attempting to make himself known. The federal funding is also based upon a matching system. For every $250 contributed by a private individual, equal federal funding is granted. To receive money, a candidate must place considerable effort on fundraising from small contributors located across the country. A result of the new funding system is the financial pinch often occurring after a primary in which the candidate did not make a good showing or a media event in which a candidate was rated as a loser and federal matching stops simultaneously. Early withdrawals from the race are a predicted result unless candidates have vast private funds of their own or can turn the tide of the unfavorable image of a loser. Those with early substantial funding may employ computer-assisted firms for fundraising. Use of national lists of party supporters and members of pressure groups may assist the nation-wide voter appeal and fundraising efforts of a candidate and assure continuance in the race. Again, the system is designed to narrow the field early whether the framers of federal campaign funding legislation intended to do so or not.

The new proportional primary selection system also tends to distort the alternatives open to the voters. Early primaries, generally occurring in the East and North Central areas of the country, narrowed the field of possible candidates by establishing early winners and losers. In effect, the earliest primaries disenfranchised the vast proportion of the voters, since their alternatives were few. In 1980 there were more primaries than ever in the history of the country and a record number of voters participating in the selection process. This should have assured the selection of candidates desired by the voters and enthusiastically supported by large numbers of Americans. Presidential candidate choice was limited very rapidly to Carter and Reagan. Strangely, neither candidate was enthusiastically supported by the voters or by members of their own party. Voters tended to be alienated by the primary selection system and the alternatives being offered to them. Poll data reveals the voters expressed their intent to vote against something or someone rather than support a platform or a candidate. Although the reforms in the smoke-filled room system and the new proportional primary system were intended to open politics to wider participation and deliberation by the populace as a whole, the new system tended to limit choice and to promote alienated voters.

Why does the new primary system seem to fail in the selection of candidates for the presidency? One explanation offered is that the primary system designers assumed that the act of voting was the essence of popular democracy. On the contrary, voting is the final act of choice among alternatives of policy and candidates. Prior to this final choice should come lengthy deliberation over alternatives and the definition of what early choices actually exist. The new expanded primary system forces early choice of candidates and limits the fields of hopefuls. Issues are not a significant part of the process. The old smoke-filled room style with all of its faults and drawbacks required the party leadership to look over all possible candidates, exchange views and issue positions with leadership from all regional and local levels of the party, clash over choices of candidates and platform positions, and eventually reach an accommodation of views or face a party walk-out at the nominating convention. The smoke-filled room style was blamed for most of the defects of the American political system prior to 1968. Among such defects were corruption, bribery, the shutting out of significant segments of the populace, bossism—to name a few. The new primary system was intended to correct these defects by opening the system to popular participation. Strangely, its results appear to be early narrowing of the field, discouragement of candidacy, promotion of celebrities, alienation of the voters, and weakening of the party structure.

The Election Mandate and the Future of the Two-Party System

The size of the Reagan victory raises a number of basic questions concerning the possible impact of the 1980 election upon the future role and relative strength of the two-party system. One question centers on whether or not the Reagan victory should be interpreted as a major realignment of the American political values toward a new conservative ideology. Elections in the past involving major shifts in political party coalition make-up and party platform positions have been accompanied generally by very diverse shifts of voters and high popular enthusiasm for a new platform position. The year 1980, to the contrary, exhibited a falling voter turnout, little impact of ideology upon voting preference, and widespread desertion by liberals from Carter as a candidate. Rather than a mass movement to the Republican ranks, the voter was against Carter but not necessarily for Reagan.

The shift to Reagan centered upon economic issues and concerns. Inflation was seen as the primary problem facing the United States by three-fifths of the voters turning to Reagan. Liberal philosophy and party loyalty paled in significance as the liberals increasingly blamed Carter for their sense of economic dilemma and potential financial hardship. Perceived economic suffering encouraged Democratic party members to defect to Reagan or Anderson and to remain in the Democratic fold only if their pocketbooks were not impacted by galloping inflation. A second factor in the voter shift to Reagan was concern over the U.S. international position and the preoccupation with freeing the hostages in Iran, and the failure of the rescue mission. However the negotiations had begun to show hope for successful resolution prior to the election. International concerns therefore tended to be less compelling than the economic concerns.

The New Conservatism?

Theodore White has concluded that every American election forces the American voter to weigh the past against the future. Although the major realignment of party coalitions has not occurred as yet, Reagan is presented with the opportunity to work for a major realignment of voters.

What might be the basis for a new Republican or Reagan coalition? Reagan's campaign rhetoric presented a picture of the future of the country that was hopeful. "Supply-side" economics suggests that the private sector, with assistance of limited government intervention, can make America once again affluent. Less taxation will produce a balanced budget and end deficit financing. Interest rates will subsequently fall. Housing, automobiles, and all consumer goods will once again become affordable for the average American worker. Military spending will increase. Finally, energy sources will be found in an energy-rich country, and the reliance on the outside and OPEC will cease. Supply-side economics paints a picture of returning to the American dream. Reagan's message is that Americans have a basic right to consume, and his programs will make sacrifice unnecessary. Voters were attracted to Reagan and his platform as an answer to the middle-class malaise and the potential of eventual economic disaster.

While the 1980 voter may have believed only a small part of the Reagan philosophy, they apparently hoped he might be able to do something to get the government "off American backs" and to protect the middle class from inflationary and taxation impoverishment.

Many voters also hoped apparently that he might be able to do something about social issues and the return to the traditional American values. Reestablishment of the stability of the family and the practice of traditional values of private life was viewed by many voters as more compelling issues than the economy. Americans tended to feel that society was crumbling around them. The Reagan campaign made an effort to project an image of social conservatism. Opposition to ERA, protest over legalized abortion, possible assistance for denominational schools, drug control enforcement and crime abatement programs were all raised to suggest the Reagan administration would encourage the return to traditional values and a secure family or private life. In appealing to the malaise expressed over American private values and life styles, Reagan has continued to employ symbols of social conservatism. In every campaign speech and address as President, some reference is made to the private values of hard work, virtue, and self-discipline that have made America great in the past. Although he publicly supports the reestablishment of the "Protestant ethic" value cluster, Reagan does not propose to employ government regulation or intervention as the means to accomplish this end. Rather, by example and symbols accompanied by "supply-side" economics in the private economic sector, the country will once again return to the glory of the past.

A third set of issues forming the Reagan voter support concerned foreign policy. Reagan was seen as a strong leader. Carter was rejected by many for a perceived inability to lead or be decisive. Although lack of decision-making ability was significant in all areas of policy, foreign affairs was seen by the voters as requiring a regime that would be less ambivalent in the use of the international power and prestige of the United States.

Foreign policy strained the Democratic coalition severely. American power and position in the world were of major concern to many voters. The Vietnam War, the Iranian hostage crisis, the rising military dominancy of the Soviet Union, and the growing interpretation throughout the world and at home that the United States had declined as a major world power were pointed to as results of the lack of leadership coming from the Democratic presidential regime. Reagan was able to capitalize upon the theme of the American humiliation in foreign affairs and to build support among significant numbers of voters.

Democratic Party coalition prospects may be less positive than the possible Reagan potential for building a new major political coalition. Prior to the 1980 election two major political trends had been weakening the old Democratic coalition for a a number of years. Economic groups that had traditionally supported the FDR New Deal coalition were defecting to more conservative positions. Labor, protected by collective bargaining, seniority, retirement and fringe benefit programs had moved philosophically toward middle-class values and life styles. A new set of economic issues related to suburbia and consumer protections as well as to the social issues of rising divorce, crime, alcoholism, drug-use rates, as a few examples, had become more significant than the old economic ties to the FDR coalition in the union member's mind. Inflation was seen as a greater threat to the union member than unemployment by the 1980 election.

White ethnic working-class communities had been the backbone of the Democratic Party strength in the United States from FDR to Nixon. These white ethnic neighborhoods formed the "safe" districts for candidates to state and congressional offices and provided the party organizational support for campaigns and fund-raising. Changes had been occurring in these neighborhoods for a long period of time. Population movements to the suburbs eroded traditional democratic support in the core center city urban areas. In addition, the United States population has been an aging population for a period of years. Those over thirty now form the bulk of the voters. Working Americans with family responsibilities, home-owners, and permanent residents of a suburban area tend to express concern and interest in a different set of issues than the young, single center-city dweller. The proportion of senior citizens in the United States population has also been increasing significantly in the last ten to fifteen years. Senior citizens tend to center their concerns politically upon protection and preservation of their accrued retirement, health, and welfare benefits. All of these population trends represented potential groups of voters concerned about inflation and the economy. Fear over the economy and personal security accrues to the benefit of "supply-side" economics and a pro-conservative position rather than toward a strengthening of the old Democratic coalition.

Further threatening Democratic Party coalition strength, the Republican Party had been quietly building a coherent party organizational structure nationwide for a number of years. While the Democratic structure had been crumbling, the Republican Party organization was growing in workers and had become efficient at voter appeals and fundraising. Reagan further strengthened this party structure by campaigning as a Republican Party spokesman. He was careful to appear on the campaign trail with Republican Party candidates for all levels of office and to stress the need for Republican control of Congress, the state houses, and at the local levels if his program was to be successfully implemented.

One major weakness of the Reagan victory may prove to be an advantage for the Democrats. The Reagan win was accomplished with the virtual exclusion of Blacks and Hispanic Americans. A white, middle-class coalition for the Republicans violates the American emphasis upon equality and opportunity for all. It not only may be exploited by the Democrats in attempting to rebuild their coalition, but it would not appear to represent a viable base for a permanent Republican coalition in the future.

Assisting the Democratic Party in its rebuilding attempts is the fact that Black and Hispanic ethnic groups already have tended to become the backbone of the Democratic Party structures in urban America. Blacks have sometimes been described as the "new Irish" in the Democratic party, forming the party regulars and straight-ticket voters. As Blacks moved to the core of the Democratic Party structure, the white ethnics deserted to the suburbs. The old New Deal coalition is ended and major rebuilding will be necessary for future success as a major party.

The above discussion of political trends and party strengths and weaknesses suggests that the 1980 election may prove to be a turning point for the future. At this point major shifts have not occurred, but the potential exists for both of the major parties to exploit the election of 1980 for future strength.

New Political Actors:

The Role of the Media in Campaigns

The news media perform the key function of communicating information to the populace. Given the complexity of modern technology, events receive virtually split-second transmittal to all parts of the world. In the communication process and its selection of what to carry or not carry, the media looms potentially as a major influence in shaping public attitudes, opinions and concerns.

The media picture themselves as playing the role of a consistent loyal opposition. They attempt to uncover hidden events, wrong-doing, corruption, or errors in information in the political arena. In the role of loyal opposition the media confront many dilemmas over their reporting functions. The desire to cover interesting and dynamic events to advance their personal careers and to "sell papers" may conflict with the protection of national values, personal ethics and societal norms.

Media representatives have spent millions of dollars surveying the public preference in regard to the "news." Results of such studies point to the public desire to be "entertained." The public wants visual reports of limited length, detail and content. Excluded are complicated and lengthy debates or discussion of the pros and cons of a given issue before the public. Television news programs attempt to limit "hard news" coverage to forty seconds and to intersperse such coverage with footage on weather, sports or the zoo. Such programming does not belabor the mind of the viewer and promotes the size of the viewing audience. Reporting of disasters, violence or terrorism is considered entertaining or interesting news by the public. The media is frequently criticized for only doing the "bad" news and encouraging violent behavior by its selection of the events to be covered and by its attempt to entertain the public with such coverage of "bad" news.

A second charge leveled at the media is that they "make" the news. It is suggested that events are distorted or events of little import are reported as significant in order to justify the expense of having sent a news crew to cover it. Editorial and reporter bias also receives considerable attention by those critical of the role of mass media as news maker. News is perceived as not being treated "straight" but subject to interpretation based upon the political or social values of the reporters and editors as to their judgments of what the public will consider entertaining or newsworthy. Media polls are accused of making opinion. Published results of winners, front-runners, and losers may set voter opinion. A serious charge is that early reports of voting results in the East on election day often discourage turnout in the West, since voters feel the election is all over. The question of whether polls "mirror" opinion or "make" opinion is unclear, but debate over media polling techniques will continue to rage.

A third charge is that the media create images of the world and American society. The media and the advertising they carry are accused of portraying society from a number of biased perceptions. One is that the "good life" and happiness are pictured as requiring a life style of consumption and affluence based on material possessions and rewards. "Small" is rarely painted as "beautiful." Veneration of materialism is reinforced by media reliance upon advertisers to fund their programs and activities. Over-emphasis upon consumption in the media is blamed for rising public frustrations when what the public expects to achieve materially is in sharp contrast to what they actually are able to acquire. A second perception said to be mirrored by the media is the view that

American society is sick. The family structure and traditional private values of work and virtue are interpreted as disappearing. Replacing them are violence, crime against persons and property, and reliance upon drugs, pills, and other unrealistic remedies for solutions of personal unhappiness or frustrations.

Finally, the media is accused of presenting false images of certain groups in society and distorting their accomplishments and value to society. One example might be the picturing of senior citizens as senile, helpless, and needing constant attention from the young.

When these charges of media bias, distortion, and over-simplification of issues are viewed in relation to the media's political role, the accusations become very significant.

The media may be playing a role beyond its capabilities when it attempts to define issues for the voters and predict what the real alternatives for the electorate may be. Unquestionably the media in the 1980 campaign did create "front-runner" candidates by its coverage of political events and the primaries. In their desire to make news exciting and break a story first, the media attempted to predict eventual winners and losers. Their decision to cover or not to cover a candidate often spelled victory or defeat for that person. Their interpretation of winners and losers often became a self-fulfilling prophecy in the subsequent primary campaign. In an attempt to turn politics into drama, the media was guilty of severely damaging some candidates by focusing on a mistake in a statement, a crying jag, or the loss of poise before a crowd.

Many of the defects of the new primary system for presidential selection tend to be exaggerated by current media roles. Celebrities gain greater coverage than the relatively unknown regional candidate. Early candidate entry in a race may be built by media coverage to discourage late entrants into the race. So-called "losers" in early primaries are described as "out of the race," narrowing the field of presidential hopefuls early to a few media survivors. Drama rather than coverage of complicated issues is the goal. Short and entertaining visual coverage rather than serious discussion of the alternatives of policy is the norm.

Added to concern over the role of the media politically is the accelerating trend toward media ownership concentration. For example, concentration of national and international reporting through United Press International and Associated Press wire services means that decisions on what news will be covered and from what angle are controlled by a very few. These wire services provide news-coverage for most newspapers throughout the country. Television coverage also is concentrated in the hands of a few major networks providing the news for their subsidiaries throughout the country. All of the charges of bias, oversimplification of issues, false imagery, and selection of entertaining events is compounded when only one or two sources set the news for the country.

A question may be raised in the face of split-second communications. Do Americans have too much information or not enough? Do the mass media mirror or make our impressions of American society and world issues and people? Has the decision-making about candidates and issues shifted from the voter to the media? These are serious questions resulting from the 1980 elections. Effective participation in the political process requires a well-informed rather than entertained electorate.

Since media coverage is so significant in building visibility for a candidate and promoting voter support, candidates feel that media coverage also must be purchased for a successful campaign. The cost of television prime time, radio spot announcements and newspaper ads are responsible in no small measure for the rising expenditures required for campaigns. A Senatorial campaign requires several million. A House seat campaign necessitates almost a million at minimum. Presidential campaigns approach one hundred million dollars or more.

Free media coverage of campaigns is crucial to most candidates unable to pay the prohibitive costs of buying time. Again media decisions of what is news and who is a "winner" play a major role in candidate exposure to the public and perhaps eventual success.

The Political Action Committees

The PAC's are not new in American politics but their number and role politically has increased in the contemporary period. The soaring cost of campaigns requires candidates to seek significant funding beyond their own private funds and possible political party support. The PAC's are formed by business, labor, professional and other pressure groups to raise campaign funds in support of candidates supporting their interests in a specific piece of legislation. For example, the used car dealer PAC has raised over a million dollars for the 1982 congressional campaigns. Money is given to the campaign funds of candidates serving in congressional committees directly handling the legislative proposals intended to regulate used car sales and require disclosure of the defects of a used car to the consumer. Those voting against the proposed legislation requiring disclosure of automotive defects to the consumer receive greater campaign funding from the PAC than those unsure of their vote.

The PAC's interest is to pass legislation favorable to its interests and defeat legislation contrary to its desires. The PAC represents a specific group and a specific set of issues or legislative proposals. Political action funds are raised from the members and used to attempt to influence congressional or presidential action on the issues or legislation. Similar activities occur at the state and local levels of government. The minimum goal is to be certain the PAC position receives a full hearing. The maximum goal is to promote the votes necessary to assure the PAC position is adopted.

Elected officials argue that contributions to their campaign funds do not "buy" their votes. However the danger exists that the PAC's with greater funding may exert more influence than those with less funding. Another danger is that positions not organized into a PAC organization may not receive a fair hearing.

Two major limitations to PAC influence exist. One is federal limits on total funding that may be spent yearly by a PAC. The second is that the large number of PAC's tend to counter each other's influence and positions and to prevent one PAC from becoming dominant.

PAC's will continue to operate in some form as long as campaign spending remains so high. Candidates attempting to buy media time and run an effective computer-based campaign are faced with heavy funding requirements. Federal funding and party funding do not meet these needs. The gap between campaign funds and the availability of funding from government and party sources provides an opportunity for the PAC's to form and to pursue a potential for political influence. PAC's will continue to grow in numbers and influence until campaign costs are governmentally funded and administered to control total amounts spent and to assure every candidate the potential for an effective campaign.

The Rise of the New Politics and New Political Alignments

Despite achievement of a high degree of material prosperity and a past history of the ability to reconcile political problems, Americans in the post-Vietnam War period have increasingly expressed doubt, fear, and uncertainty over their future. The promises of the New Deal for the "good life" have proven illusory. Political life and institutions, human behavior and social relationships have not attained the levels promised in the past. The American dream is still to be achieved. Present criticism of the profound disorders found in contemporary American society continue past traditions of self-examination and dissent reflected throughout American history. The current malaise points hopefully to renewed vitality of society rather than to self-satisfied tranquility or a stagnation of American culture.

Contemporary protest tends to be centered in the segments of the populace called the "New Left" and the "Protests of the Sixties" and the more recent "New Right" and "Moral Majority" as a phenomenon of the late seventies and the eighties.

The critics from both the Left and the Right charge that the American dream of the individual pursuit of happiness and the private development of self have gone sour. Contemporary American society is accused of producing loss of individuality, self-identity, and human dignity, resulting in alienation of the public.

Alienation has become a major preoccupation and theme of psychologists, political analysts, and literary novelists. Two general characteristics are associated with alienation. The first is estrangement from society and meaningful personal relationships. Modern urban society is pictured as turning humans into faceless mobs. Dehumanized to a mere punch on a computer card, the human is described as pursuing meaningless and boring economic activities. Living in congested areas, the human faces uncertain standards of living and unreliable employment, retirement, and welfare safeguards. Beset by inequities and prejudices, minorities follow a drab existence. Lost in the crowd, the human has surrendered both individuality and dignity.

A second condition associated with alienation is resentment. Americans perceive the world as not quite measuring up to their expectations. Society has not fulfilled their dreams. The political system has dashed hopes for the future by imposing an unexpected reality. Theodore Gurr in his study of violence in America describes alienation as a phenomenon occurring when the gap between what

Americans anticipated from the future on a rising curve of expectation confronts their frustration over the reality of what they are able to achieve.

The middle class educated American has traditionally been the political and community activist and the "backbone" of the American political system. Significant political alienation and non-participation has occurred as the middle class American confronted the economic limitations imposed by high taxation and inflation. Social and intellectual malaise increased in the face of rising divorce rates, suicides, the breakup of the family structure, suburban crime, alcoholism and drug abuse.

The middle class increasingly express their perception that they have been "ripped-off." They are unwilling to support or remain active politically or socially in community concerns following their traditional pattern of participation since there is little evidence of a payoff for them from their efforts.

American youth expresses disenchantment from a different perspective. Maintaining that humans are of great worth and capable of reason, freedom, and love, they decry present depersonalization. They conclude that contemporary America has turned its citizens into "things." Even the campus has become a computer card center rather than an arena for the development of individual potential. Education has failed to meet its goal of intellectual freedom and fails the human along with the rest of American society.

Minorities point to the hollowness of past promises in the light of the systematic, consistent, and often brutal exclusion of racial and sexual minorities from the full benefits of American life. Despite avowed good intentions and assurances, inequities continue to abound in every area of life, including the social, economic, educational and political systems.

The war in Vietnam sharply raised the issue of what should be the American role in world affairs and the proper use of American power. U.S. responsibility toward the developing world and toward the world's "have-nots" plagues the American sense of human dignity and worth. The data pointing to the threat of nuclear holocaust and the insanity of the East-West armaments race reinforce doubts over the quest for American dominance in international politics. A question besetting citizens is whether, in the name of freedom, U.S. policy operates to the material wealth of a few at the expense of American well-being and of the world's population as whole. The environmental and ecological impact of the arms race and of modern technology as a whole deepens concern. Thinking humans cannot help but wonder whether the human race faces the certain death of the planet in the future as a result of the pursuit of affluence and U.S. power dominance in the world.

The energy crisis of the seventies reinforced the doubts expressed by the alienated. The politics of scarcity is an unfamiliar concept for American society. The promised affluence and freedom for all found in New Deal slogans has been rudely shaken. A serious political question raised by the energy shortage was who would get what, when, where and how? An even sharper dilemma was presented by the realization that some Americans might be excluded from a share in resources in short supply. A picture of life raised by the crises was whether the poor and old would freeze and walk while the affluent could ride in comfort.

These growing alienations, resentments, and fears turned dissent to the political system. Reservations were expressed concerning the ability of American political institutions to achieve full attainment of the American dream. Although doubts have existed historically, such reservations have become a consistent theme in the contemporary period. Political parties have been criticized for providing inadequate channels to allow participation by the mass of the people in the party decision-making processes.

In trying to control decisions affecting their lives and futures, the New Left endorsed participatory democracy as the solution for the political exclusion of segments of the populace. Community organizations were romanticized as the structures to provide direct participation by everyone in the decisions affecting them. Participatory democracy was claimed to be the channel to achieve political responsibility and responsiveness from the system. Participation also was seen as a path to escape isolation and alienation.

Participatory democracy has as its goal that individuals will share in the political and social decisions determining the quality of their lives. It is seen as the structure to assure that society will promote individual independence and freedom. Political action is hailed as the way to individual salvation. Groups expressing their concerns over policies and conditions are encouraged to form a movement composed of "like-minded" citizens. The movement would then serve as the vehicle, to call attention, protest, and "make something happen."

Alienation and the New Left protests resulted in a second major political change. The phenomenon of "one-issue" politics became a dominant political pattern. Small groups of individuals committed to a specific and narrow political position have organized to pursue their goals by use of all political and media channels available to them. Examples of one-issue groups are the pro-abortion and the Right-to-Life movements. Both groups center on one set of issues of concern to them and have taken their programs to all levels of the political and social system throughout the country.

The growth of the phenomenon of one-issue politics makes the traditional political party coalition system difficult to operate. In past presidential campaigns, party platforms were written in vague generalities to create an umbrella under which a wide variety of interest groups could cluster comfortably. An accommodation of interests and concerns needed to be reached if the party was to assure majority support by the voters for the party's presidential candidate. In contrast to the older coalition-building style, one-issue groups search for the party or candidate firmly committed to their position. They insist the candidate promise to implement their specific demands before pledging their voting support. The result is alienation of opposing groups and positions. Abortion, ERA, drug control, and many other issues have proven major stumbling blocks for hopeful candidates. Making a public commitment to support a specific position, while not making it, is a neat maneuver if a candidate can pull it off. Promises to one group often spell defeat as opposing groups defect rapidly to candidates closer to their group interests. PAC's are one form of a one-issue group attempting to buy influence.

A second political revision resulted from the New Left movement. The series of system reforms discussed above were instituted. The expanded primary system was adopted to promote wider popular participation in presidential elections. The proportional system for selection of delegates to the national conventions was designed to protect both the representation of one-issue groups and those segments of the populace perceived to have been shut out of party caucuses. The downgrading of the role of the party leaders and party organization in candidate selection was proclaimed as the way to end corruption and elitism in the political system. The impact of these system changes upon the operation of the 1980 presidential election were discussed above and will not be repeated. However the hoped-for wider participation, open nominations, and candidate responsiveness to voters has not been achieved if the process and behavior of the 1980 elections is an accurate representation of the new system.

The New Right movements also follow the "one-issue" patterns of political behavior. The New Left or Right do not necessarily follow different political styles of behavior or group dynamics. Rather the interpretation of the issues and their conclusions about reasons for the failures of the American political system are sharply diverse.

The New Right tends to see America's salvation as embodied in a return to the Protestant ethic and the values and priorities of the past. Return to the private virtues of honesty and thrift are claimed as the means to end rising crime waves. Return to the nuclear family structures will correct soaring divorce rates, juvenile delinquency, suicide, alcoholism and drug abuse. Return to hard work and thrift and the private enterprise system will resolve questions of economic well-being and rewards. Return to traditional institutional styles and curriculum will restore correct thinking by the young and solve the problem that "Johnny can't read." Return to religion and God will reestablish the American way of life and American virtue. The New Right is actively engaged in surveying contemporary America and correcting deviance from these past virtues at all levels of society. Reagan's use of the symbols of social conservatism and his references to past glory and honor make him particularly appealing as a candidate to the right. However there is also disappointment over his failure to deliver on abortion, a Supreme Court Justice and federal regulations on school curriculum. His ability to use the New Right as a base for a future conservative coalition is unclear at the moment.

Conclusion

This brief analysis of the politics of the 1980s and the changing political environment points to a period of political upheaval and substantive debate over American values and political ethics. The defects of the "smoke-filled room" style of presidential selection has not been solved by the new primary system. Narrow choices for voters have been the result. The extended campaigns country-wide have increased the role of mass media in the political process. Expensive nationwide campaigns have offered the PAC's opportunity for more influence. Dependence upon computer-based technology to run effective campaigns increase costs further. Narrow political choices, the favoring of celebrity candidates, political discussion intended to entertain rather than inform, and increasing influence by the wealthy with the prospect of buying votes—all of these serve to deepen American alienation with the political system and American society. There are no easy solutions to these system and value crises. Many proposals for revision are suggested and available. Clearly the 80's are a period requiring serious discussion and debate by informed citizens concerned about preservation of the American political system and the values of human dignity and worth. Rather than proposing one solution or another, this discussion would suggest that alienation and the desire to only be entertained are luxuries the system can ill afford. The thinking and concerned citizen has the responsibility to analyse our political problems and to search for better answers than we have achieved to this moment.

REFORMED FAITH AND WORLD POLITICS

Alan Geyer

Some Christians, including many Presbyterians, understand very well that politics is not an optional interest or avoidable evil. They know that God has so ordered Creation that there must be a struggle for power and purpose over the conditions of our life-with-and-for-one-another. Politics is an inescapable covenant for ordering the common good. Politics is the way a nation makes decisions for itself, as well as decisions with and for other nations. Politics is a projection of our God-given human nature into the arena of conflict and community. It is a prerequisite of human fulfillment. It magnifies all our capacities for either good or evil. It's full of winning and losing and coming together, of courage and treachery. Politics is the medium for determining whether we shall have justice and peace and human survival.

Yet some Christians (including, perhaps, a few stray Presbyterians) do not understand these things very well. Even activists for peace may not grasp them adequately. In fact, peace activists sometimes seem to have special incapacities for comprehending what politics is all about. The quest for world order by Christians and others has all too often foundered on the rocks of political ignorance or political illusion or political bigotry. A theology of peace must be grounded in a well-wrought theology of politics. Ultimately, both a theology of peace and a theology of politics must spring from the most basic affirmations of Christian faith. What we believe about Creation, Incarnation, Judgment, and Redemption should enlighten the struggle for justice and peace at every point.

When the members of any Christian tribe such as the Presbyterians seek to understand the relationship of their faith to world politics, they should distinguish carefully among three dimensions of their heritage.

First, there are the *affirmations* which they more or less share with all Christians.

Second, there are the distinctive *accents* which their own particular communion has given to the Christian language of politics.

Third, there are the *affinities* which have developed historically between their religious styles and their culturally shaped patterns of social thought and conduct.

Preeminent among *affirmations* shared by all Christians are those most clearly rooted in the Bible, especially those nurtured by the integrity of prophetic theology in both testaments. Only a brief sample of familiar Biblical themes will serve as a reminder of the richness of the prophetic heritage in world politics:

1. The power and majesty of God as Creator and Sovereign over all nations and peoples.
2. The promise that nations will cease their wars and that the weapons of war will be converted into tools of food production.
3. The God-given choice of life or death for all future generations.
4. The exaltation of the poor and the oppressed, together with the humbling of the rich and powerful.
5. Security as an indivisible part of God's covenant of righteousness and peace, requiring a judgment upon all false promises of peace and security.
6. The overcoming of national self-righteousness and the honoring of aliens.
7. Love and forgiveness of enemies and the apprehension that God often works his will through enemies.
8. The follies of violence.
9. The universality of the Gospel of Jesus Christ.
10. Jesus Christ as Prince of Peace who celebrates the blessedness of peacemakers and breaks down the dividing walls of hostility.
11. The message and ministry of reconciliation, making Christians ambassadors for Christ.
12. The infinitely compassionate vision of a New Earth in which all nations come together peaceably before the Lord God and in which hunger and hurt and sorrow are no more.

Calvinist Accents

Whatever Reformed Christians may be conscious of sharing with members of other tribes, there is a pattern of distinctive *accents* in their ways of religious speaking and doing which have significant political and international implications. At the risk of indulging in impressionistic generalizations by one who has only been a sometime participant in this tradition, let me specify six of these accents.

1. There is a distinctly Calvinist expression of *universalism*. The emphasis given to the glory of God, in and beyond the whole Creation—to the absolute sovereignty of God above all nations and peoples—to the grace and goodness of God without which all human striving is nothingness—and to the fallenness and lostness of all human creatures: these accents suggest that Presbyterians are rooted in a vigorously transnational heritage.

John Calvin was, after all, the most internationalist of all the Reformers. Geneva remains a peculiarly international center, full of intergovernmental, peace, humanitarian, and ecumenical organizations as well as political refugees—although the citizenry of Geneva has never adjusted very happily to all these foreigners and alien enterprises in their small community. When Presbyterian Eugene Carson Blake became General Secretary of the World Council of

Churches, with headquarters in Geneva and with a personal passion for international peace and justice, he conspicuously incarnated the universalist zeal and energy of his fathers and mothers in the Calvinist faith. It is more than coincidental that studies of voting behavior in the United States, both at the polls and in Congress, consistently disclose a stronger internationalist sentiment among Presbyterians than among most other mainline denominations.

2. There is a stern moral emphasis on *obedience to the law of God.* It is preeminently in the Holy Scriptures that God's law is to be found. The identification of God's will with law was doubtless reinforced by Calvin's own legal studies which preceded his theological treatises. Churches in the Reformed tradition have tended to ascribe more authority to the Old Testament as a source of law than have other churches. Puritanism has been described as "English Hebraism." There is plenty of "Scotch Hebraism" in American Presbyterianism.

The place of law and order in the Reformed heritage is well-defined ecclesiastically and, in Calvin's Geneva and elsewhere, has been strenuously articulated politically. Presbyterians are firmly committed to the solemn injunction that both their beliefs and practices should be maintained "decently and in good order." They are covenantal, confessional, and catechetical (except, of course, when they are licentious, rebellious, and heretical). It is hardly surprising that they should have named as Stated Clerk a layman and lawyer, William P. Thompson, or that Thompson himself should have emerged as the authority on parliamentary law and procedure in the governance of the World Council of Churches. Presbyterian clergy, lawyers, and diplomats, in disproportion to their numbers, have rallied to a "world rule of law" as the basic approach to peacemaking.

3. There is a preaching of *salvation through both faith and works.* To be sure, Calvin shared Luther's insistence on justification by faith and the worthlessness of all human works apart from the indwelling of the Holy Spirit which leads to repentance and true faith in Jesus Christ. Yet Calvin had a double-edged doctrine of works which set the Reformed churches on a course somewhere between Lutheran and Roman Catholic traditions. In his *Institutes,* Calvin declared: "We are justified not without, and yet not by works."

It is this imperative to good works, if not as the way to salvation then as the sign of salvation, that has done most to energize Presbyterians into a zeal for moral character and a life-style of public activism. Presbyterian leaders have almost always had a sensitive nose for moral evils. They have just as regularly insisted that we must *do something* about those evils. Any broad-based American movement for peace, human rights, economic justice, or world food policy is bound to have conspicuous Presbyterian leadership. Presbyterians are readier to serve as God's anointed instruments in redeeming the whole world than are the lower-energy types in most other denominations.

4. There is a lingering doctrinal heritage of *predestination.* In this as in many other matters of belief, modern Presbyterians tend to be sundered from their roots and various in their opinions. But the conviction that some are chosen while others are not, some are elected and others rejected, some are saved but

others lost, has hardly disappeared from American religious and political behavior.

Presbyterians have often moved in ecumenical circles, both nationally and internationally, with a mixture of theological and social confidence which mere Methodists and Baptists have envied. That confidence stems in part from the assurance of being fortified by sound doctrine and in part from the high socioeconomic status of median Presbyterians. Presbyterians also tend to take their own history more seriously than do most other tribes. In short, whatever the continuing theological adherence to predestination, the sense of destiny remains well-developed.

The transfer of such sentiments of destiny from theology to politics—from confessional identity to national identity—is a topic which will be further discussed as a problem of affinities.

5. In no Protestant tradition is the dynamic sanction of *calling* more fruitful than in the Presbyterian communion. The idea of election is not simply a matter of identifying a religious elite: it supposes that God elects particular individuals to do particular works, whether in church or society.

This vocational sense of mission has vital consequences for both clergy and laity, not least with regard to Christian missions and foreign policy. Two Presbyterian preacher's sons, Woodrow Wilson and John Foster Dulles, had a monumental sense of diplomatic calling which contributed both to dramatic achievements and to fateful political failures. Early in the Cold War, two Presbyterian ambassadors held the most sensitive diplomatic posts: John Leighton Stuart (a missionary and the last pre-Mao ambassador to China) and George Kennan (author of "containment" policy and ambassador to the Soviet Union). Still another Presbyterian, Dean Rusk, followed the precedent of Dulles and graduated from the Rockefeller Foundation to become Secretary of State during the Vietnam War years of the Kennedy and Johnson administrations. A very large share of the diplomatic history of the twentieth century is thus focused in the careers of these five Presbyterians, all of whom brought extraordinary personalities and the most earnest commitments to their careers.

This doctrine of calling was reinforced recently in the very title as well as the contents of the formidable Presbyterian document, *Peacemaking: The Believer's Calling.* It may be doubted whether any denomination, apart from the historic peace churches, has done more to generate vocational commitments to foreign policy.

6. There is a Calvinist theology of politics in which *civic duty* represents a profound integration of religion and politics. If modern American Presbyterians tend to be careful custodians of the constitutional boundaries between church and state, they can find little warrant in their heritage for separating their religious beliefs from their political behavior. Other communions tend toward a more schizophrenic faith in these matters.

Twentieth century Lutherans, even a young Dietrich Bonhoeffer, have remained heavily burdened by Luther's sharp dualism between the two realms of faith and politics. As Bonhoeffer's brother-in-law, Gerhard Leibholz, has reported, it took the ascendant evils of a barbarous Nazism to shake Bonhoeffer out of that compartmentalized theology:

> In the earlier stages of his career, Bonhoeffer accepted the traditional Lutheran view that there was a sharp distinction between politics and religion. Gradually, however, he revised his opinion, not because . . . he refused to give Caesar his due, but because he came to recognize that the political authority in Germany had become entirely corrupt and immoral and that a false faith is capable of terrible and monstrous things.[1]

Yet Bonhoeffer's theological reorientation was a minority view in the German churches of the 1930s. It was precisely Adolf Hitler's appeal to traditional Lutheran dualism that attempted to silence dissent from some church leaders. Martin Niemoeller has told of his summons by Hitler when Der Fuehrer was becoming increasingly aggravated by any signs of Christian protest against Nazi terror. Hitler shrieked: "You leave politics to me! You mind your own business! You just prepare people for heaven!"

Latter day Calvinists do not have to return to theocratic Geneva to admit that they have less theological excuse than do Lutherans and many other Christians for neglecting to make politics their religious business. They should not require the reappearance of barbarism or a holocaust or a world war to remind them of the sovereignty of God and the integrity of faith in all areas of life. Yet the fact is that Presbyterians share in an American Protestant sub-culture in which the mixing of religion and politics is still viewed with suspicion.

To assert that religion and politics cannot be legitimately separated, either as a matter of faith or a fact of history, is not to dull the perception that some peculiar mixtures of religion and politics are extremely problematical at best—especially when they are projected into politics among nations.

Our attention to some of the Calvinist *accents* in the American religio-political heritage must now be supplemented by a review of some of the cultural *affinities* which have developed alongside them.

Cultural Affinities

1. One of these affinities with the most perverse tendencies is *messianism:* a sense of predestination with regard to one's own nation or political program. The metaphysical passion with which the American nation was born has various roots, all of which were well-watered by a Calvinist sense of destiny. Here, at last, was the New Israel, God's Chosen People, those who for centuries would regard themselves as the "darlings of Divine Providence" (the term is Reinhold Niebuhr's).

Perry Miller's study of Calvinist influences upon "the New England Mind" led him to this characterization:

> The Puritan state was seen by Puritans as the incarnation of their collective will; it was driven by an energy they had acquired in their conversion, it was the embodied image of their power, of their resolution, of their idea. . . . New England political theory made the state almost a kind of second incar-

nation, a Messiah fathered by God and born of the people. Mortal men, being visited by God in the Covenant of Grace, conceive a will to moral obedience; when they covenant among themselves, when they combine their several regenerate wills into one all-inclusive will, the state becomes another savior, the child of God and man, leading men to righteousness and preparing them for the final reckoning.[2]

If "the New England Mind" is hardly identical with Presbyterian heritage, Presbyterians have partaken deeply of a Puritan ethos which has profoundly shaped these covenantal images of American nationhood.

Sure the very passionate secular sense of being a "superpower" and yearning to be Number One in everything powerful and good owes much to these metaphysical conceits about American origins and destiny. The problem, of course, is that so many other nations are decked out with similar metaphysical conceits. The heritage of Holy Mother Russia has hardly been annulled by the Soviets' insistence that they must remain the center of world history. The Chinese identity as the Middle Kingdom has not dissipated under Maoist or Dengist ideology: China remains the homeland of the New Man and the True Revolution. French nationalism shows no signs of losing its mysticism. Religious fundamentalism remains a political fundament for South African apartheid-nationalism. Reverence for the Emperor is renewing its strength in Japan. Khomeini's Iran is awash in theocratic arrogance.

Both ancient and modern Israel have been caught up in an almost unbearable tension between universalism and messianism. It has been the tragedy of modern Israel that its messianism has driven it increasingly to militarism and paranoia toward the outside world, at the expense of its universalist and peacemaking vision. And so it has been with the United States of America through the 1970s and early 1980s: we are being driven to the most regressive chauvinism and a simultaneous frenzy of hostility toward much of the outside world. This is the newest form of an old cultural syndrome: isolationism. It is an inversion of the old isolationism which sought to be disentangled from the world. Now Americans are being urged to take on the whole world. We are being harangued by the New Right not only to stick it to the Russians and the Poles—but to the Libyans, the Nicaraguans, the Cubans, the United Nations, the entire Third World, and even to scold Japan and our European allies for not seeing the world through American eyes. And how dare our neighbors, Canada and Mexico, criticize our righteous foreign policies!

Christian universalism, as all good Calvinists know, is not founded upon some abstract global idealism: it is driven by a sense of solidarity with the whole of humanity in its creatureliness and lostness and alienation. The reconciliation which the world requires has an inescapable prerequisite: repentance for the evil and the suffering which result from violating God's laws. It means turning away—or being turned away—from what Herbert Butterfield called the "gravitational pull in human nature" which drags down our capacities for imagination, sympathy, and self-analysis, all precious traits demanded by peacemaking. Butterfield's classic study, *Christianity and History* (1949), insisted that Christianity address itself precisely to that crust of self-righteousness which, by the nature of its teaching, it has to dissolve before it can do anything else with a man. . . . And though conflict might still be inevitable in history even if this particular evil did not exist, there can be no doubt that its presence multiplies the deadlocks and gravely deepens all the tragedies of all the centuries. At its worst it brings us to that mythical messianism—that messianic hoax—of the twentieth century which comes perilously close to the thesis: 'Just one more little war against the last remaining enemies of righteousness, and then the world will be cleansed, and we can start building paradise.'[3]

There is a more personal dimension to the excesses of messianism which is painfully familiar to veteran participants in and observers of the peace movement. It is the problem of egomania: the absolute projection of one's selfhood into the cause of peace so that other selves and opinions are trivialized or abused. In some extreme cases, a pathological person becomes totally absorbed in promoting a scheme for peace or national security as an escape from coping with more intimate personal problems—and imposes his scheme upon others with extravagant claims of urgency and an aggressive intolerance for alternative proposals. More common is simply a personal arrogance which thrives on global conflict, apocalyptic visions, and inspired audiences. This pattern is so common that the peace forces of America are typically afflicted with wasteful proliferation and even fratricidal competition.

It is when this personal messianism gets compounded by metaphysical nationalism that peacemaking becomes doubly difficult. Competence and wisdom may yield to fantasy and demagoguery. C. B. Marshall, veteran policy-maker and political scientist, has written:

The sweep of its problems gives foreign policy a special attraction for those . . . born with a passion to reform the world. Foreign policy appeals to those inspired by identification with large and high-sounding public causes. Its complexities and subtleties are rich with opportunities for generalizers and obfuscators.[4]

These warnings suggest that individuals with a fervent sense of calling and election to peacemaking must constantly be on their guard against confusing their own ego-gratification with the salvation of the world (Those of you who think of yourselves as messiahs are especially annoying to those of us whom God has really chosen to be His special agents.)

Secretary of State Dulles, as portrayed in Townsend Hoopes's massive biography *The Devil and John Foster Dulles,* was a man who did not always succeed in separating his own messianism from the Kingdom of God. Reinhold Niebuhr said of Dulles that his "moral universe makes everything quite clear, too clear" and led to a dogmatic self-righteousness. His rigid absolutes, especially set forth in his preachments against "atheistic communism," combined with an extraordinary self-certitude. Aides at the State Department said Dulles acted as if he had "a pipeline to God." Colleagueship was difficult: "to cross him was to cross the deity."

2. Another problematical affinity with Calvinism is *legalism:* a preoccupation with the making and enforcing of laws as the solution to human conflicts, to the neglect of political, cultural, moral, and other factors.

Given the Calvinist emphasis upon law as the foundation of righteousness, it is hardly to be wondered at that the Protestant ethos of the USA should resound again and again to the moralistic harangue: "There ought to be a law against that!" Law can indeed be a vital instrument of social change and of moral suasion: the question is a matter of proportion and prudence. Americans are a people who lobby, legislate, and litigate more intensively than any other people the world has yet seen. There are more lawyers per square inch in the US than in any other country. Lawyers often seem to have a professional monopoly upon the legislative process and bureaucratic decision-making.

There are very few lawyers, comparatively, in many other countries. Japan has attained a high level of economic and cultural development with a very small company of mostly modestly-paid lawyers. In some societies, especially in Asia and Africa, the law is a last resort, not a first resort. Latin American governments for many generations have made and remade constitutions in the image of Anglo-Saxon constitutionalism—but documents which have typically borne little correlation with social and economic realities.

Much of the diplomatic history of the United States concerns the export, if not the imposition, of legalism. In the first three decades of this century, the US negotiated, with fervent religious support, 97 bilateral and multilateral treaties of arbitration on the presumption that peace was primarily a legal and judicial problem—yet neither world war nor totalitarianism was prevented thereby. War was "outlawed" by the Kellogg-Briand Pact of 1928—but that treaty lacked any practical means of implementation and the US remained outside the collective security obligations of the League of Nations. Some political leaders who publicly supported the treaty privately viewed it cynically as a sop to the peace movement. While the Federal Council of Churches and *The Christian Century* were primary promoters of the treaty, a diplomatic historian has recounted that it "exercised a harmful rather than a helpful influence on the cause of world peace. The outlawry of war served to satisfy the conscience of the American people without requiring of them any positive action, and also created the illusion of safety which seemed to obviate the need for any more direct participation in world affairs."[5]

If American tendencies toward legalism sometimes derive from the illusions of idealists, there is a more manipulative approach to international law in the service of superpower interests which marked the tenure of two Presbyterian secretaries of state, John Foster Dulles in the 1950s and Dean Rusk in the 1960s. Dulles was the architect of such insubstantial regional instruments of anti-communism as CENTO (the Central Treaty Organization in the Middle East) and SEATO (the Southeast Asia Treaty Organization), both now defunct because they lacked solid regional participation.

On February 18, 1966, Secretary Rusk testified before the Senate Foreign Relations Committee that US intervention in Vietnam was legitimate under the

SEATO Treaty. He was remarkably candid in informing the Senators that the Treaty's language permitted the US to act unilaterally but with a sort of multilateral license:

> It is this fundamental SEATO obligation that has from the outset guided our actions in South Viet Nam. . . . The finding that an armed attack has occurred does not have to be made by a collective determination. . . . Nor does the treaty require a collective decision on actions to be taken to meet the common threat. If the United States determines that an armed attack has occurred . . . then it is obliged to act . . . without regard to the views of any other treaty member.

The case for peacemaking through a world rule of law was hardly bolstered by this testimony. For an American official to cite this legal document when even treaty allies refused to support US policy may have helped his case before Congress but surely did not strengthen the US case with other governments. This is a kind of legalistic legerdemain which may result more in deceiving the American public than in persuading non-Americans. The SEATO Treaty was thus exposed as a very feeble and mischievous instrument of international law and would die soon thereafter.

Such cases tend to reinforce the suspicion throughout the Third World that much of what purports to be international law is a facade for the rich and powerful to maintain the status quo and to resist vital social change. That suspicion has been further reinforced by more recent US behavior in the United Nations in such matters as human rights and the Law of the Sea. United States representatives have been preoccupied with Anglo-Saxon concepts of political and civil liberties, while Third World and socialist representatives have emphasized social and economic rights, especially for the poor. During the Reagan administration, this contrast has been drawn even more sharply, with US resistance to any legal codification of such rights as health, nutrition, employment, and shelter. Yet there has been stubborn pressure on behalf of the rights of American corporations to loosen health and safety regulations on their exports and to exploit the mineral resources of the seabed without recognizing those resources as a common heritage—thus frustrating the commitment of most of the world's nations to the functional development of a new global order of shared sovereignty.

The wider the gap between law and social justice, the more must Christians press for the transformation of law itself. To keep invoking obedience to inadequate laws without changing them is to risk the ultimate overthrow of the rule of law altogether. American Christians should continue to be advocates for world law, human rights, and at least minimal world government in some form—but only on foundations of social justice.

3. There is an historic affinity between Calvinism and *capitalism*. That is the principal theme of Max Weber's 1905 study, *The Protestant Ethic and the Spirit of Capitalism*. In a startling reversal of Marx's economic determinism which reduced religion to an epiphenomenon, Weber portrayed Calvinism as the dynamic force which generated the psychological preconditions of capitalist de-

velopment. Weber fixed primarily on the doctrine of "calling" as the energizing force behind the worldly asceticism, rationalism, individualism, spirit of enterprise and profit-seeking as signs of God's election. Thus did asceticism lead, ironically, to acquisitiveness and materialism. Weber noted that business leaders, owners of capital, and skilled workers were overwhelmingly Protestant.

R. H. Tawney's *Religion and the Rise of Capitalism* (1926), while differing in detail from Weber's account, saw the ascendant English bourgeoisie of the 1600s as being under the spell, the religio-economic inspiration, of the Puritan Revolution:

> There is a magic mirror in which each order and organ of society, as the consciousness of its character and destiny dawns upon it, looks for a moment, before the dust of conflict or the glamour of success obscures its vision. . . . For the middle classes of the early seventeenth century, rising but not yet triumphant, that enchanted mirror was Puritanism.[6]

Weber and Tawney thus offered provocative theories of history concerning which eminent scholars can be most argumentative.

Modern Presbyterians, with a middle-to-upper class profile and high median incomes, are not unanimously happy to be called "the Republican Party at prayer." Their prophetic sensitivities may be measured, in part, by the question as to how uncritically they support the dogma that capitalist economics is a blessing to the poor. Secretary Dulles evangelized for free enterprise as the answer to Third World poverty (and Marxist-Leninist revolution) in the 1950s, a mission now revived by the Reagan administration. But Third World Christians (and their governments) have increasingly insisted that private enterprise cannot and will not provide the capital and employment needed for the infrastructure of economic development and basic human needs. Third Worlders, whose economies for generations have been severely damaged by First World booms and busts, are also pressing hard for a New International Economic Order in which the terms of trade, aid and money are not dictated by First World corporations, banks, insurers, and shippers. And Third Worlders vigorously protest against the US government's current tendency to recast North-South economic issues into anti-Soviet East-West issues and to portray all indigenous liberation movements as tools of the Kremlin and Castro.

If American Christians fail to perceive the elements of justice in such Third World perspectives, the Weber-Tawney theses will have been vindicated more resoundingly and more harshly than those renowned scholars could have anticipated. Whether Americans turn to a more enlightened form of capitalism with a long-term view of its own stake in lifting the living standards of the poor, or to some alternative economic philosophy, they are being pressed by much of the world to match their commitment to political democracy with a new commitment to economic democracy, both domestically and internationally. On the other side, however, they are being propagandized by the new campaigns of some American corporations and corporate think tanks to cloak the grossest of interests in new theologies and to discredit the churches' social action programs.

4. There is a likely affinity between Calvinism and *scientism*. By "scientism" we mean a profound faith in the power of science and technology to solve basic social problems. If twentieth century America has experienced the most advanced brands of scientism, its origins have been traced to the Puritan ethos of seventeenth century England.

Robert Merton's 1936 essay on "Puritanism, Pietism, and Science" suggested that religious faith was not so much an obstacle to the emergence of modern science as the very stimulus to it. It was the Calvinist creed of an orderly nature under the laws of a Sovereign God which imparted to Puritanism its potentials for rationalism, utilitarianism, and empiricism—the prerequisites of modern science and technology.

While the Puritan ethos thus gave impetus to the inventions and industrialization of England, it was transported to a New World whose material resources and opportunities would far exceed those of the imperial islands. Calvinism would energize the most ambitious schemes of education as a virtual path to salvation: an article of faith conspicuously espoused by Presbyterians. Thus would American messianism and materialism, conspicuous religiosity and capitalist prosperity, develop side-by-side in a society dominated by technocratic utopianism. In no other society has there been such a powerful drive to dominate and exploit nature for the sake of economic progress—and to see such progress as providential evidence of God's favoritism.

Such a heritage helps to explain why Americans in the 1970s were so shocked to discover the limits of their technical prowess. Energy suddenly became a finite and costly commodity. Non-renewable resources were threatened with exhaustion. Ecocatastrophies multiplied and loomed ahead as much greater disasters waiting to happen. The Green Revolution in Third World agriculture, promoted largely by American foundations, increased productivity but produced vast social dislocations. Economic growth in the US itself slowed severely. Real income leveled off—and even declined for millions of families. The technologies of other societies caught up with, and even surpassed, many American technologies. Foreign trade deficits appeared, and mounted, for the first time in generations. Inflation and recession, heretofore regarded as mutually exclusive, became constant companions. As new marvels of military technology developed, the Soviet Union somehow kept pace and national security diminished: as the superpowers' destructive capacities multiplied, their political influence diminished. In both countries there was a bitter revelation: military scientism was devastating civilian economies.

In short, the dynamisn of a Utopia-bound technocracy seemed to run out of gas. Theologians began to rethink the whole religion-and-nature relationship. The United Nations sponsored a series of global consciousness-raising conferences on the environment, population, food, habitat, disarmament, development, and women in which US policies were constantly on the defensive. Public interest groups won major legislative and judicial victories for environmental protection, public health and safety, and energy alternatives. Technology assessment became a major function of government at all levels. Third World demands for a greater share of industrial know-how and equipment were qualified by a new commitment to appropriate technologies for the transition from abject poverty to a basic human needs strategy of development: there were growing doubts as to whether American know-how really knew how. There was a mounting concern that scientists and engineers not become the tools of military technology to the neglect of civilian needs. All these trends found expression in two landmark international events in the summer of 1979: the World Council of Churches Conference on "Faith, Science, and the Future" at M.I.T. and the United Nations Conference on Science and Technology for Development (UNCSTD) in Vienna.

The challenge to American Protestant theologies in these trends was not to repeal technology but to turn away from the idolatry of scientism. It was to come to a more modest, humane, and ambiguous assessment of what technical change could do to improve the predicament of Planet Earth and our own society. It was to invite a new quest for harmony between humanity and nature as a religious imperative for the survival of our species.

Messianism, legalism, capitalism, scientism: these are several of the problematical cultural affinities for American churches in the Reformed tradition. All these affinities tend to shape religious postures toward politics. All have profound implications for foreign policy. The capacity to transcend and transform such isms is essential to peacemaking.

The New Right in American religion is essentially an uncritical and regressive rallying around just such isms, now that they are under attack. It is a wallowing in messianism, especially against such ideological enemies as the "godless Soviets." It is an obsession with legalistic moralisms on "social issues" and a campaign for new constitutional amendments as the solution to such divisive controversies as abortion, busing for school integration, and school prayers. It is heavily financed by, and aggressively apologetic for, corporate interests. It revels in the technologies of computers and electronics, even while it beats the drum for every new product of military technology. In short, the New Right is bound by the severest chains of cultural captivity, even while it appeals to religious absolutes. It is a campaign to reclaim the American dream. It is an invocation of nostalgia. It is a reaction to racial and religious pluralism. It represents the manipulation of all the traumas and frustrations which proud Americans have endured in the past decade, especially the shocks of lost power and economic decline. As such, the New Right is more the symptom of cultural distress than the cause of it. Church leaders in the mainline denominations are too easily tempted to scapegoat the New Right without perceiving these deeper stresses of history and culture upon which it feeds.

By contrast, liberation theology is the prophetic cry of the poor, the powerless, and the oppressed, in both the Third World and the US, against all these cultural affinities which mainline Christians have tended to assimilate into their faith. It is a rejection of imperial messianism and militarism, although it proclaims a messianic vision of its own in Christ as Liberator and it may proceed to justify violence in the name of revolutionary justice. Liberation theology tends

REFORMED FAITH AND WORLD POLITICS

toward a repudiation of capitalism and multinational corporations, if not necessarily an embrace of Marxism or other forms of socialism. And it is marked by radical criticism of Western scientism and technocracy.

Theological truth is not exclusively to be located at the exact midpoint between the New Right and the New Left, between neo-fundamentalists and liberationists, or with the leadership of the mainline denominations. Such faith orientations are all partial and parochial expressions of Christianity which are deficient in that radical universalism found at the heart of prophetic theology. The Oxford historian and philosopher, R. G. Collingwood, declared four decades ago that Christian faith cannot sanction any chosen people or privileged race: "The Christian cannot be content with Roman history or Jewish history or any other partial and particularistic history: he demands a history of the world, a universal history whose theme shall be the general development of God's purposes for human life."[7]

The Cold War

There has never been a more formidable challenge to American Christians to transcend their own partial and particularistic history than the long twilight struggle of the Cold War with the Soviet Union. That struggle has been intensified by precisely those affinities between Protestant heritage and American culture which we have been reviewing.

The collision between American and Soviet brands of messianism was described a quarter of a century ago by Butterfield:

> The greatest menace to our civilization today is the conflict between giant organized systems of self-righteousness—each system only too delighted to find that the other is wicked—each only too glad that the sins give it the pretext for still deeper hatred and animosity. The effect of the whole situation is barbarizing, since both sides take the wickedness of the other as the pretext for insults, atrocities, and loathing; and each side feels that its own severities are not vicious at all, but simply punitive acts and laudable measures of judgment.[8]

If it had seemed for a few years that détente had at least cooled the rhetoric of this titanic struggle, the late 1970s and early 1980s have experienced a regressive chauvinism and "rearmament" on the American side and unrelenting propaganda and military buildups on the Soviet side. If legalism and capitalist ideology, with strong religious sanctions, have been polarizing elements in this conflict, Americans and Soviets have increasingly shared a scientistic and technocratic set of priorities in both domestic and foreign policy.

In some respects American churches are ill-equipped for the work of peacemaking with the Soviet Union. They have never made US-Soviet relations a missional priority comparable to the attention, reflecting missionary investments, they have devoted to China and some Third World countries. Protestant dialogues with the Russian Orthodox establishment have been difficult at best. The "Choose Life" consultations in Geneva in 1979 and 1980, in which

REFORMED FAITH AND POLITICS

denominational leaders from the US and USSR for the first time framed common theological statements, may have marked a vital turning point in the orientation of those leaders but remain to be substantially implemented programmatically. A Presbyterian church historian and specialist in Russian studies, Bruce Rigdon of McCormick Seminary, has played a particularly resourceful role in this process, as has William P. Thompson who gave a major paper at the 1980 consultation. The theological language of the 1979 "Choose Life" statement, which astonishingly was published in the Soviet newspaper *Izvestia*, was largely the product of two men: Dr. Arie Brouwer, General Secretary of the Reformed Church in America, and Metropolitan Juvenaly of Krutizy and Kolomna, then chairman of the External Church Relations Department of the Moscow Partriarchate. A Presbyterian, Dr. Claire Randall, has given leadership in these dialogues through her office as General Secretary of the National Council of Churches.

What really matters in such bilateral events is not simply ecumenical rhetoric or personal friendship: it is the prospect that church constituencies may be led to overcome some of the hostile stereotypes which obstruct the progress of diplomacy. The new peacemaking programs launched by the United Presbyterian Church and the Presbyterian Church in the US in 1980 have featured a major effort to do just that.

When American Christians say that Soviet government is repressive and abuses human rights, they are surely correct—but Soviet society in the 1980s is hardly as brutal as it was in the Stalinist 1930s to 1950s.

When we claim that Soviet industry, consumer goods, and agriculture are chronically in trouble, we know a bitter part of Soviet reality—but when we think not simply of ideologies and systems but of longsuffering people, the waste of a scorched earth war, the burdens of the arms race, and the harshness of Soviet climate, we may muster some compassion to offset our contempt. We may even arrive at the prudent judgment that an increasingly self-confident and prosperous Soviet economy is more conducive to our own security than a frustrated and faltering economy whose weaknesses we try to aggravate and exploit, to the intensification of Soviet paranoia and aggressiveness.

When we point to the harshness of Soviet policies in Afghanistan and Poland we are rightly outraged by much of what we see—but we would do well to temper our rage with a perception of the defensive desperation to which Soviets have felt driven by their bloody history. And we would also do well to recall the suffering caused by American interventions in such countries as Vietnam, Iran, Guatemala, and Chile.

If, however, we succumb to the alarmist notion that Soviet power has been expanding relentlessly all over the globe, we shall have blinded ourselves to the truth: Soviet political power, like that of the United States, has been declining over most of the world for many years. The Soviets have experienced the loss of hegemony in China, Yugoslavia, Albania, Ghana, Guinea, Egypt, Sudan, and Somalia, and their presence in many other countries is much more precarious than the New Chauvinists in America have admitted.

If we interpret the USSR's military buildup since the 1960s only as evidence of Soviet aggressiveness, supposing that the US has been weakening its defenses all the while, we shall have misread history very badly. The truth is that the Soviets have essentially followed a relentless American momentum in the arms race, with most of the innovations on the US side, the quintupling of independently targetable nuclear warheads during the 1970s, and the simultaneous development of cruise missiles, Tridents, Mark 12-A warheads, MX, Pershing IIs, and other counterforce weapons.

If we ascribe only propaganda, intransigence, and treachery to Soviet diplomacy in disarmament, we shall find it hard to believe that Soviet leaders and citizens (including millions of Christians) have their own historic and very human reasons for wanting to avoid nuclear war and to relieve the economic burdens of the arms race. Unless we engage in careful study of the public record, we may find it very hard to credit the Soviets with making more than their share of concessions in negotiations over SALT (strategic arms limitations) and a Comprehensive Test Ban. Indeed, we may soon perceive that Soviet leaders, feeling understandably pushed past the point of further compromises, have become just as intransigent as we always "knew" they were, instead of perceiving them as feeling newly threatened by the recent upsurge of American hostility. The arms race has been full of self-fulfilling prophecies on both sides.

When people are trapped by their own messianic self-righteousness, their capacity to grasp the truth is destroyed. Peacemaking is not primarily an exercise in the promotion of sentimentality and charity: it is a struggle for the deepest truths which may be obscured by hostile prejudices.

At a superficial level, Gospel imperatives to peacemaking and especially to the love of enemies may seem like idealistic and perfectionist counsels which have little to do with the "realistic" domain of world politics. The sentiments of too many American Christians are reflected in the cartoon which shows a preacher advising his congregation: "Of course, in case of national security, disregard everything I have previously said." When conflict comes and the crisis is upon us, we are urged to forget the New Testament and get on with the arms race or the war. The enemy is dehumanized and even demonized. The faith that Christ is alive and at work, even among communists who despise and reject him, too readily dissolves before our own arrogance and aggressiveness.

At a deeper level, the imperative to love our enemies is grounded in the truth that, in hating them, we blind and destroy ourselves. That is a truth that must lead Presbyterians and all other faith communities into a more profound encounter, not only with their own tribal heritage, but with him in whom we have One Lord, One Faith, and One Baptism. This is the Christ who is our peace, who is breaking down the dividing walls of hostility. This is the theology of the Cross— and the love and power beyond the Cross. It's all there in St. Paul's letter to the Christian congregation at Colossae:

> For in him all the fullness of God was pleased to dwell, and through him to reconcile to himself all things, whether on earth or in heaven, making peace by the blood of his cross.

Endnotes

1. Gerhard Leibholz, "Memoir," in Dietrich Bonhoeffer, *The Cost of Discipleship* (New York: The Macmillan Company, 1963), 30.

2. Perry Miller, *The New England Mind: The Seventeenth Century* (New York: The Macmillan Company, 1939), 409.

3. Herbert Butterfield, *Christianity and History* (New York: Charles Scribner's Sons, 1949), 41.

4. Charles Burton Marshall, *The Limits of Foreign Policy* (New York: Henry Holt and Company, 1954), 12.

5. Foster Rhea Dulles, *America's Rise to World Power: 1898-1954* (New York: Harper and Brothers, 1955), 160.

6. Richard Henry Tawney, *Religion and the Rise of Capitalism* (New York: Harcourt, Brace and Company, 1926), 175.

7. R. G. Collingwood, *The Idea of History* (New York: Oxford University Press, 1956), 49.

8. Herbert Butterfield, *Christianity, Diplomacy, and War* (New York: Abingdon-Cokesbury Press, n.d.), 68.

A PERSPECTIVE FROM
THE UNITED STATES SENATE

David Pryor

A scene midway in the current award-winning film, "Chariots of Fire," makes a telling point on the subject of political involvement. Harold Abrahams, the English runner obsessed with victory, has just lost a 100-meter race to Eric Liddell, the only man in the kingdom who is faster than he. Abrahams is sitting dejected in the empty bleachers, going over the race in his mind and wondering how he could have lost it. He has cut himself off from everyone around him.

His fiancee joins him in the stands and reproaches him for taking his loss so hard. She tells him he's acting like a child. "After all," she says, "if you're going to run you have to learn to take a beating."

Abrahams turns on her angrily. "I don't run in order to take a beating," he explains. "I run to win. And if I can't win I won't run."

"But Harold," she says, "if you don't *run* you can't *win.*"

Surely this is a point considered by every politician at some time in his public life. How often, in fact, has anyone involved in the political system grown disenchanted with things as they are and vowed to quit the game, to stop running? How often has he wanted to remain detached out of sheer uncertainty, or because of a lack of confidence in himself to do the job at hand?

I'm reminded of a conversation between Franklin D. Roosevelt and his wife Eleanor following his serious attack of polio when he was considering whether to enter the race for Governor of New York. Roosevelt was going through a long and painful convalescence and the re-entry into public life promised to be a major gamble, probably the most crucial risk he would take in his political life.

"I'm afraid," he said to his wife, "that if I try, I'll fail."

"Then don't," she said.

"You mean don't try?" he asked.

"No," his wife said. "Don't fail."

A similar question of involvement is raised in many of today's institutions, and particularly the church. Faced with a bewildering spectrum of concerns, does the church marshal its forces and enter the mainstream—or in self-isolation tend to the private concerns of its own flock? The problem is hardly new, having occurred as early as Paul's letters to the Romans where, in the 13th chapter, he admonishes followers of the new church to obey governing authorities, pay taxes, and resist the fear of magistrates. But somehow the question of involvement occurs in the 1980s in such graphic and dramatic terms that it seems more crucial than ever before.

World peace has seldom been quite so threatened, social programs never so necessary to the elderly citizens of America. The economy is probably in worse shape than at any point in the last half-century. Forces divide us on such issues as birth control, abortion, school prayer, and what many refer to as the sexual revolution. Drugs are prevalent even in small towns, and crime rates are up throughout our major cities.

I mention these concerns not out of some dreary need to dampen our spirits but because most of us are affected by one or more of them at every moment in our lives. We wonder how to deal with them: through the church, or political parties, or neighborhood alliances, or self-help support groups. Or do we face this litany of problems alone and detached from those around us?

In an essay published recently on personal values and their place in public policy, Richard A. McCormick reminds us that social and global concerns, in the final analysis, are personal and human: "One need not be a Christian," he says, "to be concerned with the poor, with health, with the food problem, with justice and rights. But if one is a Christian and is not so concerned, something is wrong with that Christianity. It has ceased to be Christian because it has ceased to be what its founder was—human."[1] McCormick echoes here an evaluation of Christian concern expressed by John C. Bennett, who points out that Christ cared most for those unable to defend themselves. As Christians, we are therefore charged with the obligation to seek justice for "the people of greatest need, the people whom respectable society neglected or despised."[2]

If our approach to the concerns of modern society is through politics, then we have to remember that we are working with ideals. This is a very loose term frequently bandied around by politicians and philosophers, along with "goals," its companion word. The two are seldom defined to good purpose. In its basic sense, ideals have to do with the way we want things to be—and not the way they are. Ideals give us something to work *toward* but not necessarily *with*. It's the *with*ness that we find in the political system, the nuts and bolts of everyday striving that may eventually lead toward those ideals. Both are necessary—the reality of today's trench warfare, plus the far horizons of tomorrow where we hope to arrive.

The mention of ideals in politics always reminds me of a story involving my colleague Senator Russell Long of Louisiana. When he was a young student, Senator Long went to his uncle, Earl Long, the Governor of Louisiana, and asked for help in preparing a debate for his high school class. The Governor asked his nephew the topic.

"Resolved," said the young man, "that ideals should be used in politics."

"Which side are you taking?" the Governor asked.

"The affirmative," Russell replied.

"Why hell yes you use ideals," the Governor said. "In politics you use any damn thing you can get your hands on."

No matter what our ideals may be, or however lofty our goals, they are useless and wasted unless we are willing to take action. In saying this we come to the center of a typically American point of view. In his classic essay, "The American Scholar," Emerson said the final obligation of man thinking is action. We must be about the daily chore of living and making our lives complete, our world better than we found it. In fact, the primary task confronting us in politics today is that of being informed and alert, and of guarding against a tendency to substitute moral rhetoric for hard work.

A useful legacy of what is known as existential theology is its three responses to human experience. We're given three possible choices to the question of involvement in social and political questions. They are simple and elementary, but they provide an approach to the dilemma of political participation in today's world. I want to mention two of these in the briefest way since neither is, in my opinion, an acceptable choice for any of us. The third is not only acceptable, it is also in line with the direction the church seems to be taking in the 1980s. This third area of experience—or what is called "authentic existence"— is one that I wish to discuss in some detail.

The first of our choices is hardly a choice at all. In many ways it constitutes a non-choice. It admits no awareness of human involvement or concern but is defined by a certain contented indifference to the world. So rarefied is the air this person breathes, and so self-contained is his experience, that it would be hard to refer to this position even as selfishness. It is more like blissful ignorance.

An effective description of this willful isolation appears in Tennyson's treatment of the Lotus-Eaters, those melancholy people who elect to stay where they are. As they put it: "We will no longer roam."[3] Yet the act of "roaming" is exactly what the modern crisis of participation is all about. Unless the modern citizen leaves the comfort of his protective shell, he might as well have no virtue at all. There is no chance of victory, as Harold Abrahams' fiancee explains to him after the race. And I like the idea, implicit in the word "roam," that we might not always be certain of our direction. There is a definite and appealing sense of wandering, a willingness to explore. Few leaders in our world have known for sure exactly where they were going or how they planned to get there. But they knew that standing fast would produce nothing at all.

The second choice open to us is hardly more responsible than the first, although it does admit the possibility of involvement. At this level the person is aware of political realities and the needs of others around him. If he is not ready to commit his time and interest to the pursuit of accomplishment, he is nevertheless awakened to the fact of choice. He is not frozen into a state of inaction or indifference.

Ten years ago I lost an election and was tempted, like Harold Abrahams, to withdraw from any future race. I wasn't in the arena of politics in order to learn some valuable lesson about the necessity of taking a beating with heroism. I was in it to win, and if I couldn't win I saw no good reason for running. My text was taken from Vince Lombardi: "Winning isn't everything—it's the only thing."

Some friendly spirit, acting as a conscience, perched on my shoulder and nagged at me about the childish error of my ways. It reminded me of the most basic of truths: that a runner, in order to win, must first enter the race. It stressed the necessity of risk, the danger that all might be lost, the challenge of balancing my life between failure and success. How was I to know the joy of victory if I sat it out on the sidelines?

So I became involved again by being elected Governor of Arkansas. Another factor, in addition to that voice of conscience, entered my decision to get back into action. Only a year before, I had become involved in nursing home legislation, and if there was ever a project still unfinished it was this one. I could hardly turn my back on people and programs that had occupied my time for the past three years.

Here is what had happened. In 1969 and 1970, we had heard reports of abuses against the elderly who lived in nursing homes across the country. The problem was that most of our information was rumor. We needed hard evidence in order to convince others in the Congress that federal legislation was necessary. Then in my second term as a member of the House of Representatives, I volunteered to work as an orderly in several nursing homes in the Washington area. My duties included activities that ranged from changing beds to taking patients for walks. The evidence gathered during my days and nights as a volunteer had been partially responsible for the first hearings in the House on problems of the elderly in nursing homes. Eventually this activity, and the time and commitment of many concerned people, led to initial elderly legislation and the establishment of the House Select Committee on Aging.

My recollection of this activity was important in the decision to work within the system and get back into politics. Certainly it was in part the awareness of a job left undone, the frustration of seeing a needed project still incomplete. Whatever the particular stimulus might have been at the time, my choice was re-entry. If I didn't become involved again no one could be blamed but myself when things were not turning out as they should. I might not be able to accomplish much, but as a full non-participant I knew it was impossible to accomplish anything.

Which brings me to a third and preferred level of experience—the fully engaged and committed member of society who knows the risks and dangers and accepts them as part of the world around him. This is the ever-alert participant, the political realist, the finely-tuned and informed public citizen. It may be that no one can maintain the intensity of this commitment throughout a lifetime, but I have known those who have made a try. In recent American history we have the examples of Roosevelt and John F. Kennedy. Both men plunged into the often tedious and protracted world of politics and government, taking clear pleasure in making those choices and decisions called for in their positions of leadership.

Perhaps it is easy to point out the grand and famous President as a model of political commitment. But few citizens are given the chance to hold high responsibility. What about the others, the vast populace who may never be elected to office? And what about those not interested in holding such a position them-selves, but who want to feel a part of the body politic? The truth is that they have an equal hold on political duty and commitment, a charge to engage in life around them at least as serious as those elected to office.

There was a man in my hometown of Camden, Arkansas, who embodied the kind of commitment I have in mind. His name was Wiley Rogers, and by mod-ern definitions he was the operator of a public landfill. In 1940s terms he was a junk man and a house-mover. But what determination and resolve he brought to his job! In fact, I have known few people who took their public trust more seriously. We saw his truck all over town, collecting garbage, gathering what needed to be thrown away, cleaning neighborhoods, performing what was surely a thankless but necessary task. He could pick up and move anything, no matter how large or heavy or awkward. And on top of the cabin of his truck was a sign that expressed his dedication to public service: IT CAN BE DONE. In all those years we never knew Wiley Rogers to give up on a job.

My childhood in Arkansas was a patchwork of grass-roots participation. In fact, one of the givens of my early years was the awareness of politics my family expected of me, a grasp of public issues that affected our county and state, as well as the entire country. We were fully engaged in the political system, never questioning whether we had a choice in the matter or not. My father and grandfa-ther were both sheriffs of the county. My mother was the first woman to seek public office in the State of Arkansas. And when we were not directly engaged in races of our own we worked in those of relatives and neighbors.

As a Presbyterian, I was aware of Calvin and his insistence that secular government is a proper activity for all Christians. It appealed to my sense of order that even the governing bodies of the church were set up in a manner strikingly similar to the American system of states. And it was clear to me that universal suffrage, as Calvin taught, is good for all people, along with the elec-tion of officials by the public and the maintenance of a regulated and enduring liberty of speech and thought. It was also clear that church and state should remain separate, and that they function best when operating in spheres of their own. Yet within these two distinct worlds I saw the need for a common commit-ment to fairness and devotion to one's duty.

In my experience, the people of the church have not abandoned this call to public responsibility. They continue to demonstrate the "authentic" existence I have tried to define. Let me offer an example of this concern. Surely the most serious issue facing us today is the prospect of nuclear war and the pressing need for arms control. Unless concerted action is taken on both sides, I am afraid that civilization as we know it is doomed to extinction. Yet we are able to do some-thing about it. Our country, and the world, is threatened by the willful refusal of major powers to negotiate an effective agreement. The unthinkable, even in the past year, has become all too thinkable and familiar.

This alarm was the thrust of a speech I made twice during the fall of 1981, first in Little Rock at the Rotary Club and later on the Senate floor. In both instances I objected to mistakes being made by public policy-makers in defense spending and cost overruns at the Pentagon. I also pointed to the curious reluctance of our negotiators to move peace talks at a faster pace and with more accountability to the American public. Most of what I said dealt less with policy and more with a visceral concern over arms buildup and our reckless plunge toward oblivion. My final point was a plea for direct negotiations between Presidents Reagan and Brezhnev and, if necessary, without the diplomatic protocol that might complicate and delay personal discussions.

Reactions came primarily from people in Arkansas, most of it favorable. I have been particularly encouraged and heartened to find that nearly all of the organized expressions of support—in the form of petitions and letters—have come from the Presbytery of Arkansas. Acting individually and as a group, the members of the church have been consistently strong and vocal in their endorsement of arms limitations and their expressions of concern over the proliferation of nuclear weapons.

A similar participation by church members is also occurring on the issue of chemical weapons. In January of this year, President Reagan certified the production of nerve gas as essential to national defense, thereby authorizing the resumption of its manufacture at the arsenal in Pine Bluff, Arkansas. His announcement reversed a 13-year policy of the United States not to engage in the manufacture of chemical weapons.

My opposition to the President's decision extends back at least five years when, as Governor of Arkansas, I requested of President Carter that the production of binary weapons not be produced in Arkansas or anywhere else. Evidence I have seen shows that our country has adequate supplies of nerve gas to last for years to come. Yet we embark on a project that will cost more than $6 billion during the next five years. What's more, our allies in Europe—where the weapons will have to be stored—have informed us in very clear terms that they will not have them on their soil.

It has been interesting to see where opposition to this move by the government has originated. Almost without fail, it has come from the churches of America and, particularly in Arkansas, the Presbyterian clergy and lay people. One of the most supportive petitions I received from Arkansas was signed by members of the community at Arkansas College in Batesville, a Presbyterian school.

These expressions of concern are taking place nationally as well. Last November a conference on nuclear disarmament was held in New York, where the Rev. Robert Davidson, moderator of the United Presbyterian Church, defined the role of the church in these terms: "Peacemaking," he said, "is an issue where we can mobilize the churches."[4]

The manner in which Presbyterians express themselves is exemplary. It is a credit to the church that those involved are rational in their expression of dissent and willing to work for programs only as members of the system of government. They avoid the temptation to let their social and political views control their religion. And while their religion provides a moral framework for their views, it does not blind them to the constitutional separation of church and state.

The difference between voicing opinions on nuclear armaments and the sort of political campaign waged by others is essentially threefold. One, the action of the church in making peace efforts is a positive direction. It is not based on the negative and narrow assumptions that define public interest groups of a different stripe. Second, it is not vindictive. Its purpose is not to target and defeat this or that elected official, but instead to raise questions and expand the horizons of everyone who cares to listen. The third distinction grows out of the first two: the church is not in pursuit of one-issue concerns. It is careful to put its questions—defense, social spending, or education—in a larger context. In my experience, the church has never lost its grasp of the big picture, and it is not likely to yield in its efforts to bring about social and political progress.

Which brings me back to "Chariots of Fire" and a scene resonant with meanings and implications. Eric Liddell, the runner who later becomes a missionary to China, preaches a sermon in the Scottish Church in Paris on the Sunday before winning a gold medal for the 100-meter race in the Olympics. He reads from Ecclesiastes the description of runners and the importance of the race in their lives:

> I returned, and saw under the sun, that the race is not to the swift, nor the battle to the strong, neither yet bread to the wise, nor yet riches to men of understanding, nor yet favour to men of skill; but time and chance happeneth to them all.[5]

He goes on to say that the consciousness creating national lines and barriers, and separating man from man, is an artificial one and doomed to fail. Finally, we are all one people under God. This is what all of those in politics are trying to say. This is why we chose to run.

Endnotes

1. "Does Religious Faith Add to Ethical Perception?" *Personal Values in Public Policy: Conversations on Government Decision-Making,* ed. John C. Haughey (New York: Paulist Press, 1979), pp. 171-172.
2. Quoted in John Brademas, "Christian Responsibility in the Political Order," *Congressional Record,* July 2, 1980, p. E3361.
3. *The Poems and Plays,* Modern Library Edition (New York: Random House, 1938), p. 102.
4. *New York Times,* Tuesday, November 17, 1981, p. B8.
5. King James Version, 9:11.

A POLITICAL LIFESTYLE AND AGENDA FOR PRESBYTERIANS IN THE NINETEEN-EIGHTIES

Donald W. Shriver, Jr.

Several years ago *The New York Times* ran an editorial on the theme of religion and poverty. A Manhattan church had announced its intention to devote a large part of its resources to the needs of poor people, and the newspaper commented that this was hardly a purpose that a religious organization should worry about. Tell the poor about the spiritual salvation of another world, the paper counseled; but leave the problems of poverty to other agencies that know what they are doing.

Quite opposite to this advice, in the spring of 1981, came the word of newly-elected President Ronald Reagan, that churches and other "private" sectors of American society would have to pick up the slack in social programs whose funds the federal government would soon have to cut.

Which of these two free bits of counsel is supposed to instruct the churches on this matter? We can answer preliminarily that both counsels are wide of the Christian mark. Each is a seduction of the spirit, from the point of view of a group of Protestant Christians who call themselves Reformed and Presbyterian. As I read that naive, historically-untutored, Biblically illiterate *Times* editorial, I wondered to myself, "How many Presbyterians, titular heirs to John Calvin's reading of the Bible, laughed out loud when they read this opinion in America's most prestigious newspaper? And did some appreciate the irony that the *Times* was assigning religion a role in society exactly like the one assigned by Karl Marx?"

In fact, one does not have to go to church often to acquire some minimal critical response to such a secularist claim in the media. A more sophisticated response is required, however, to President Reagan's call for more church and other voluntary ministry to the needs of poor people in this society. There is something wholly American about such a call. After all, we believe in the "separation of church and state." We do not want a government that presumes to preside over every aspect of human life—that is the definition of totalitarianism. Precisely because "doing justice" to the poor is so regular a theme of both the Old and New Testaments, few well-educated church members want to turn over the churches' concern for the poor entirely to government. Why not accept the Reagan challenge, mobilize our own institutional resources, and prove once again that human salvation comes not wholly from government?

But this also is a seduction of the spirit, at least the spirit that Presbyterianians should have caught from Calvin and all his faithful successors in our segment of the Christian movement in history. Other Christians may read the Bible and draw "sectarian" conclusions about the role of the church *vis à vis* government: "Let the church organize its own life apart from the secular powers, which are likely to be the instruments of Satan anyway. If there is to be a ministry of social justice to the poor, let the church carry it on inside its own structures. Let religion remain uncontaminated with the world, including the world of conflicting human powers in the processes of government."

But this version of the sectarian spirit is alien to the spirit of John Calvin and Reformed Christianity generally. There are other versions of distinction and link between faith and culture—H. Richard Niebuhr's book *Christ and Culture* remains a classic statement of the various historical options; but the Calvinist version contrasts to the others chiefly in its complexity and comprehensiveness. Perhaps only in Roman Catholic thought can be found so complex, so comprehensive a tradition relating the life of the church to the life of all human society. The German theological historian Ernst Troeltsch said that, in its original form, Calvinism had the most elaborate social ethic in the history of the Christian movement.

Other papers in this series will have made this point at greater length; but, against the background of contemporary secularist and governmental claims about the church in American society, these classic Calvinist convictions are worth summarizing:

—God is the Creator, the Judge, and the Redeemer of the whole world; nothing in reality is outside the sovereign, active rule of God.

—The church exists by the grace of One who is active in all history, in the life, death and resurrection of Jesus and in the power of the Holy Spirit. No government or other human power legitimates or creates the church. It is the free creation of God.

—The Gospel and the scriptures have meaning for the whole of human life. The ministry of the church, while beginning with "the equipment of the saints," must concern all those ties that link humans together in a society. God sends the church on a mission, to be light and leaven, to all society. Just as nothing human is outside the rule of God, nothing human is outside the potential concern of the church.

—But the church is not government, which has its own direct relations to the true Sovereign of this world. Church and government are both called to "serve the Lord." They can each be used as God's instrument of guidance, judgment, and help to humanity; and if both become so corrupt as to be unfit as divine instruments, then God will raise up other instruments.

—The individual Christian serves God in both the church and the rest of society. Discipleship consists in the awareness that "during one's whole life one has to do with God" (Calvin).

—But such discipleship is not primarily a personal, individual calling. The Sovereign Lord works not only in the depths of individual souls but as well in the organizations, the institutions, and the movements of human history. The struggle of Christians to glimpse and to obey the will of God must go on everywhere—in the church, in society, in the most secular of contexts. "Everywhere that man can be, thou God art present there" was a hymn-line written (by Isaac Watts) from the world-view of Calvinism.

Troeltsch summarized his understanding of the Calvinist world-view as a vision of a "holy community." The phrase rings as antique in our ears these days. To recover its meaning would be to remember the contribution of John Calvin to the building of the first textile industry in sixteenth century Geneva; his concern for sanitation law, the licensing of dentists, and the restriction of interest rates. It would be to remember how Presbyterian ministers played a role in the American Revolution, much to the discomfort of those who wanted to "keep politics out of the pulpit." It would be to acknowledge that a modern secular society makes it natural and tempting for religion to be put into its own pigeonhole. And it would be to pray again, with all those faithful to this Reformed tradition, "lead us not into this temptation"—of separating our faith in Thee from *anything* "in the world as it is or the world as it shall be" (Romans 8:39).

Is it possible to serve God in the politics of a secular land?

We should not underestimate the *spiritual difficulty* imposed upon modern members of the Reformed-Presbyterian churches when their ministers and other teachers tell them: "Remember John Calvin, and go thou and do likewise." We are a long four-and-one-half centuries from John Calvin's Geneva. We have had much reason, in the meantime, to become aware that there are no easy connections between faith and politics, churches and governments, local and global justice, religious reasoning and the new technological powers of organized human society. American history alone is littered with grotesque attempts to carry "the will of God" into political action. In our own time, Christians have offered their public support to such diverse causes as World Wars I and II, the Eighteenth Amendment, segregation laws, prayer in public schools, anti-abortion legislation, Civil Rights laws, women's rights, restriction of women's rights, support of the Vietnam War and opposition to the Vietnam War. Where in this patchwork of allegedly Christian reasoning about human political causes is there something that "has to do with God?"

The only way to be a serious Christian, in the Calvinist mode, is to treat this as a serious question. Where indeed? Are we to lapse into the practical atheism of believing that God in fact does not care, act, or speak to human beings in their concrete life together? This lapse into practical atheism characterizes the real lives of many church members of our time. Who among us must not confess to having practiced just such an atheism? We read the news headlines about the latest moves of the Soviets; and we assume that, if the Americans do not do something, nothing good will be done in response. We note the latest interest rates and applaud (or condemn) the "free market," assuming that an economic question has nothing to do with a theological question. And we discuss politics at cocktail parties, being quite careful not to make any references to last Sunday's sermon or any ancient quotation from the Bible. Wouldn't people think that we were odd if we talked as if faith in God had anything to do with political policy?

This temptation, to think and live in utter conformity to the perspectives of a secularized society, confronts most American Christians today; and, in the 1980s and 1990s, it will probably confront them more starkly yet. Some, like the followers of fundamentalist television preachers, are already scrambling rather frantically to recover "old time religion" and "old time Americanism" in ways wildly at odds with the Calvinist tradition as described above. But there is one thing which both the new political evangelicals and the old Calvinists have to teach some of us bewildered, middle-of-the-road American Presbyterians: *You can't live the Christian or the political life alone.* You cannot long remain a believer in God alone. You cannot discover or serve the purposes of God alone. You need a community of faith, action, reflection, and struggle, if you are to serve God in the politics of a secular land, or any other land.

The truth of this statement came home to me, with renewed force, in the midst of a community research project in my home town, which was then Raleigh, North Carolina. (The results of that research are recorded in a book, *Is There Hope for the City?*, written with my colleague, Karl A. Ostrom, published in 1977 by Westminster Press.) The question at the heart of our inquiry was: Under what conditions does a citizen of this community become most active in political affairs? We defined "political" broadly as any activity that involved a group of citizens in an effort to influence the course of some public policy, event, or structure. Our interviews with almost a thousand carefully sampled citizens of our community indicated that scarcely more than 25% of our neighbors had any involvement at all in public, political life. Hardly more than 25% of church people had it, either. What makes the difference, we asked, between "active" and "inactive" citizens? The answer we derived from our various stacks of interview records was complicated; but it was nonetheless instructive.

The people most likely to be active influences in the public life of their communities are people who have:

(1) *A strong faith or philosophical view concerning the human drama.* People active in politics, we found, tend to be people who believe deeply in a vision of what human life is meant to be. They are capable of a "sense of intolerable wrong," not simply from an experience of personal outrage but from something they believe about the very nature of the world. Most often, this sort of motive-power was expressed to us in terms of religious faith.

(2) *A group of friends with whom they share their joys and sorrows, including their political joys and sorrows.* Such friends might be a very informal set of associates in business, the neighborhood, or a church. The important difference

between these citizens and others was twofold: politics was a *subject* of their talk together, and they felt free to share their mixed frustration and fulfillment in public life. Quite in contrast to these active citizens were others who either were sure that "politics and friendship don't mix" or simply lacked a trustworthy cluster of friends.

(3) *At least an introduction to political life in some concrete experiences.* People who say, "Politics is not for me," are often, we found, people who have never had a political experience. Once one signs a petition, writes a letter to a Congressperson, receives an answer, attends a rally, or visits a city council meeting, one has experiential reason to think, "Politics is for everybody." Nothing reinforces a commitment to political *ethics,* we found, so much as some concrete political *participation.* Faithful Bible-reading is not enough to sustain a political vision. You can read all the books on swimming, take classes, and acquire all the right concepts. But you will never think that swimming is really a good idea until you hit the water.

The most important of our research findings was the three-dimensional nature of this pattern of "citizen activation." If you lack any one of these three characteristics—philosophy, friendships, or political experience—each of the other characteristics is likely to be weaker. If you have a high sense of how human society needs to be cured of its evils—racism, sexism, war, poverty—but never talk about these things with friends and never do anything politically about them, your very convictions are likely to wither. On the other hand, if you are frantically active in a series of political causes but have few friends and little religious or philosophic convictions to sustain you along the way, you are not likely to last long in political life. This is a strong explanation for why some liberals grow "tired." We discovered a subgroup of people among our interviewees who were exactly that: tired liberals. They had tried a political cause or two, felt the pangs of failure, and retired from the fray. A striking correlary about these people is that they were the people in the sample most likely to suffer from insomnia and stomach ulcers! Their unrealized high ideals proved bad for their health.

The New Testament, as usual, puts the human truth of all this in pithy form: "Faith without works is dead." (James 1:26) "There is nothing love cannot face." (I Corinthians 17:3) "Courage! The victory is mine; I have conquered the world." (John 16:33) Grounded in our vision of the world as greatly loved by God in Jesus Christ, our faith, love, and hopeful works compose our human social-political lifestyle. Like the clothes on our backs, the strands of this fabric are inseparable.

The 1980s are a time for the rediscovery of this wisdom by Presbyterians of all political persuasions. The Moral Majoritarians, and their like, have given the American public the impression that Christians move from the certainties of their faith to equal certainties of political claims. Thus, in one leap, the Gospel of Jesus Christ seems to send its emissaries to city councils and state capitols to lobby religiously for laws on abortion, school prayer, national defense, and lower welfare expenditures. ("I have a divine mandate to go right into the halls of Congress and fight for laws that will save America," says Jerry Falwell.) Some liberal Christians of the past have given a similar impression about the relation of their faith to their own favorite causes. Experienced citizens know that the leap from faith to politics is not really that simple. The Christian way to deal with political complexity is the practice of a complex lifestyle that combines faith, friendship, and political struggle. Many a patriotic supporter of the Vietnam War learned to revise his or her opinion about that conflict by talking to its veterans, listening to students, and sharing their own doubts with a few close friends. The good and the evil in human societies are usually more complicated than any of our *early* political opinions. People who serve the community best are usually those who know from sustained experience how social good and evil really work.

A Political Agenda for the 1980s: Peace, Justice, the City

I have my own sense of the key political issues of the next few years of the human story on this earth. I can tag these issues as peace, justice, and the life of cities. To conclude this essay with a few "counsels to Presbyterians," regarding their part in the human struggle with these issues in the 1980s, is not merely to recommend to my neighbors-in-the-faith a slick set of my own political opinions. You will see some of the opinions plainly enough, but the above context should make this point the clearest of all: *You will never know the truth or the error of any connection of faith and politics unless you subject yourself regularly to the combined disciplines of prayer, Bible study, church-going, conversation with friends, and participation in collective political activities.*

The Christian life is not a set of concepts and opinions. It is a pilgrimage, done with companions, and directed towards ends in the hands of our sovereign Lord. Better to be sure of *this,* than to know yet just whom you should vote for in the next election!

1. *Holding back the terror of nuclear war.* Like the Lutherans and Catholics, Presbyterians have never had a reputation for being a "peace church." National patriotism and a certain respect for the role of coercion in human affairs have kept us suspicious of pacifism and the pacifist churches. But in the late 1970s both the Presbyterians and the Catholics of the United States began in impressive numbers to agree that nuclear weapons are an unprecedented threat to the future of the human race. For virtually the first time in its history, the United Presbyterian Church designated "peacemaking" as every "Believer's Calling"; and the Presbyterian Church U.S., against the background of a militaristic regional tradition, began in 1978 "to confess that we Christians in the United States have not been serious enough in our work for disarmament" (1978 General Assembly, P.C.U.S.).

In calling all its members to take up their calling as peacemakers, these General Assemblies were setting out a long, complex, difficult political agenda for their members. Remarkable in their statements about this agenda was their combination of spiritual and political language. For example:

"How will peace be achieved? By disarmament? Certainly . . . By global economic reform? . . . By change of political structures? Basically, at the heart, it is a matter of the way we see the world through the eyes of Christ. It is a matter of prayer and yearning." ("Peacemaking: The Believer's Calling," p. 5.)

In effect, this General Assembly was saying that the issue of world peace, seen from the perspective of a disciple of Jesus Christ, calls for active involvement of churches and their members in the full spectrum of prayer, worship, study, thought, discussion, organization, demonstration, campaigning, legislation, and institutional restructuring, from a local to a global scale. What an intimidating agenda! But the forces that put the world at nuclear risk are more intimidating. The question for Christians is whether they will hear again the word of Jesus— "Be of good cheer. I have overcome the world!"—and throw themselves into the struggle for peace between nations.

The turn of "mainline" churches towards serious engagement with the threats of global war is already a development of enormous political consequence. Everyone who stood under the Presbyterian banners in Central Park on June 13, 1982 for example, alongside 500,000 other human beings from all the United States and many foreign countries, knew that here was one place on earth where the disciples of Jesus belong: in political movements seeking to hold back the terror of nuclear war.

The thought that an ordinary citizen, an ordinary Christian, has a "calling" to get involved in issues of global significance, remains an intimidating thought. How *will* the world be delivered from World War III? It is not required of Christians, Presbyterian-style, that they know exactly. It is required that they be found among the political folk who are trying to find out.

A footnote about what it means to be a political folk: it may mean something as simple as asking a neighbor to come with you to a community meeting on a nuclear freeze resolution, or an initiative, decent and in order, to get the Session of your congregation to endorse the same. Jesus said that he would be present "where two or three are gathered together in my name." Politics can begin in a group just that size. In the end, like the Gospel, it involves our neighbors to the uttermost parts of earth.

2. *Justice for the poor.* If peacemaking is a relatively new fixture in "the believer's calling" in the Calvinistic tradition, *work* and *wealth* are old fixtures. As the writings of Max Weber early in this century made clear, Calvinists have always believed that God's "glory" can be expressed in the material world of farms, factories, commerce, and material human improvement generally. A corrolary to the old Calvinism was that wealth must never become the idol of human effort. Getting rich was not John Calvin's idea of fulfilled human nature and destiny. He himself died a relatively poor man.

On no subject, however, must Presbyterians, especially American Presbyterians, subject their inherited thoughtways more strenuously to new Bible study, new observation of social reality, and new politics. Of all people on earth, Americans, perhaps, are most vulnerable to the thought: "Rich people are better." Of all countries on earth, the poor in America are made to feel most miserable. In no other culture does the phrase "on welfare" ring so much with tones of pity and disdain. And in no other culture, perhaps, is it harder for Bible-believers to hear and understand the clear message of the prophets and Jesus himself: "Blessed are the poor, for yours is the kingdom of God!" (Luke 6:20)

As the authors of so-called liberation theology have been discovering anew, the God of the Exodus, the prophets, and Jesus of Nazareth is one who exercises sovereignty on earth *especially* in "lifting up the humble" and "satisfying the hungry with good things" while "sending the rich empty away." (Luke 1:52). Large numbers of secularist Americans and embarrassing numbers of Christian Americans are genuinely mystified at this scriptural theme. "A government policy that actually *favors* the poor? Government should help those who help themselves!" "Spend hard-earned tax money for welfare rather than national defense? No country can grow strong that way!" This is the ordinary talk of many Americans with regular jobs, income, and economic security. In a time of inflation and recession, such talk may be muted, especially among those of us who see our income, jobs, and economic security threatened for the first time in our lives. But the culture of the United States is pitched against the idea that society must help the poor. For many members of a largely middle class Protestant church, the threat of *being* poor resembles the threat of death.

The 1980s are ripe for reflection, prayer, discussion, disagreement, struggle, and political involvement of middle class Presbyterians around the issues of wealth and poverty in the modern world. For example, the notion that wealth comes chiefly by individual effort went out of date with the industrial age. Agriculture, manufacturing, commerce, investment, and systems of economic reward to individuals are all profoundly cooperative human inventions; and, in a day when economic gain and loss involve global competition and cooperation, the wealth or poverty of individuals is often a result of how a society is organized. *Organizing society so that none of its members lack the basic resources for survival with dignity must be a basic political goal of Christians.* To start one's political *thinking* with this principle must become a central point in the social teaching of churches; and American Christians, in particular, must recover their Biblical heritage of justice for the poor if they are to be Christian and not merely American in their political identity.

How does a society so organize itself? What should the richest country in the world, the U.S.A., do about its own poor? And how shall the corporations, government policies, and political power of this country benefit, rather than ignore or exploit, the poor of the earth? American Christians, Presbyterians among them, may not carry any sure answers to these questions into the legislatures, the corporate boards, and the political parties of the land. But they will carry the questions into all these places; and with as many allies as they find, they will look for ways to make these systems serve the poor as one sure way they can serve our Lord. On this point the Biblical word is so clear yet so hard for many middle-class Presbyterians to hear, that the first step towards Christian political discipleship is likely to come, for many, *inside the church,* as we decide if we can tolerate sermons, Bible studies, stockholder actions, and legislative recommendations consistent with such teaching. Weariness with this word may impel some church members to seek the sanctuary of a congregation where the minister deftly skips over this theme when it appears in either Testament. Indeed, the problems of poverty may become so severe in America and elsewhere on the 1980s that congregations and denominations may face splits over just this issue: Will we be a church that sides with the poor, or not? To be weary with this question is to be weary of believing in the God and Father of Jesus Christ.

3. *The livable city.* Presbyterians should have no difficulty remembering that Christianity is fundamentally an urban religion. Not only in its early history was the church associated with cities like Jerusalem, Rome, and Corinth; but the Reformed church's great founder, John Calvin, exercised his ministry chiefly as pastor to an entire city—Geneva. The vision of a "holy community" in which neighborly relations are subject to the justice, mercy, and power of God remains the heart of the Calvinist social vision. It is no exaggeration to suggest that the first test of the Calvinist lifestyle is the willingness of the Christian and the church to "seek the welfare *(shalom)* of the city to which I have carried you," as Jeremiah instructed the Jewish captives in Babylonia (Jeremiah 29:7).

Most Americans live in communities that might best be called "small cities," not unlike Geneva in size. Quite unlike Geneva, our cities, small and large, are knit together and torn apart by economic, technological, and political forces that link millions of people together, for good and ill, on a global scale. What citizen of Detroit today can fail to think almost daily of its economic decline in competition with the cities where Japanese and German automobiles are manufactured? What city in America is not shaped daily by mortgage interest rates, investment decisions, industrial site transfers, and governmental tax policies, many of them little controlled by residents of the city itself? What knowledgeable city mayor (like Republican-Presbyterian Mayor William Hudnut of Indianapolis in December of 1981) could help recognizing that the federal government's decision to raise its national defense budget would have immediate effect on American cities' ability to fix their sewer systems, maintain their public transit, and repair their streets? Someone has said that the modern city is like a plate of spaghetti: wiggle a strand of it on one side, and you get wiggles all over the plate. So intertwined are the forces shaping modern city life that many citizens despair of having any real influence on the future of their own communities.

Faith in God, the fellowship of the church, and courage gathered from political experience must fortify Christians against such despair, in cities and everywhere else in today's world. Especially in the large cities of America, where world languages, cultures, economies, and communications come into contact and conflict, we really do experience Marshall McLuhan's "global village." In its intensity this is a new human experience in the history of the world. The nineteen-eighties will see the cities of the U.S.A. fill with an ever-denser mixture of people born in Asia, Latin America, Africa, Europe, and other distant places. Can the church make a positive contribution to the cultivation of a new political community between "all sorts and conditions" of humans in cities? Can we learn in our very congregation that the church is not a social club based on

[189]

similarity but a community based on God's love for sinners? Can we learn from the connectional Presbyterian system to be connected with people whom *God* chooses as our neighbors? And can we learn from the ecumenical, world network of the church to recognize an ecumenical promise, a secular analogy to the church-universal, in the sea of diverse faces crowding our city streets? Rhetorical questions all: God means all parts of the human race to live in reconciliation. The merest congregation-on-the-corner can be an organized embodiment—a political signal—of that divine purpose. In the struggle for justice and community in our pluralistic cities, we can demonstrate if the signal is a false alarm or a sign of "the city which is to come" (Hebrews 13:14).

NEW AND OLD ASSUMPTIONS
ABOUT POLITICS

Anne Austin Murphy

Christians must help establish new assumptions for the society's political life. The gap between Christian ethics and the assumptions operating in U. S. politics is enormous. In the light of this, it is not enough simply to vote. We are called to join the struggle to create a different climate of expectations, to engender a healthy political will in the body politic.

One contribution that the churches have made is to be critical of current policy and processes; this has often taken the form of "debunking" and ridiculing government and politics. Current political science provides a number of insights about the lack of fit between the conventional wisdom of popular civics and the realities of everyday politics. Theology and church history provide insights into the non-Christian aspects of some political movements that arrogate the term "Christian." Informed church people need to reassess their own expectations and assumptions about what is going on and what can happen in politics. Part I of this paper will make some suggestions about the misguided "conventional wisdom" of civics, and the idolatry, arrogance and blasphemy of some "Christian" political activism.

Beyond skepticism and debunking, there is the need for developing some workable ideas for assessing the worldly work of policy-recommending. Political science has just been going through a radical shift of defining what the important questions are, what the appropriate focus of analysis is, and generally, a whole reordering of the way in which politics and policy can be understood. In order for Christians to engage in fruitful conversation with others who are concerned about the polity, some of us need to join the conversation with the professionals. The second part of this paper will show why this shift took place, and using one of its concepts, sketch how the church and churches can benefit from a systems analysis of politics.

The agenda and style of Presbyterians active in the political arena is the assignment to be addressed. The followers of Jesus should be able to "be there" in the public arena, to stand the heat, to share one another's burdens, and to be a force for the upbuilding of the human community even though Heaven is our

Home. Beyond providing the social lubricant of healthy presence, the Christian communities are potential "agenda setters" for the whole polity. We should do that with humble intentionality. The last section of this paper is addressed to that task.

Political Misconceptions

The following examples of the misconceptions widely shared in the United States serve to suggest directions in which basic civic education needs all the wisdom and energy of people of goodwill, especially Christian educators. This section draws heavily on a textbook written by Marian D. Irish and James W. Prothro.[1]

Politics is Dirty.

This is a puzzling misconception. Since the only way people can hope to influence public policy is through the pursuit and exercise of power or politics, we might assume that politics would be as respected as democracy itself! The disrespect comes about because the political process inevitably disappoints people anticipating any given outcome: everybody has some disappointment, others have great dismay. The necessity of compromise to enable people to live together is uncomfortable to private individuals who can afford the luxury of holding to inflexible principles and who feel superior because of their cherished purity. The media generally encourages anti-political viewpoints. The crooked politician must be exposed, and that gives publicity which makes the crook appear typical. Thus highly private values are encouraged by investigative reporting and exposés. Public-regardingness in media reporting is rare, not dramatically expressed, and does not appear to be normal.

The Government as an Impersonal "It," or "They."

Heavy seas and rocks loom ahead for a democracy where the citizens regard the government as hostile, as "they, not us." Yet, we talk as if decisions were made by self-appointed aliens or faulty robots. There is little sentiment for insisting that we act as if top policy makers are either elected or appointed by president or governors. "We" the people seem to be willing to cop-out. It is called alienation. But in this case it is a form of self-inflicted powerlessness. This attitude spreads an irrational factor into political decision-making akin to astrology, lucky charms and voodoo.

The National Government is Worst.

Many Americans have the impression that all politics is dubious, but local government is best, county and state governments are second or third rate, and national government is worst of all. Despite the legacy of Thomas Jefferson, which asserts that local government would be the most efficient, honest and responsive to broad public needs, that statement is a reversal of the facts of modern political life. Inefficiency, non-performance, dishonesty and special interest domination are found most often at the county and municipal level. Such conditions at the national level are most likely to be challenged and exposed. Moreover, the constituencies of national officials are more diverse, neutralizing narrow interests. The pressure of politics can encourage a more statesmanlike performance from governors than from city councilmen, from presidents than from governors.

Government Should be Run Like a Business.

What is the "bottom line" for government? What is the product? The nature of the service of governments is frequently those necessities and amenities so uneconomical that no entrepreneur can afford to provide them. Investment in plant and inventory is always called an "asset" in the private sector: even if it is tied up in deodorant, hula hoops or race horses. But activities such as vocational rehabilitation, desegregating a racist society, or preserving wilderness are "investments" that are hard to parallel in double-entry ledgers or even to evaluate in the newer social program accounting.

The American Forefathers were Above Politics.

Conventional wisdom urges good citizenship by presenting a depoliticized picture of our founding politicians. Even in Sunday School one gets the idea that George Washington, Thomas Jefferson, Alexander Hamilton, Patrick Henry, and James Madison were great *because* they were "above petty politics." Only in advanced courses does one learn how tough and able was the opposition to ratifying the federal Constitution. Those people argued publicly, clearly, even angrily, throwing themselves into power struggles and alliances and risks similar to ours today. They understood special interests, conflicting commitments, strategy and compromise. "The idea that a statesman should be 'above politics' is as ridiculous as the notion that the Pope or the Archbishop of Canterbury should be 'above religion.' "[2] This misperception of the noble heroes leads moderns to disillusionment as they try to assess our contemporary "mere politicians."

I vote for the Man and Not the Party.

Or as the Ad Council seems to say, "We don't care how you vote, but vote!" Without relevant information a voter can do himself and his nation untold harm! Where is one to get relevant information in a context one can use? If the political parties were doing their job, they would provide what is needed. The widespread slandering of parties and of "partisan politics" is depriving voters of the links they need to make rational choices.

The American Way is the Only Democratic Way.

A moment's thought reveals the blind provincialism in political discussions and suggests a healthy distinction between love of the familiar, the strange, the new. "Such practices as unitary government (instead of federalism), parliamentary supremacy (instead of separation of powers), multi-party politics (instead of the two-party system), and socialism (instead of capitalism), for example, may be "unAmerican" and even undesirable without being undemocratic."[3] On the other hand, to picture everything American as essential to democracy is also misguided. If our rulers are responsive enough to the desires of the ruled, our government can be classified as a democracy and none of our critical patterns is absolutely incompatible with democracy. We have achieved a remarkable degree of democracy in spite of barriers such as a racial caste system and cumulative injustices for specific groups, and spreading social violence.

The Individual Doesn't Count.
Politics are Dictated by Pressure Groups.
Free Elections Alone Translate Public Opinion into Policy.

You have heard these canards. Yet, an individual who is willing to expend energy and resources politically can make a difference. No one will ever get exactly what one wants. Even pressure groups don't get just what they want. As Reinhold Niebuhr said a generation ago, the only reason we can accept the approximations to good policy, or accept the defeats during the policy process is because we are convinced in a democracy that we can reopen the process and try for something more acceptable at a later date. Democratic solutions to issues are both proximate and temporary.

The simplistic model of the rugged individual and the impersonal "government" as the only actors in politics leads to cynicism. In the United States it is very far from describing our polity. As a society of "joiners," U.S. citizens have the pattern of belonging—potentially each one of us—to several face-to-face groups. Not enough has been made of this basis for American democracy. It provides the human-scale interaction that is so needed in complex society with entrenched institutional forces. Voluntary associations provide a ready-made skeleton for healthy political communication, for compromise, for generating alternatives and for introducing new ideas into the polity. The church is particularly prominent in this network; but the churches have not consciously seen the healthy potential for working this way to act politically upon Jesus' charge: Love your neighbor.

The notion that "talking politics" is unAmerican leads to the undemocratic nonsense that policy should reflect the findings of survey research about attitudes and opinions held by the whole population. Wise policy comes from widespread *debate*. Having relevant information is essential, and part of that should be knowing who supports a measure, and who is against it; relevant information includes learning about feasible alternatives. The arena of the debate should be among acquaintances who have experience in evaluating one another's wisdom, not between the passive viewer and the all-powerful for the moment TV commentator.

Policy is, and should be, the product of a complex process—called politics—that stems from conscious debate among groups and individuals, modified by negotiation, compromise and creative alternatives evaluated in the light of feasibility.

Policy Reflects Consensus.

Policy in the U.S. reflects the victory of one coalition of interests over another, with the losers protesting loudly. The victorious coalition is made up of an alliance of minorities. "Majority" rule is a *procedural* description. The majority that wins represents a temporary set of diverse interests. We have "minorities rule" insofar as *substance* is concerned. It is important to note that the easiest coalition to mobilize is the "nay-sayers," the "agin-ers." To fashion a majority alliance for substantive change is almost a miracle; politicians at their best do this occasionally. Minorities can veto change; an intense minority can be very effective over against a mildly-interested numerical majority. An intense minority thus can create policy: minority control. What Americans have agreed upon or have a high degree of consensus about has been a method of governing that represents a very diverse society: regionally, economically pluralistic, of conflicting religious commitments and rich differences of ethnic values. The consensus on procedure has made government possible without destroying the right to disagree. Procedural consensus is notably different from the idea that specific policy reflects consensus, or even that it should.

Government in Neutral.

Is it? Should it be? What is the case? Who gets hurt, who feels hurt by legislation or policy. Evaluating government in terms of effect, rather than of its declared purpose is a useful way to evaluate politics. Using this measure we can see that someone is always benefitting, some always being disadvantaged by policy decisions even though the dream of any politician is to make a decision that will reward everybody! If government were neutral, how long would it stay neutral? Social justice suggests a process of correcting for bias, "tilt," or oppression. Should government be on the side of the unfortunate, actively redressing hurt?

Now turning to a different sort of critique, look at the tempting effort to use the power of religious conviction to make a difference in government policy. There are at least three temptations. To simplify politics by focussing on a *single issue*; to envision politics as a *dichotomy* in which the only acceptable outcome is unconditional surrender by the opposition; to identify one's position with the Word and *Will of God*. The single issue flaw is idolatry; to define a win-lose line is arrogance, and to identify the Eternal Creator with a human political platform is blasphemy.

Single-issue politics is not peculiar to religious folk; it is a demonically successful strategy in the short run for any political group. But for Christians who know that God's Creation is more wonderful than we can imagine, politics can be seen as the arena for multiple possibilities and new solutions. This view of Creation leads to seeing possibilities as a continuum and evaluating proposals and positions as "more than," or "less than" we want. To see possible alternatives along a continuum produces language like "better" and "worse," rather than Good and Bad. It enables the political observer to ask, "In this case is half a loaf better than none?" One may decide the half-loaf is tainted, or may be grateful for a partial victory. The taint may stem from evil allies. That is part of the goodness or badness of the outcome. The politically astute always continue to ask, "What are the goals of my well-wishers? Who is pulling the strings?" To know that the single issue can become an idol illuminates this problem.

Dichotomous political demands that demand unconditional victory are arrogant. Even that most arrogant Puritan, Oliver Cromwell, is quoted as addressing his fellows: "By the bowels of Christ, Gentlemen, has it never occurred to you that you might be wrong?" Aside from that terrible possibility, dichotomous win-lose politics excludes the creative array of alternative solutions that can emerge in the face of urgent negotiations. Democracy cannot survive when there is no room for compromise.

The human tendency to mistake our own will for the will of God is so well documented that each of us must guard against the substitution of our own insights for God's Will. It is amusing to see someone else mistake his own tradition for the Kingdom of God. Christians must be alert to this in ourselves and our allies, as well as our opponents.

Two other issues run through the rhetoric of many religious activists: one is the substituting of a Christian legalism for other ideologies, the other is to point the finger at "enemies." The misguided assumption that politics has to rest on an ideology leads to the legalistic syllogisms of much that has passed for Christian political activism. That legalism ill fits democratic politics, and leads the faithful believer to muse, "What was the Good News all about?" Compassion, humility, trust . . . The singling out and labelling of "enemies" is not limited to religious activists, because it is such an effective mobilizer of the lukewarm and inattentive citizen. Who, what is the enemy? "Communism!" "Humanism!" "Impeach Earl Warren!" still appears on a billboard on a farm-to-market road I know. Robert Bilheimer calls us to account: "Jesus clearly taught [that] a person's handling of the enemy reveals the person himself. . . . Jesus' teaching about the enemy stands squarely against indiscriminate and therefore depersonalizing of the enemy."[4]

Changes in Political Science

Since the middle of the twentieth century, political scientists have made radical changes in how they view their work. The understanding of politics was once a branch of history and biography. At that time, growing along with the success of the nation-state as a way of mobilizing resources, the study of politics assumed that it was the "science of the state." Variations included political philosophy which tried systematically to explicate how that "ought" to work, and spun webs of prescribing citizen responsibility, literacy, public-regardingness, etc. Subtly the prescriptions were transformed into the expected norm. Citizens were to calculate the appropriate relation between ends and means—and ideology was launched. Historians looked for the unique; "Great Men," battles, earthquakes and churchquakes were said to be the causes of policy for the nation state.

Then the nation state became less useful as the focus for understanding what is going on around us. During World War II ordinary people became familiar with far away places with strange-sounding names, places that had no central government, whose basic decisions were better understood by anthropologists than by political scientists. Our culture met other peoples who were subservient to far away imperial decisions which were alien and wrong-headed for local needs. Communal-based politics, or religious conviction better explained what was needful to such peoples than a theory of the state. Saudi Arabia and the United Arab emirates have no interest in becoming a nation state. How can we study them? Another inconvenience arose: we needed to understand what was happening in the U.S.S.R. To look at the government institutions, the party, the Constitution—the nation state—not only was useless, it was counter-productive, misleading! How could the State Department assess what might happen next? The "Kremlinologists" had to scrounge through a whole new set of variables to explain what political science once expected from a scientific study of the state. Is this not a most instructive parallel to what the church committee has to do to try to decide how to correct an injustice in its neighborhood? The scientific theory of the state or city government just doesn't give much guidance. The upheaval of the entire globe getting into the act at the United Nations, with tiny nations getting one vote equal to the U.S. in the UN General Assembly happened at the same time that the prototype nation states in Europe became destabilized. The final blow to the old paradigm for studying these matters is the permeability of the boundary lines of the nation states: airplanes fly across them (carrying bombs, or tourists), broadcast waves ignore the Atlas lines carrying ideas that appeal to people who overhear things not intended for them, or people are cruelly mislead by hearing things that are dishonestly tailored for their consumption. The movement of peoples—visiting, migrating, fleeing—started with the human race and now defies the nation state unit unless artificially impeded. Trade, business, commerce, finance—and multi-national corporations—gesture solemnly in the direction of the established governments, but legally do what can only be extra-legal because there is no power to hold them accountable. As political science shifted its thought, everything had to be defined anew. "Power," "democracy," "Citizen or subject?" A healthy questioning of the basis for legitimate authority emerged, as did the issue, "By what criteria does one evaluate policy?" How does one prescribe, "Somebody ought to . . . ?" What are the building blocks of power? What are the political units to study? State? voter? workforce? ethnic groups? wards and precincts? political parties? factions? cabals? PACs? network newsrooms?

Attentive Christians should follow this development, because they will find the new variables more in keeping with their own arena. There is renewed interest in the action of overlapping human groups, of political communication, of how individuals acquire their commitments and whether they act upon those commitments, or not. There is less attention paid to intention and rhetoric, more to the measurable impact of policy on identifiable groups or types of citizens. The "public arena" is seen as including all human communication groups—not just elective office and voting. Instead of analyzing power, political science now studies resources: what resources can be translated into influence? Who has access to those resources? What potential resources are lying fallow, unused? Who might exercise those resources and for what reasons? Who takes the time and trouble to mobilize resources and commit them for impacting public policy? Where do they apply the resource? In the lobbies of Congress? In the New York Times? On the steps of City Hall? Getting a law or journalism degree? Organizing a Political Action Committee? Church groups and Christians surely can see these human activities as relevant to their Christian concern. An easy way to epitomize this is to ask, "What have you got to use? What have you got to lose?"

Contemporary political science finds the purported ideologies of left-right, or liberal-conservative, or even planning vs. laissez faire to be useless for understanding most of what is going on. One ideological conflict has emerged as pertinent: what is the appropriate scope of government? Minimal? Compensatory? Positive? Neutral? But that is more of a background, metaphysical issue whereas the old familiar liberal-conservative split has been overwhelmed by the bundles of issues that defy the labels still used. Americans are confronted with "cross-cutting cleavages" where they have some allies on one issue, and are in league with different forces, even opponents on Issue #1, on another issue. Following Robert A. Dahl,[5] many political scientists find this a healthy situation, which enhances stability of a democratic political regime.

This shift in theory has introduced so many important variables that it is hard to find a substitute focus for the nation state. There are many candidates for organizing principle for studying politics. All social scientists have found systems analysis very useful in conceptualizing a variety of human processes. The model has flaws, but if one avoids reifying (idolizing) the metaphor, one can begin to see how groups of concerned people, including Christian groups, can affect the process, the system itself, and the product. The system is dynamic—a change in any of its parts has consequences for the whole. What a powerful metaphor! It is both exciting and terrifying. Forces at work in the society *do* make a difference in the polity. Concerned Christians can better mobilize their energy and resources if they use a realistic notion of how to bring about change: changing attitudes and expectations; encouraging and aiding candidates and leaders, accepting nomination to election and appointment—not only as individuals, but recognizing they represent a human group; active and conscious articulation of needs for the inarticulate, the powerless, the oppressed; building alliances and coalitions by sifting the wants and wishes, organizing the myriad demands upon the system according to some faithful set of criteria, that means subordinating some wants to other, more urgent, needs, in order to get some things done when everything cannot be done due to scarce resources; and finally, providing a wholesome arena for political communication and debate. All of these factors are essential inputs to make the political system work. Our whole culture has become inordinately dependent upon the mass media of communication for these essential tasks: the media are ill-adapted for healthy political communication, representing the peoples' needs and alliance building. The electronic media, and even the press are anti-political by their very nature of "broadcasting" to isolated individual receptors who can only say "Wow!" or "Ugh!"

Politics is for People

Politics is a human activity. We need to recapture it on a human scale. Policy, in a democracy, is to be accessible to the people. The church, both local and connectional, is a political network of sorts. More attention should be paid to the messages that flow and converse in that network. *Conscious* caring for the body politic (the polity) is part of the mission of the church according to Reformed theology. Christians have a high moral obligation to know what is going on, to "do our homework," to base decisions on the best available information, and to check that information with one another. Part of that knowledge base is to know how the process presently works, to be aware of the institutions and the patterns of policy proposals, policy deliberation, policy decisions. Knowing the political patterns, however, need not dictate acceptance of them as given; to believe that the policies, the processes, the patterns themselves might change takes powerful Hope. Hope probably is the only factor other than pride or greed that could make people willing to expend the energy needed to make significant change.

Traditionally American churches have been very abstract in our preachments about politics (the exceptions regarding beverage alcohol, gambling, and other moralistic issues prove this rule), mouthing "oughts" and "shoulds" that were unrelated to what was going on. All this moralism had to be demythologized as much as the visions of Ezekiel in order to be made into political insights. Much of American rhetoric about politics has assumed that one must first have some ideology "in place," from which one deduces the correct political move and policy. Many Christians and non-Christians assume that Christianity is an ideology. Thus the whole analysis veers off into cloud-cuckooland. Christianity is *not* an ideology, although it has over the centuries spawned many, conflicting ideologies.

The Christian church is not an idea, rather it is a flawed working model of human caring and action. Political processes are human networks, human decisions, based in and affecting groups. Is not the church experienced in this nexus? Even the most individualistic, private faith has a sense of the fellowship. The strength of those bonds can be a model for the life political: a model particularly of disagreeing in love, and also pressing ahead to get a task completed even when there is not unanimity.

How can one assess the policy process without an ideology or a sure vision of "what must now be done?" Too much Christian analysis of policy has been exclusively evaluative without a sense of the feasible, or a useful description of how to make changes. It is thought all must be swept away in order to start with a clean slate. To influence the process, however, is to engage the process: to be active in the public arena. It is a particularly Christian insight that things need not necessarily turn out the way they seem to be heading: predictions can be

[199]

nullified, age-old patterns do change. God is at work in our time, in our institutions and processes. Christians can be change agents.

The church could be more of a conscious participant in the pluralist society. If we are strong in our faith and our fellowship we will not be threatened by disagreement, nor hostile to those who hold other values. While there is great debate and disagreement about the idea of "pluralism" as a healthy or unhealthy way to envision American society and politics, some of the disagreement is because of different definitions or understandings of what "pluralism" means. A useful way of thinking about the diversity of the U.S. experience is to assert the wisdom and dignity of a variety of heritages and of new attempts to make sense of human experience. This is the insight of "Roots," of ethnic festivals, of Flower People, and also of Presbyterian celebration of the Reformation, the Scottish Covenanters, and the Methodists' delight in the outrageous "enthusiasm" of the Wesley brothers. "Melting pot" may have been a useful idea at one time, but now our sense of powerlessness in the face of principalities and powers may stem from accepting the notion that each of us is "a cog in a machine," or a faceless globule in an homogenized mass society. Commercial market researchers know better. Politicians seeking a viable constituency know better. James Madison in the Federalist Papers knew better. There are legitimate, honorable bases for disagreement, for differing commitments. These subgroups give their members identity as full persons. Christians may be the rare people who can welcome those differences and celebrate the pluralism of our land. Too often we have demeaned "toleration" by shrugging our shoulders and turning our backs in disapproval of "the other," rather than learning how the variety of God's creation: enhances our life together, provides dignity, and encourages a sense of self worth to individuals.

This celebration of our pluralist variety, despite the difficulties, conflicts, and dismay it causes all of us, suggests that Presbyterians could honor politicians, could find ways to support politicians, and realize that Presbyterians can be politicians and thus be present where proximate and temporary decisions are made that affect each one of us.

The Salt of the Earth. The Leaven in the Lump. The Saving Remnant. Old and New Testament teachings give us language and metaphor for the activity of those who accept the vocation of enhancing the life of the whole society. Right now there is need for face-to-face political discussion to leaven a bureaucratic and technical age; there is need to recapture political discussion, action and decision on a human scale over against the complex, remote and impersonal image of government to salt the earth. In our congregations and study, worship and prayer groups we have networks for mutual comfort and support. We may not have much confidence, our Hope may be dim, but we can be obedient to God's will. Jesus called his followers to be in the world, witnessing to him. Political witness never wins a final victory, it is never-ending, often discouraging. Paul understood the importance of the fellowship to support the downhearted, to encourage the defeated, to comfort the troubled, and to build one another up. This, too, is the agenda and style of Presbyterian political action.

Endnotes

1. Marian D. Irish and James W. Prothro, *The Politics of American Democracy,* third Edition. (Englewood Cliffs, N.J.: Prentice-Hall, Inc., 1965), pp. 656-665.
2. Ibid., p. 660.
3. Ibid, p. 660.
4. Robert S. Bilheimer, "Christian Political Analysis." United Presbyterian Board of Christian Education, 1972.
5. Robert A. Dahl, *Democracy in the United States, Promise and Performance,* 3rd Ed. (Chicago: Rand MacNally, 1976), pp. 287, 347, 374.